Free to Move

*Foot Voting, Migration,
and Political Freedom*

ILYA SOMIN

OXFORD
UNIVERSITY PRESS
A CATO INSTITUTE BOOK

Contents

Acknowledgments

I have accumulated many debts in the process of writing this book, which I first envisioned several years ago. Among the scholars who provided valuable comments, suggestions, and criticisms are Bruce Ackerman, Jonathan Adler, Larry Alexander, James Allan, Jason Brennan, Terry Anderson, Michael Blake, Bryan Caplan, Michael Clemens, Shikha Dalmia, Stephen Davies, Bobby Duffy, Fred Foldvary, Heather Gerken, Michael Greve, Marie Newhouse, Alex Nowrasteh, Lant Pritchett, David Schleicher, Troy Smith, Kevin Vallier, and two anonymous reviewers.

I must also thank participants at the Kadish Workshop in Law, Philosophy, and Political Theory at the University of California at Berkeley and the Law Faculty at Hitotsubashi University in Tokyo, which organized dedicated seminars where I presented early versions of parts of this book. Susumu Morimura, Masahito Tadano, and Tetsuki Tamura provided thoughtful comments at the event at Hitotsubashi University, a seminar that Professor Morimura generously conceived and organized. At Berkeley, I must acknowledge R. Jay Wallace and Joshua Cohen, who hosted the seminar, and Melissa Carlson, who provided excellent comments on my presentation.

I am also grateful for the opportunity to have presented parts of this project at Boston University School of Law, the Georgetown University conference on "The Ethics of Democracy," Jesus College at Oxford University, King's College (London) conference on "Case Studies in Self-Governance," the Institute of Economic Affairs, Osgoode Hall Law School at York University (Toronto), the University of Calgary Faculty of Law, the Stranahan Lecture at the University of Toledo College of Law, and the University of San Diego School of Law conference on "The Travails of Democracy," and the College of Business at the University of Central Arkansas.

David McBride of Oxford University Press, deserves enormous credit for all the wonderful work he did in editing this book. The project would not have been possible without him.

George Mason University law students, Nicole Chammas, Michael Sebring, Taylor Alexander, and Tierney Walls provided excellent research assistance. My assistant Katie Hickey did her usual excellent job of handling a variety of logistical issues. Esther Koblenz and Ashley Matthews of the George Mason University law library were extremely helpful in tracking down a variety of research materials.

Dean Henry Butler and the rest of the administration and faculty at the law school have provided a wide range of institutional support that was essential to this book and indeed to all my work since I came to George Mason University in 2003.

I am very grateful to the Cato Institute for its support of this book. John Samples and Jason Kuznicki helped arrange and oversee the collaboration between Cato, Oxford University Press, and myself.

Rob Tempio of Princeton University Press came up with the title "Free to Move." I am more than happy to acknowledge that contribution here, as I promised I would do!

I am grateful to Cambridge University Press, the *European Journal of Political Science*, the *Minnesota Law Review*, the University of Nebraska Press, Nomos (NYU Press), and the *San Diego Law Review* for permission to reprint parts of previous publications. Elements of chapters 1 and 2 were adapted from "Foot Voting, Federalism, and Political Freedom," *Nomos LV: Federalism and Subsidiarity*, ed. James Fleming and Jacob Levy (New York: New York University Press, 2014). Chapter 1 also includes material from "Foot Voting vs. Ballot Box Voting: Why Voting with Your Feet Is Crucial to Political Freedom," *European Political Science* (2019), and from "How Foot Voting Enhances Political Freedom," *San Diego Law Review* (forthcoming). The Introduction and Chapter 2 incorporate material from "Foot-Voting Nation," in *Our National Narrative: The Search for a Unifying American Story*, ed. Joshua Claybourn (Lincoln: University of Nebraska Press/Potomac Books, 2019). Chapter 1 and Chapter 6 include material from "Foot Voting, Decentralization, and Development," *Minnesota Law Review* 102 (2018): 1649–70. Chapters 5 and 6 include a few passages adapted from "Foot Voting and the Future of Liberty," in *Cambridge Handbook of Classical Liberal Thought*, ed. M. Todd Henderson (Cambridge: Cambridge University Press, 2018). In Chapter 8, I have incorporated much of "A Cosmopolitan Case against World Government," *World Orders Forum*, August 2017 (published by the World Government Research Network). In several passages in Chapter 5, I have adapted and expanded material previously published on the Volokh Conspiracy law and politics blog, hosted by the *Washington Post* until 2017, and *Reason* magazine since then.

In this book, more than any previous one, I must thank my parents Yefim and Sofya Somin. Their decision to "vote with their feet" to leave the Soviet Union for the United States made not only this work possible but virtually everything else I have been able to accomplish in my life and career.

My children Adam and Lydia patiently put up with the disruptions to their lives caused by this book; Adam also helped by learning to sleep through the night at the precociously early age of two months, much as big sister Lydia did when I was working on a previous book! Willow the golden retriever helped by providing her usual abundant good cheer, and by demonstrating some impressive foot-voting (or, perhaps, paw-voting) techniques of her own.

Finally, my greatest debt—as always—is to my wife Alison, who dealt with the many inconveniences caused by this book, offered invaluable advice on many issues related to this project, and provided unwavering support for all of my personal and professional endeavors.

Free to Move

Introduction

We often take it for granted that ballot box voting is the essence of political freedom. In liberal democracies, it is generally considered the main way for the people to choose what sort of government policies they will live under.

The ballot box indeed has great value. But it also has significant flaws. As a mechanism of expressing political choice, it leaves much to be desired. The individual voter almost never has more than a minuscule chance of making a difference to the outcome of an election. And for that very reason, he or she has little incentive to become well-informed about the issues at stake in any election.

Voting with your feet—or "foot voting"—is in many ways a superior alternative. You can vote with your feet by deciding to move to a different city or state because you prefer its government policies to those in force where you currently reside. International migration is also often a form of foot voting. And, as we shall see, many people can vote with their feet in the private sector, as well.

Foot voting offers individuals a chance to make decisions that actually matter. And precisely because their choices do matter, foot voters have every reason to seek out information and use it wisely.

If you are like most people, you probably spent more time seeking out information the last time you bought a television or a smartphone than the last time you voted in an election, whether national, regional, or local. That is likely because the decision on the TV really makes a difference. The one you buy will actually end up in your living room. But when you turn it on and see the president or prime minister of your country, the chance that you can actually influence the selection of that person is utterly insignificant.

This logic applies with even greater force to foot-voting decisions. Like the decision on which TV or smartphone to buy, they allow individuals to make decisive choices, ones that are usually far more important than any decision to buy a particular consumer product, and therefore create even stronger incentives to seek out information and use it wisely.

The purpose of this book is to show how these two advantages of foot voting—the opportunity to make a decisive choice and the associated stronger to make well-informed decisions—make it a powerful tool for expanding political freedom. This logic applies to all three types of foot voting prevalent in the modern world: foot voting between jurisdictions in a federal system, foot voting through international migration, and foot voting in the private sector. Each of these has been the focus of much controversy. But they are rarely considered together in a single unified framework, and never one that explores their implications for political freedom.

Nobel Prize-winning economist Robert Lucas famously said that "[o]nce you start thinking about [economic] growth, it's hard to think about anything else."[1] He was referring to the ways in which even modest cumulative increases in economic growth can have an immense impact on human welfare because of the way the effects of growth compound over time. Even a 1 percent increase in annual gross domestic product (GDP) growth can make a massive difference over a period of decades.

The same can be said for foot voting and its impact on human freedom. Even modest increases in opportunities for people to vote with their feet can have an enormous impact in expanding liberty and well-being. For both internal and external migrants—especially those who are poor or fleeing oppression—foot voting is often a life-altering experience that massively improves their situation for the better. Even a 1 percent increase in the number of people who have access to major foot voting opportunities can fundamentally transform the lives of millions of people.

Few if any other policy changes can help so many people so much as breaking down barriers to foot voting. A recent World Bank report concludes that "ignoring the massive economic gains of immigration would be akin to leaving billions of hundred dollar bills on the sidewalk."[2] Free migration throughout the world could potentially double world GDP, a far larger gain than from any other possible reform.[3]

As Harvard economist and former secretary of the treasury Larry Summers puts it, "I do not think there is a more important development issue than getting questions of migration right."[4] What is true of development is also to a large degree true of human freedom and well-being more generally. Increasing opportunities for internal foot voting can also potentially generate enormous gains, both economic and otherwise.[5]

The arguments advanced this book do not prove that foot voting should be unconstrained in all conceivable circumstances. Political freedom and related issues considered here are not the only ones that need be weighed in assessing policy on foot voting. But the massive potential gains considered here do counsel in favor of expanding foot voting far more than we might otherwise.

To the extent we value political freedom in any significant sense, we should also assign a high value to foot voting. Freedom of choice through foot voting—and the freedom of movement that makes it possible—cannot be absolute principles. But there should be at least a substantial presumption in their favor.

My analysis also emphasizes the fundamental similarity between three different types of foot voting that are usually considered to be very different from each other: interjurisdictional foot voting in federal systems, foot voting in the private sector, and foot voting through international migration. Despite some important differences, the three have common virtues and help advance political freedom in similar ways.

In assessing foot voting, I define "political freedom" as the ability to choose the government policies one wishes to live under. As we shall see, some theories of political freedom place inherent value on the ability to choose. For others, it is part of a broader conception of liberty, which focuses on the potential impact of such choices, as well as the ability to choose, in and of itself. Both types of conceptions are considered in this book, and both provide support for expanding foot-voting opportunities.

Concluding that foot voting is vital to political freedom and often a better mechanism of achieving it than ballot box voting does not amount to a call for the abolition of democracy. Far from it. Democratic government is still superior to alternatives such as dictatorship and oligarchy,[6] and choosing political leaders by election has value that does not depend on its effect on political freedom.

Similarly, my analysis does not provide anything approaching a comprehensive theory of what the powers of government should be and how they should be distributed between different levels of government in federal systems. But it does demonstrate that there are good reasons to constrain and structure democracy in ways that increase opportunities for foot voting.

This book also does not attempt to assess foot voting from the standpoint of all conceivable approaches to political theory. It focuses primarily on considerations associated with various interpretations of political freedom. It does not, for example, assess foot voting from the standpoint of utilitarianism or virtue ethics.[7] I also consider foot voting primarily from the standpoint of potential voters' ability to exercise political choice for themselves and their families. I therefore do not assess claims that they might have to use political power to control the lives of other people, except insofar as such claims might be used to justify restrictions on foot voting.[8]

Notwithstanding these limitations on the scope of my analysis, some of the approaches to political freedom considered here also have implications for other theories of political morality. For example, the "positive freedom" approach clearly has affinities with consequentialist theories that seek to enhance human happiness and well-being. As we shall see in Chapters 2 through 6, my arguments are also consistent with a wide variety of stances on issues such as the appropriate level of redistribution to the poor. While my analysis will not appeal to adherents of every possible approach to political theory, neither is it restricted to one narrow conception.

Frederick Douglass and Freedom of Movement

I am far from the first writer to recognize the similarity between different types of foot voting. The great nineteenth-century African American abolitionist and political leader Frederick Douglass intuitively grasped it long before me. In an 1869 speech "On Composite Nationality," Douglass took white Americans to task for their growing hostility to Chinese immigration:

> I submit that this question of Chinese immigration should be settled upon higher principles than those of a cold and selfish expediency. There are such things in the world as human rights. They rest upon no conventional foundation, but are external, universal, and indestructible. Among these, is the right of locomotion; the right of migration; the right which belongs to no particular race, but belongs alike to all and to all alike. It is the right you assert by staying here, and your fathers asserted by coming here. It is this great right that I assert for the Chinese and Japanese, and for all other varieties of men equally with yourselves, now and forever.[9]

Later in the same speech, Douglass compared "[r]epugnance to the presence and influence of foreigners" to "chattel slavery" and "prejudice of race and color."[10]

It is no accident that Douglass, who first became famous because of his escape from slavery and subsequent work as an abolitionist, saw parallels between racially based enslavement and laws barring immigration. Despite some notable differences, both restricted "locomotion" and "the right of migration" on the basis of arbitrary circumstances of birth—in one case race, in the other geography.[11]

In his early career, Douglass eloquently argued that slaves should be allowed to leave the authority of their masters. In the 1880s, after the rise of early segregation laws and other forms of repression deprived southern blacks of much of the freedom they hoped to gain after the Civil War, he argued that internal migration could help alleviate their oppression. In 1886, he contended that "*diffusion* is the true policy for the colored people of the South," that as many blacks as possible should be encouraged to move to "parts of the country where their civil and political rights are better protected than at present they can be at the South," and that "[a] million of dollars devoted to this purpose [of assisting black migration out of the South] would do more for the colored people of the South than the same amount expended in any other way."[12]

Douglass understood what too many people today have forgotten: the importance of the right to mobility, and the ways in which different types of mobility are interconnected. Domestic and international freedom of movement often serve similar purposes and have similar justifications. Their denial inhibits human freedom and well-being in many of the same ways.

Two Examples of the Power of Foot Voting Today

My own life is far from being as dramatic as Douglass's, and I cannot even begin to compare anything I have done to his many achievements. But my experience is nonetheless a small but telling example of the transformative power of foot voting.[13]

I was born in the Soviet Union in 1973. The life of most residents of that totalitarian state was one of poverty and oppression. My family was materially better off than the average Soviet citizen, but still lived in awful circumstances by Western standards. Several of my relatives had at various times been victims of the government's repressive policies. In addition, as Jews they often felt the weight of the regime's institutionalized anti-Semitism.

I was freed of all that because my parents were able to leave the USSR for the United States in 1979. I am, as a result, vastly better off than my peers who stayed in Russia, a reality driven home to me whenever I have visited Russia in the years since. But virtually all of that difference is the result of the difference between American institutions and Russian ones, not any special merit of mine.

Had we stayed in Russia, I would likely still be poor, and still have to live in fear of repression, if I dared to speak out publicly against the government. The authoritarian regime of President Vladimir Putin is less oppressive than that of the communists, but still persecutes—and occasionally even kills—dissenters. The Russian nationalism that has replaced communism as the government's official ideology still includes elements of anti-Semitism and hostility to minority groups perceived as potentially hostile to the regime or sympathetic to the West. I avoided the poverty, repression, and bigotry only because my parents were able to vote against it with their feet.

At least initially, J. D. Vance's life story may seem almost as remote from mine, as Frederick Douglass's. Vance's compelling 2016 memoir *Hillbilly Elegy* captivated the nation with its account of his upbringing in a poor Appalachian-white community in Ohio.[14]

Much of the public debate triggered by the book focused on his descriptions of the social dysfunction and pathology that surrounded him there. But reading *Hillbilly Elegy* makes it hard to avoid the conclusion that Vance's life was transformed in large part by moving: leaving home to join the Marine Corps, getting a college degree at Ohio State University, and eventually attending Yale Law School opened up opportunities that he probably would never have had if he had not left home.[15] As a result, Vance bettered his lot and became a far more productive member of society than he likely would have been otherwise.

Vance, unfortunately, does not include the need to enhance mobility among the "policy lessons" that might be drawn from his experiences, and that of others in similar circumstances.[16] But his ability to "escape the worst of my culture's inheritance" by becoming a "cultural emigrant" from a dysfunctional setting (as he puts it) was greatly facilitated by the ability to move to an environment that offered greater opportunity.[17]

Aside from our having eventually attended the same law school (at different times), our backgrounds could hardly be more different. But there is this important commonality: both our lives were transformed for the better through the power of mobility. That is what has enabled each of us to lead lives that, in Vance's words, were "the stuff of fantasy" in the communities we were born into.[18] And, as we shall see in later in this book, much can be done to extend similar opportunities to millions of other people who would otherwise languish in poverty or oppression—as Vance and I likely would have done had we been forced to remain where we were born.

Three Types of Foot Voting

This book focuses on three types of foot voting.[19] First, people can vote with their feet by deciding what jurisdiction to live in within a federal system, such as a state or local government. In the United States alone there are fifty states and thousands of local governments that foot voters can choose among. Both historically and today, millions of people move from one jurisdiction to another at least in part because of preferences over public policy.

A second mechanism for foot voting is international migration, where migrants choose what type of government they wish to live under by moving from one country to another. Such nations as the United States, Australia, Argentina, Canada, and New Zealand were largely populated by immigrants who chose to vote with their feet in hopes of finding greater freedom and opportunity due in large part to superior government policies in the destination country.[20]

Foot voting across international boundaries potentially expands choice even more than domestic foot voting, because of the vast differences between national governments. The differences in policy and quality of institutions between, say, Mexico and the United States are vastly greater than those between any two American states or any two Mexican ones.

Finally, foot voting also occurs in the private sector, when we decide what goods and services we wish to purchase in the market or what civil society organizations we wish to join. Such private sector foot voting is particularly clear in the case of private planned communities and other organizations that carry out functions traditionally associated with local or regional governments, such as security, environmental amenities, and waste disposal.[21] In the United States alone, some 69 million people lived in private communities as of 2016.[22] Such organizations have spread elsewhere as well.[23] Private planned communities have increasingly taken on a wide range of functions historically performed by government.[24] The three types of foot voting are distinct, but they also interact with each other. In many situations, as well shall see, their benefits are mutually reinforcing.[25]

Foot voting can often be undertaken even without physically moving from one place to another. In the private sector, for example, one can change schools, join a new civil society organization, or purchase a new product or service without ever changing one's place of residence.

The key attribute of foot voting that differentiates it from conventional ballot box voting is not movement, as such, but rather the ability to make an individually decisive choice. Unlike the ballot box voter, whose vote is just one of many thousands or millions and generally has only a tiny chance of affecting the outcome, the foot voter can make decisions that have a high probability of making a difference.

As described in Albert Hirschman's famous theory of political choice, people dissatisfied with a political regime can use either "voice" or "exit" to address the situation.[26] Ballot box voting is the principal form of voice in democratic societies, while foot voting is the most significant type of exit.[27] This circumstance makes it easy to confuse the distinction between foot voting and ballot box voting with Hirschman's distinction between exit and voice. But the two are nonetheless distinct. Unlike Hirschman's theory, the distinction between foot voting and ballot box voting focuses on the presence or absence of opportunities for individuals to make a decisive choice, as opposed to one where they have only a tiny chance of affecting the outcome. By contrast, Hirschman's framework does not distinguish between exit and voice mechanisms that offer opportunities to make a decisive choice and those that do not.

The theory developed here is also distinct from economist Charles Tiebout's classic analysis of interjurisdictional choice,[28] which outlined potential advantages of mobility between local and regional governments. Tiebout considered only movement within a federal system and did not analyze either private sector foot voting or international migration. He also focused on the effects on economic efficiency and human welfare without analyzing issues of political freedom of the sort that are at the heart of this book.[29]

Foot voting need not always be completely individualistic. Families and businesses, for example, make foot-voting decisions that require the assent of more than one person.[30] But in most such cases, there are individuals who can either make the choice all on their own or at least exercise a high degree of influence.

The exact point at which an individual's leverage becomes too small for the decision to be considered a case of foot voting rather than ballot box voting may be hard to identify. The distinction between the two is, in close cases, more a matter of degree than kind. But the difficulty of drawing a precise line should not divert attention from the key fact that there is an important difference between them and that most important real-world cases clearly fall on one side of the divide or the other.

Plan of the Book

Chapter 1 provides an overview of the reasons why foot voting outperforms ballot box voting as a mechanism of political freedom. Foot voting has two fundamental advantages over its more traditional counterpart: it enables individuals to make choices that have a decisive impact, and it gives them much stronger incentives to make well-informed decisions. These advantages are significant in themselves, and also translate to stronger performance in terms of several widely accepted normative theories of political freedom, including consent theory, negative freedom, positive freedom, and nondomination.

The latter part of Chapter 1 argues that the disadvantages of ballot box voting cannot be offset by mechanisms for improving deliberation or by methods of political participation that go beyond voting. This chapter also rebuts claims that foot voting is not a meaningful alternative to ballot box voting, because it is not a genuine exercise of political choice.

In Chapter 2, I consider foot voting between jurisdictions in federal systems. This is perhaps the most widely recognized form of foot voting. It has important advantages in terms of increasing political freedom, including for the poor and disadvantaged. At the same time, however, it also has notable potential downsides, including possibly high moving costs, "races to the bottom," inequalities between different people's abilities to move, and the exclusion and oppression of unpopular minorities. Each of these problems could potentially undermine the utility of foot voting under federalism as a mechanism of political choice. I suggest ways in which these disadvantages are overstated by critics but also propose strategies for mitigating them in cases where the problem is genuine.

Chapter 3 focuses on foot voting through international migration. This is perhaps the most controversial type of foot voting, one that has attracted the ire of nationalists around the world. But it is also one whose expansion promises perhaps the greatest gains for human freedom and welfare. That is because the differences between nations are often so great, far eclipsing those between regional jurisdictions in federal systems.

This chapter outlines the enormous potential benefits of international foot voting, while at the same time addressing some of its key shortcomings, most notably its relatively high moving costs. Chapter 3 also criticizes claims that foreign aid is preferable to migration rights as a tool for expanding political choice for citizens of poor and oppressive societies.

In Chapter 4, I consider foot voting in the private sector. Private organizations can offer many of the same services as governments do, especially local and regional governments. These include education, environmental amenities, waste removal, and even security. This is especially true in the case of private planned communities, such as condominium associations and others. Private organizations can potentially offer a wider range of choice than regional and local governments, often with much lower moving costs.

Many may reject private sector mechanisms for expressing political freedom out of hand because such choices are by definition not genuinely "political." I argue that they nonetheless can be viable alternatives to government services, and that the objections to them are flawed for many of the same reasons as are similar objections to foot voting in federal systems. Critics also argue that private sector options are only a meaningful alternative for the wealthy and certainly of little use to the poor. But such claims are, at the very least, greatly overstated. While some inequality is unavoidable, it does not negate the value of private sector foot voting.

Chapter 5 examines claims that foot voting actually destroys, rather than enhances, political freedom. It potentially does so by undermining the self-determination of current residents of areas to which migrants move. Many believe that current residents and their governments have a right to exclude potential newcomers. Such arguments sometimes take the form of analogies to individuals' freedom of association, as when nations are analogized to private clubs or homes, whose owners have a right to exclude strangers for almost any reason they wish.[31] Other claims are founded on group rights to a territory, based on culture, ethnicity, or other similar characteristics.

I argue that both group and individual rights claims of this sort are seriously flawed. If accepted, they have deeply illiberal implications for natives no less than potential migrants. For example, if national governments have the same rights over their territory as homeowners have over their houses, they would have broad power to suppress speech or religion they disapprove of. I also reject claims that a general power to reject migrants must be accepted because it is supposedly inherent in the very nature of national sovereignty.

Chapter 5 also considers claims that foot voting must be constrained in order to protect the rights of the jurisdictions from which migrants depart. Perhaps would-be migrants have a moral duty to "fix their own countries" or stay home to avoid "brain drain." I criticize these types of arguments on both moral and pragmatic grounds. Forcing unwilling people to stay in their home jurisdictions is likely to cause great harm. And the idea that they have a moral duty to do so has profoundly illiberal implications.

While self-determination arguments against freedom of movement are usually used primarily to justify restrictions on international migration, Chapter 5 explains why most can also be used to justify restrictions on internal migration. Those who wish to use such claims to justify restricting the former, but not the latter, cannot avoid serious internal contradictions in their theories.

In Chapter 6, I consider several standard justifications for restricting foot voting that are not based on concerns about self-determination. These include fears that migrants will increase crime and terrorism, create "political externalities" by voting for bad government policies, overburden the welfare state, displace native workers, spread harmful cultural values, and destroy the environment. Some who do not necessarily believe there is a general right to exclude migrants on grounds of self-determination nonetheless argue that such exclusion is sometimes justified in order to prevent "political externalities"—harmful influence of migrants on public policy. For example, migrants might favor policies that violate the rights of natives or otherwise harm them. Alternatively, perhaps governments should restrict the exit rights of some people so that they would be more likely to reform flawed institutions by exercising "voice," as famously argued by economist Albert O. Hirschman.[32]

This book cannot provide a comprehensive evaluation of all such concerns. But I do develop a three-stage framework for addressing them. First, it is important to ask whether the claimed problem actually exists and on what scale. Concerns about the effects of migration often turn out to be groundless, or at least overblown. In some cases, the issue in question may be one that does not justify coercive measures at all, even if the issue is a real one. For example, it is wrong to conclude that governments have a general power to use force to keep in place currently dominant cultural values.

Second, if the problem is real, it is important to consider whether it can be addressed by a "keyhole solution," a fix less harmful than keeping out migrants entirely. For example, concerns about overburdening welfare systems can be addressed by restricting migrants' eligibility for redistributive programs.

Finally, where the problem is a genuine one, and there is no viable keyhole solution, we should consider whether the issue can be mitigated by tapping some of the vast wealth created by increased migration or by redirecting resources currently devoted to immigration enforcement. For example, increases in crime might be forestalled by using some of these resources to increase the number of police officers on the street. Similarly, political externalities can be mitigated by restricting migrants' access to the franchise, as the United States and other countries already do to a considerable degree.

As with the issues addressed in Chapter 5, many of those dealt with in this chapter apply to internal migration just as readily as the international type. This should make us wary of theories that hold they are sufficient to justify imposing severe restrictions on one type of migration but not the other.

The topics covered in Chapters 2 through 4 necessarily overlap to some degree with those analyzed in Chapters 5 and 6. Both deal with a variety of objections to different types of foot voting. But, as a general rule, the former chapters consider claims that foot voting is ineffective from the standpoint of would-be migrants themselves, while the latter focus on claims that restrictions on foot voting are necessary to protect the rights and interests of other people, particularly natives of receiving jurisdictions and those whom migrants "leave behind" in their former homes.

In Chapter 7, I assess some implications of foot voting for constitutional design. No one constitutional framework is ideal for all nations. Nonetheless, there are some general principles that can help maximize opportunities for foot voting while helping to mitigate its potential downsides. Most notably, foot-voting options can be enhanced by systems of decentralized federalism that leave considerable autonomy to regional and local governments, while at the same time preventing those authorities from restricting freedom of movement themselves. Federal systems can also be structured in ways that increase the incentives of subnational governments to compete for migrants, thereby further enhancing foot-voting opportunities.

In some areas, foot voting can be enhanced by constitutional rights that provide a wide range of liberties to private individuals and associations. These too can expand opportunities for foot voting—some directly and some by more indirect means. Constitutional design can also help mitigate the potential dangers of foot voting for people who lack mobility or own valuable immobile assets, such as property in land.

There are several ways in which constitutional design can be used to expand opportunities for foot voting through international migration. Constitutions can limit the power of the central government to bar migrants. They can also give subnational governments the authority to accept migrants and guest workers without prior approval from the central government.

Chapter 8 describes some implications of the argument of this book for international law and "global governance." The massive advantages of expanded foot voting across international boundaries strengthens the case for broadening the class of refugees whom national governments are barred from expelling. Under current international law, such an obligation applies only to "[a] person who owing to a well-founded fear of being persecuted for reasons of race, religion, nationality, membership of a particular social group or political opinion, is outside the country of his nationality and is unable or, owing to such fear, is unwilling to avail himself of the protection of that country."[33]

I contend that this should be expanded to include at least some other types of victims of oppressive regimes. We should also reconsider the standard distinction between "economic" and "political" refugees, with the former being subject to routine exclusion. In many cases, "economic" refugees are actually victims of oppressive governments and have no other way to exercise meaningful political choice.

While the importance of foot voting weighs in favor of expanding the scope of refugee law, it counts against major expansions of "global governance," particularly those that require the establishment of world government. A political institution that spans the entire world is one that no one can escape by voting with their feet.

In addition, there is a significant risk that a world government could become severely oppressive over time, perhaps even to the point of totalitarianism. These points do not by themselves resolve the debate over global governance and world government. But they are important considerations that deserve to be given greater weight than has so far been the case in the debate over the future of world politics.

In the Conclusion, I briefly consider prospects for the future of foot voting. Particularly in the case of international migration, we are unlikely to see foot-voting opportunities expanded as far as I would prefer at any time in the near future. But there are numerous opportunities for significant incremental progress. A number of political and technological developments offer hope in that respect. At the same time, there are countervailing negative trends. These include the growth of nationalism and—in some countries—of barriers to internal movement.

Recent events provide many examples of both the enormous benefits of foot voting and the dangers created by growing obstacles to it. Over the last several decades, more people than ever before have found greater freedom and opportunity by voting with their feet. Modern transportation, communications, and information technology make foot-voting potentially easier than in any previous era of human history.[34]

But at the same time, there are also growing political obstacles to effective foot-voting. In both Europe and the United States, powerful nationalist movements have arisen, seeking to massively reduce immigration and refugee admissions.[35] In the United States and elsewhere, policies such as restrictive zoning and regional occupational licensing have made it much harder to vote with your feet even between different regions of the same country, thereby cutting off millions of people from valuable housing and employment opportunities.[36]

These trends have arisen even as many millions of people desperately need opportunities to find refuge from poverty, war, and oppression. Over the last few years, the repressive and economically destructive policies of Venezuela's authoritarian socialist government have created some 4 million refugees, the biggest refugee crisis in the history of the Western Hemisphere.[37] Many of them have been unable to start new lives, as the US government refuses to accept more than a small fraction of them.[38] Millions more have fled war and oppression in Syria, Yemen, and North Africa,[39] even as Western nations have taken steps to make migration more difficult, including by severely restricting refugee admissions.[40]

Empowering more people to vote with their feet can save millions from lives of poverty and oppression, and expand opportunities for meaningful political freedom for many more. Despite the very real obstacles to its expansion, foot voting holds great promise for the future of humanity. I hope this book will contribute to the debate over how to realize that promise as fully as possible.

1

How Foot Voting Outperforms
Ballot Box Voting

Ballot box voting is a valuable institution. But, as a mechanism of political choice, it has serious shortcomings relative to foot voting.

In most contexts, few would suggest you have meaningful freedom if your decisions have only a minuscule chance of making a difference. Imagine you are deciding what kind of car to buy. Do you have meaningful freedom of choice if you can cast a vote choosing between a Honda and Ford, but those are your only two options, and your vote has only a 1 in 1 million chance of determining which one it will be?

Things are even worse if you have to make the decision in a framework where it is highly likely that you will know very little about the relative merits of the two cars. You are surely much more free if you can choose between a wider range of options; your choice will definitely be decisive, or at least have a high probability of being so; and you have at least some substantial knowledge of your options.

What is true for a choice of cars is also true for many much more important decisions, including those at stake in elections. Freedom is enhanced by the voter's ability to make decisions that actually matter and are well-informed. This chapter outlines the key reasons why foot voting often achieves that goal better than ballot box voting.

The shortcomings of ballot box voting are only modestly mitigated by "information shortcuts," which potentially enable voters to use small bits of knowledge to substitute for larger bodies of information they do not know. The same goes for "miracle of aggregation" theories claiming that the electorate as a whole can be well informed, even if most individual voters are not.

Similarly, the disadvantages of ballot box voting are not likely to be overcome by various mechanisms proposed to make it more "deliberative." Such approaches may have merit, but they are unlikely to overcome the twin problems of ignorance and the insignificance of individual votes to political outcomes.

Ballot box voting is not the only way ordinary citizens can exercise influence over democratic political processes. They can also engage in various forms of political activism. But these mechanisms cannot remedy the disadvantages of ballot box voting relative to foot voting. In some respects, they even make them worse.

Some critics devalue foot voting because it is not truly a form of "political" decision-making. Such critiques are largely off base. To the extent that they are valid, they are equally applicable to ballot box voting and therefore fail to provide a good reason for preferring the former to foot voting.

Foot voting cannot completely displace ballot box voting. In some respects, the two are mutually supporting complements rather than substitutes.[1] But the advantages of foot voting as a tool for enhancing political freedom should incline us to give it a much broader scope than we might otherwise.

Meaningful, Informed Choice

Effective freedom requires the ability to make a decisive choice, or at least have a high probability of doing so. It is difficult to claim that a person has meaningful freedom if the individual has only a 1 in a million or 1 in 100 million chance of making a decision that changes an outcome. For example, one does not have meaningful religious freedom if she has only a 1 in a million chance of being able to determine which religion she wishes to practice. Similarly, a person with only a 1 in a million chance of deciding what views she is allowed to express surely does not have meaningful freedom of speech.

What is true of freedom of speech and freedom of religion is also true of political freedom. A person with only an infinitesimal chance of affecting what kind of government policies he or she is subjected to has little, if any, genuine political freedom. And that is exactly the position voters find themselves facing in all but the very smallest of elections. In an American presidential election, for example, the average voter has only about a 1 in 60 million chance of affecting the outcome.[2] In smaller elections, the odds are higher but still generally very low.

As political scientist Russell Hardin put it, "most citizens do not typically have the ability to actually to make any difference to their own welfare through politics."[3] Hardin notes that "if my vote is worthless . . . having the liberty to cast it is roughly as valuable as having the liberty to cast a vote on whether the sun will come up tomorrow."[4] In fairness, casting a vote in an election is not *completely* worthless. There is a small chance that your vote really will change an electoral outcome, and situations where an election was tied or won by a single vote have occurred a few times in history.[5] But such cases are extraordinarily rare.

The individual voter's infinitesimally small odds of affecting electoral outcomes also undermine political freedom in a second way: they ensures that most will not make the effort to acquire the information necessary for well-informed decisions.[6] On many normative views of freedom, its effective exercise requires at least a reasonably informed choice, at least when it comes to important issues.

Widely accepted standards of medical ethics, for example, require physicians to secure the patient's informed consent before performing an operation. As the American Medical Association's Code of Medical Ethics puts it, "[t]he patient's right of self-decision can be effectively exercised only if the patient possesses enough information to enable an informed choice."[7] Like many medical decisions, political choices also are often literally matters of life and death. For millions of people, the outcome of an election might make the difference between war and peace, wealth and poverty, or sickness and health.

Unfortunately, few electoral decisions meet the standard posited by the AMA. Ballot box voters have strong incentives to be "rationally ignorant," because there is so little chance that their votes will matter. In a situation where there is little or no benefit to acquiring additional knowledge, it is often perfectly rational for individuals to remain largely or completely ignorant about the questions at issue.[8]

Survey data show that voters often lack even very basic knowledge about the candidates and policy questions at issue in any given election.[9] They also often have little incentive to analyze whatever information they do learn, in a logical, unbiased way. To the contrary, voters have incentives to fall prey to "rational irrationality": when there are few or no negative consequences to error, it is rational to make almost no effort to control one's biases.[10] For example, many routinely overvalue any evidence that supports their preexisting views while downplaying or ignoring anything that cuts the other way.[11]

Rational ignorance and rational irrationality affect the decisions of altruistic voters as well as those who are narrowly self-interested. Even a citizen who is strongly motivated to help others still has little incentive to devote more than a small amount of effort to acquiring political knowledge and trying to rein in his or her biases. Whether her purposes are self-interested or not, the odds that her efforts will pay off are extremely low. This makes it rational for both egoists and altruists to severely limit the time and effort devoted to acquiring and analyzing political information.[12]

Rational ignorance does not necessarily require careful, calculated decision-making. In many cases, it involves merely application of crude rules of thumb or an intuitive sense that there is little benefit to seeking out additional knowledge. Thus, the idea is not dependent on the assumption that voters are hyperlogical or capable of making complex calculations about odds. Indeed, such a detailed calculation may itself be irrational, since it may require more time and effort than can be justified given the likely benefit.[13]

Decades of survey data indicate that voter knowledge levels are low and have experienced little or no increase despite rising educational attainment as well as the development of the internet and other modern technology that makes information easier to access.[14] Often, the majority of the public does not know even basic information, such as which party controls Congress, what major policies have been enacted, or which elected officials are responsible for which issues.[15] Just before the 2014 election, in which the main stake at issue was control of Congress, only 38 percent of voters knew which party controlled the House of Representatives, and a similar percentage knew which controlled the Senate.[16] Another 2014 survey found that only 36 percent of Americans can even name the three branches of the federal government: the executive, the legislative, and the judicial.[17] Despite growing fiscal problems, most of the public also has little understanding of how the federal government spends its money—greatly underestimating the percentage of the budget that goes to major entitlement programs (among the biggest categories of federal spending), while massively overestimating that allocated to foreign aid (which is only about 1 percent of the budget).[18]

Survey data indicate that there is similar ignorance in other democracies. It is not a problem unique to the United States, and also occurs in a wide range of democratic nations in Europe and elsewhere, including those that have larger welfare states and more redistribution than the United States.[19] This undercuts claims that the problem can be significantly alleviated by reducing economic inequality.[20]

An informed electorate is a public good, in the economic sense of the term:[21] people benefit from its production even if they have not contributed to its creation, each individual's contribution is infinitesimally small, and the benefits are "nonrivalrous"—my enjoyment of them is not reduced by that of other members of society and vice versa. Like many other public goods, it tends to be underproduced, because individuals have strong incentives to underinvest in it. Informed foot voting, by contrast, is largely a "private" good that avoids this problem: individuals have strong incentives to produce it for themselves, because they stand to reap the benefits.

Foot voting is superior to ballot box voting on both decisiveness and the incentive to make an informed decision. It enables the individual decision-maker to make a meaningful choice. For those who must move with family members, that choice may not be completely decisive. Family members (at least those who are adults) must generally reach a joint decision of some kind. But each individual still has vastly greater leverage than in almost any ballot box vote. He or she can still make choices that actually matter, or at least have a high probability of doing so.

And precisely because their decisions do matter, foot voters have strong incentives to acquire relevant information and use it wisely.[22] The person deciding where to live or what choices to make in the marketplace and civil society knows that her decisions have real consequences. She therefore generally makes more effort to acquire information. Extensive empirical evidence backs these theoretical predictions, showing that foot voters outperform ballot box voters even when laboring under difficult conditions.[23]

Some political theorists critical of the effectiveness of exit rights worry that indoctrination and socialization through upbringing might prevent people in unjust circumstances from realizing that they would be better off elsewhere.[24] This is a legitimate concern, but one that is actually much more severe in the case of ballot box voting, where incentives to consider new information and arguments that run counter to one's own preexisting views and the dominant orientation of society are much weaker.

Historically, even many citizens of totalitarian societies that engage in comprehensive censorship and indoctrination have come to understand that they would be better off in relatively freer nations—as witness the need for such states as the Soviet Union, North Korea, and East Germany to forbid and severely punish attempts at emigration to prevent their population from fleeing. By contrast, ballot box voters, even in relatively free societies, often cling to serious errors in the face of opposing evidence, refusing to consider information that runs counter to their preexisting views.[25]

Neither foot voters nor ballot box voters come close to complete objectivity in assessing new information that challenges their preconceptions. But the former generally come closer to that ideal than the latter.

Adam Przeworski, one of the world's leading academic experts on democracy, laments that "no rule of collective decisionmaking other than unanimity can render causal efficacy to equal individual participation."[26] In other words, short of requiring every decision to be unanimous, it seems difficult or impossible to come up with any decision-making system under which each individual has both an equal vote and a significant chance of affecting the outcome.

Foot voting is not perfect on this score. Among other things, equality of participation is constrained by moving costs—a problem to be considered in more detail in later chapters.[27] But it comes far closer than any other alternative. Foot voting can be made available to a very wide range of people. And, unlike ballot box voting, each individual choice has a high probability of being causally effective.

The informational advantages of foot voting loom even larger if we believe, as some political theorists do, that voters should engage in "deliberative democracy"—carefully considering opposing arguments and moral values, and not merely casting ballots based on their preferences.[28] Deliberative democracy demands a higher level of knowledge and analytical sophistication than more modest versions of democratic theory do. Rationally ignorant voters are even less likely to meet those standards than the less severe ones imposed by "aggregative" theories of democratic participation, which seek only to ensure that election results roughly reflect voters' preferences.[29]

Foot Voting and Theories of Political Freedom

In addition to its general advantages as a tool for meaningful informed choice, foot voting also trumps ballot box voting under four leading standard accounts of political freedom: consent, negative freedom, positive freedom, and nondomination. In this book, I do not attempt to resolve the long-standing disagreements between advocates of these different views. The case for foot voting is strong under all four approaches, though less unequivocally so in the case of positive freedom.

Consent

At least since John Locke and Thomas Hobbes in the seventeenth century, many political theorists have argued that the authority of the state is legitimized by consent.[30] Consent theory places intrinsic value on the ability of a person to choose the government he or she lives under, even aside from any consequences thereof, such as living under improved government policies.

Many claim that living in a territory controlled by a government constitutes "tacit consent" to its authority. Some theorists argue that the consent becomes more binding if residents accept the benefits of various government services, such as police, fire protection, welfare payments, and others.[31] This argument has a venerable history, dating back at least to Plato's *Crito*.[32] But it is ultimately unsound. As the saying goes, tacit consent is not worth the paper it isn't printed on.

The key flaw in the theory is that it assumes the validity of the very point that it is meant to prove: that government has the right to enact laws of a particular type in the first place. If mere physical or political control of a given territory gives government officials the power to issue commands as they wish, then of course residents are required to follow those laws. But the existence of such a right is in no way demonstrated merely because individuals have chosen not to leave the area, or because they benefit from some of the services the government offers.

Consider the case of an organized crime boss who has established a "territory" and has the power to punish residents of the area who disobey his decrees.[33] Assume, further, that the residents benefit from some "services" he provides, such as suppressing rival mobsters. Do residents have a moral obligation to obey his dictates or pay taxes to him whenever he demands it, because they have "consented" to it?

Obviously not, since the boss never had a moral right to issue such commands in the first place. The fact that people choose to live in the territory he claims does not establish that they have consented to obey him in any morally significant sense. What is true for organi lzed crime bosses is also true for governments: the mere fact that a government establishes control over a territory and at least some residents do not choose to leave does not prove that they are required to obey the government's dictates.

Perhaps the tacit consent argument becomes stronger if the government in question is democratic, and residents can express their will at the ballot box. Even if mere residency is not enough to prove consent, perhaps a combination of residency and participation in democratic elections is. Ballot box voting is often seen as an indicator of consent.[34]

This narrower version of tacit consent theory is more appealing than one that would give carte blanche to authoritarian rulers as well as democratic ones. But it still suffers from the same flaws as its more sweeping cousin. It too assumes the validity of the point it is intended to prove. The fact that a majority of residents have voted for a government that enacts a particular set of laws does not prove that either the majority or its representatives were morally entitled to make such decisions in the first place. As critics have pointed out, voting does not truly signify meaningful consent because, among other things, those who choose not to vote are not thereby exempted from obeying the state's laws.[35] If refusing to vote does not count as a legitimate rejection of the state's claims to authority, then the opportunity to cast a ballot does not qualify as acceptance.

This is particularly true if at least some of the residents never agreed to be ruled by the winners of the election, and never had a chance to vote on the logically prior question of whether they accept the underlying structure of the electoral system. Consenting to take part in an already established electoral process does not mean that the voter consented to allow the winners of the election to control any specific set of decisions if he or she never had any opportunity to reject the process.

Once a political system is established, one can rationally choose to vote for the "lesser evil" among the available candidates even if one would prefer that the relevant government not exist at all or have much more limited powers.

Consider a modification to the crime boss scenario. Imagine that the Corleone and Barzini Mafia families of *Godfather* fame each claimed to control a "territory" somewhere in New York City[36] but agreed among themselves that the right to reallocate property rights in the area would accrue to whichever of the two crime families won a majority of the residents' votes in a referendum. Let's say they allow a new referendum to take place every four years. Maybe they even permit other Mafia families to compete in their elections so long as they follow the electoral rules initially established by the Barzinis and Corleones. Few would contend that the Barzini–Corleone cartel is justified merely because their willingness to hold occasional elections proves that the residents have consented to let them tax, regulate, and punish at will.

Democracy is a useful tool for imposing a degree of accountability on government. The democratic Mafia cartel is likely to be less oppressive than the more authoritarian system described earlier. But democracy does not by itself justify the state's claims to authority over anyone who happens to live in a given area.

Foot voting is superior to ballot box voting as an indicator of consent, because those who move out of a jurisdiction really can escape all (or at least most) of its laws. It is still not entirely clear what, if anything, gives the government the right to claim initial authority over the territory it controls. But such authority is more consensual (or at least less coercive) the more those subject to it have opportunities to avoid its reach.

The degree of consensuality here is significantly reduced by moving costs. But greater decentralization can mitigate that, at least to a substantial degree. Foot voting is less costly when moving from state to state than internationally, and less costly still when choosing between localities or between private sector alternatives.[37]

Private sector foot voting potentially offers even greater options, and even lower moving costs than decentralized government. In many cases, we can switch providers of private sector services without physically moving at all.[38] When choosing between private planned communities, there can often be numerous options within a short distance of each other.[39]

While expanded foot voting might not make political power fully consensual, it comes closer than ballot box voting. The more foot-voting options we have, and the greater the ease of exercising them, the more consensual government becomes.

Negative Freedom

Another possible approach to political freedom links it to "negative" freedom more generally: people have greater political freedom to the extent that they can minimize unwanted coercive government interference with their choices.[40] On this view, the ability to choose the government you live under is important in part because it may reduce coercion in and of itself, and partly because it helps the decision maker escape specific coercive policies.

Foot voting generally offers greater protection for negative freedom than ballot box voting: the ability to completely, or at least largely, avoid unwanted interference creates greater negative freedom than the ability to cast a vote that has only an infinitesimal chance of having an impact.

It is also important to remember that restrictions on freedom of movement are themselves a major imposition on negative freedom. When governments block would-be migrants from entering or leaving, they prevent millions of people from freely contracting with willing residents who wish to employ them, rent property to them, and otherwise interact with the would-be migrants.[41] In the case of restrictions on international migration, they forcibly confine large numbers of people to a lifetime of poverty and oppression in less-developed nations. Few government interventions in the market and civil society restrict the negative freedom of so many people so severely.[42]

To a greater extent than consent, negative freedom is not just about the ability to choose the government policies we prefer to live under but also about the impact of those policies and the extent to which they constrain the negative liberty of those subject to them. But enhancing the ability to choose one government over another through foot voting can help greatly reduce exposure to such coercive policies.

Positive Freedom

Many modern political thinkers argue for a more "positive" approach to freedom that focuses on "capabilities." On this view, freedom is not just noninterference but the actual ability to exercise autonomy, pursue your preferred projects, and enhance your capacities.[43] From the standpoint of positive freedom, individuals' relationships with government should be judged by the extent to which living under those states' policies can help increase their capacities and opportunities. Like negative freedom, the positive variety focuses on the impact of government policies on individuals rather than on the origins of the relationship between them and the state.

From a positive freedom standpoint, the ability to choose the government policies one lives under has primarily instrumental rather than intrinsic value. Nonetheless, here too, foot voting often offers better prospects than ballot box voting. Admittedly, the connection here is much more equivocal than with consent, negative freedom, and nondomination.[44] At least in theory, a policy enacted through ballot box voting could potentially enhance positive freedom for many people to a much greater extent than is possible through any realistically feasible foot-voting options. Nonetheless, foot voting often offers better opportunities than ballot box voting.

A foot voter can potentially choose between a wide variety of governmental and private alternatives that might help him or her develop capabilities and pursue a range of possible projects. By contrast, most ballot box voters have almost no control over options available to them. Moreover, foot voters are more likely than ballot box voters to make well-informed and unbiased choices.[45] Widespread political ignorance—which is even greater among the poor and disadvantaged than among other voters,[46] often prevents the enactment of policies that might genuinely enhance positive freedom, while incentivizing many that perversely undermine it.

Some poor and disadvantaged people may need redistributive programs to develop their capabilities and to help them exercise positive freedom more fully. This book does not try to address the extent to which redistribution is desirable or morally essential. But, as discussed more fully in Chapter 2, robust foot-voting opportunities are potentially compatible with extensive redistribution. Expanding foot-voting opportunities is compatible with a wide range of views on redistribution.

It is also important to stress that foot voting is itself a powerful mechanism for increasing the income and economic well-being of the poor, often a more powerful one than any form of redistribution. Foot voting opportunities have been of special value to the poor and oppressed and tend to benefit them even more than the relatively well-off.[47]

International migration is a particularly potent tool for enhancing positive freedom. Economists estimate that allowing free migration throughout the world would likely double world GDP.[48] Much of that benefit would go to migrants from poor nations where opportunities to enhance their capacities would otherwise be severely limited at best. As in the case of negative freedom, the effects are enormous, often doubling or tripling the income of the migrants in question.[49] It is difficult to think of any other policy change that would enhance positive freedom for so many people so quickly.

John Rawls' theory of political liberty can be seen as a special case of positive freedom.[50] He argues that a just state must protect the "fair value" of the right to participate in the political process, in order to promote "just legislation" and ensure "that the fair political process specified by the constitution is open to everyone on a basis of rough equality."[51] To achieve these goals, all citizens must "have a fair opportunity to hold public office and to influence the content of political decisions."[52]

This qualifies as a theory of "positive" freedom because it requires more than just noninterference with personal autonomy, such as the right to freedom of speech, but also potentially affirmative measures to ensure a positive opportunity to influence the political process on a roughly equal basis.

Rawls's discussion of "fair value" is somewhat imprecise and focuses mainly on ensuring that all have relatively equal opportunity to influence policy.[53] But if "fair value" of political liberty is truly important enough to be a core element of liberty in Rawls' theory,[54] it seems strange to conclude that it can be achieved by a process in which the individual citizen has almost no chance of actually affecting the content of the policies he or she is required to live under. Even if the citizen's influence is equal or close to equal to those of others, its "value" remains utterly insignificant. Equality in near-powerlessness has, at best, only extremely limited "fair value."

Even if we include opportunity to hold public office along with the right to vote, as Rawls indicates we should, most citizens will have only a tiny chance of ever achieving either the former or the latter. This is particularly true of important offices in the central governments of large nations, such as the United States. For example, at any given time, only 535 out of over 300 million Americans can be members of Congress, only one can be the president, and only a tiny number of others can hold high-ranking policymaking positions in the executive branch.

A much higher degree of genuinely fair value can be achieved by ensuring broad opportunity for foot voting, which can combine at least a considerable degree of equality with an opportunity to exercise genuinely meaningful influence over the policies the citizen lives under.[55] Rawls wrote that one of the purposes of the "fair value" principle is to "enhance the self-esteem and sense of political competence of the average citizen."[56] If so, surely that can often be better achieved by a mechanism where the average citizen knows that her decisions are highly likely to make a difference to the outcome, as opposed to one where that likelihood is infinitesimally small.

Even if "fair value" is purely a matter of equality, as opposed to substantive influence over policy, foot voting still should be an important component of Rawls' theory of political liberty, properly understood. As discussed later in this chapter, substantial inequality in political influence is likely unavoidable in a ballot-box voting system. Foot voting opportunities can be particularly valuable to those whose political influence is likely to be weakest, such as those who are unpopular, lacking in political skills, and have other disadvantages in the political process. Historically, foot voting has been especially valuable for politically weak and unpopular groups.[57]

For both positive and negative freedom, the benefits of foot voting go far beyond the narrowly "economic." Expanded foot-voting opportunities can also massively enhance migrants' freedom and well-being more generally. Consider, for example, women fleeing patriarchal societies, religious minorities fleeing oppression, and people fleeing repressive tyrannical regimes of various kinds.

From the standpoint of enhancing positive freedom by expanding human capabilities,[58] the noneconomic benefits of foot voting may be just as important as the enhancement of productivity, conceived in narrow "economic" terms. In many cases, escaping noneconomic oppression enables migrants to enormously enhance their capacities in a variety of ways. The full scope of these effects is probably impossible to quantify. But there is little doubt that they are massive.

Nondomination

Some political theorists argue that the true essence of political freedom is "nondomination": the state of being free from the arbitrarily imposed will of others.[59] Phillip Pettit, a leading advocate of nondomination theory, describes its objective as the absence of "involuntary exposure to the will of others" and the securing of "the freedom that goes with not having to live under the potentially harmful power of another."[60] Like consent theory, nondomination places intrinsic value on the ability to choose the government policies we live under. Even if domination is benevolent, it is still—on this view—wrongful.[61]

By this standard, too, foot voting trumps ballot box voting.[62] In most cases, the individual ballot box voter finds herself under the complete domination of whichever political forces prevail in electoral competition—at least with respect to whatever issues come within the control of democratic government. And she generally has only an infinitesimal chance of changing any of their policies. If a dictator controls important aspects of your life, but gives you a 1 in 100 million chance of changing his decisions, it is pretty obvious that you are dominated by him. The same is true if a democratic majority controls your life in the same way.

Domination by a democratic majority is likely be more benevolent and less onerous than domination by a dictator. But relatively benevolent domination is domination nonetheless. A benevolent dictator who honestly seeks to improve the lot of his subjects still exercises domination over them. Nondomination theorists explicitly emphasize that benevolence does not vitiate domination—indeed, that domination is present even if the ruler merely has the ability to exercise power over his subjects, but never actually uses it.[63] The same is true of a democratic majority that similarly strives for benevolence, or even one that simply chooses not to exercise its authority, despite having the power to do so.

This point also applies to situations where a democratic majority is likely to promote an individual's interests because the electorate includes many people with similar interests and identities. For example, an electorate that includes women and racial minorities is, other things equal, more likely to protect the interests of such people than one in a society where these groups are barred from the franchise.[64]

An inclusive franchise can play a valuable role in protecting various social groups (though it can also, of course, sometimes result in a tyranny of the majority).[65] But it does not dispense with the problem of nondomination. The individual voter is still dominated by the views of the majority political coalition and still has almost no chance of influencing the policies adopted by the government.

Those policies may be more favorable to the voter's interests than they would be in a regime with a more restricted franchise. But, as we have already seen, the benevolence does not vitiate the problem of domination. If representation of various social groups in a democratic electorate prevents domination because it helps ensure those groups' views have an impact on government policy, then we could also eliminate domination through government by a small but demographically representative oligarchy, in which women, minorities, and other social groups are represented in whatever proportion is considered proper under the "correct" theory of nondomination. Indeed, such an oligarchy might be even more demographically representative than a democratic electorate, in which there are sometimes differences in turnout between groups.

Philip Pettit contends that a democratic regime can avoid domination if its citizens enjoy "equality of influence" and the exercise of power is limited by institutional constraints, such as separation of powers, judicial review, and various political norms.[66] Each of these institutional features of a political system has value. But none actually avoids the problem of domination.

It is difficult to see how equality of influence can prevent domination. Even if each citizen has exactly the same amount of political influence, each is still dominated by the political majority in so far as he or she has little or no chance to change policy. The fact that everyone else is similarly dominated does not change this basic situation.

Institutional constraints on the exercise of power can potentially reduce domination by making it more difficult to enact laws and regulations and—in the case of judicial review—by potentially eliminating some issues from the scope of governmental authority entirely. For example, judicial review could forbid restrictions on freedom of speech or religion.

Nonetheless, individual citizens are still dominated within whatever sphere the government remains able to pass laws. In the case of separation of powers or supermajority rules, the institutional constraints in question merely increase the number of people who must agree to a given exercise of authority. For example, in a bicameral system, a law might have to be passed by both houses of the legislature. In a presidential separation of powers system, it might also be subject to veto by the executive. Such limitations may have great value in improving the quality of decision making and curbing some types of harmful policies. But they do not necessarily reduce the scope of state power, nor the extent to which those who wield it exercise domination over the citizenry.

For Pettit, the institution of slavery epitomizes domination, because the master enjoys vast power to interfere with the slave's choices "with impunity and at will," and the slave has no ability to avoid the master's authority.[67] Presumably, the slave is still dominated even if she is not owned by an individual master but by a group who make decisions by majority vote, or—say—by a two-thirds supermajority. Within slavery, domination is likewise still present even if the master is limited by laws and norms that restrict the range of punishments he can inflict on those who refuse his orders. Some restrictions of this type actually did exist in the pre-Civil War American South,[68] yet surely no one could seriously claim that the slaves were thereby freed from domination.

Similarly, the fact that the powers of a democratic state may be constrained by institutional limits or norms does not eliminate domination within whatever sphere the government still controls. Separation of powers, bicameralism, and other similar institutions might make it more difficult to exercise power, but they do not eliminate its existence. Pettit's appeal to the importance of "norms"[69] actually has much in common with defenses of dictatorship and oligarchy that rely on the benevolence of the rulers to protect the people. Kings, aristocrats, oligarchs, and other nondemocratic rulers are also usually constrained by norms of various types, including some that may be strongly internalized. Yet that is not enough, on Pettit's theory, to free their subjects from domination. The same is true of democratic governments that are constrained by norms.

Democracy is superior to dictatorship in many ways, and ballot box voting plays an important role in maintaining that superiority. Among other things, democracy leads to better outcomes on a wide range of economic and human rights dimensions than dictatorship,[70] and it can impose important constraints on the power of political elites.[71] But it cannot ensure political freedom defined as nondomination. Domination by a democratic majority is generally less onerous than domination by a slaveowner or despot. But it is still domination nonetheless.

By contrast, foot voting does much better. If extensive opportunities for foot voting are institutionalized, the foot voter can often use exit rights to escape unwanted impositions and thereby greatly reduce conditions of domination, even if not completely eliminate them.

If a foot voter can choose from a variety of options, he or she is no longer subject to domination by the will of any individual ruler, employer, or political majority. At the very least, he faces far less risk of domination than a person whose only recourse is ballot box voting.[72] The slave who can refuse the master's orders and escape his control is no longer a slave at all and is thereby freed from domination—at least to a large extent. The same goes for a citizen who can use foot-voting to avoid the dictates of democratic government.

Information Shortcuts and "Miracles of Aggregation"

Some scholars argue that we need not worry much about widespread political ignorance, because voters can use "information shortcuts" to make good decisions—small bits of knowledge that substitute for larger bodies of information they do not know. Alternatively, even if individual voters tend to be ignorant, the electorate as a whole might still make good decisions because of its high level of aggregate knowledge: the so-called miracle of aggregation."[73] If true, these theories might diminish voter-ignorance concerns about ballot box voting. Unfortunately, however, they are not nearly as compelling as advocates claim.

I have criticized both shortcut theories and "miracle of aggregation" arguments in detail in my previous book, *Democracy and Political Ignorance*.[74] Here, I will only go over a few key points.

Information Shortcuts

There are many types of information shortcuts that advocates claim can substitute for more extensive political knowledge. Perhaps the best-known example is so-called retrospective voting, under which voters can choose to reelect or remove incumbents based on whether things have improved under their rule or not. In theory, retrospective voters need not know anything about the details of government policy or party platforms. As one advocate puts it, "[i]n order to ascertain whether the incumbents have performed well or poorly citizens need only calculate the changes in their own welfare."[75] Ronald Reagan effectively captured this idea in during the 1980 presidential election, when he famously said that in order to figure out who to support, voters need only ask themselves, "are you better off than you were four years ago?"[76] Other shortcut theories emphasize the potential value of knowledge gained from everyday life,[77] identification of candidates with political parties,[78] and cues from trusted "opinion leaders"—people with values similar to those of the voters, but superior knowledge of policy issues, and therefore can potentially function as trusted intermediaries guiding voter decisions.[79]

Despite their variety, shortcut theories share two common flaws: they often require considerable preexisting knowledge to use them effectively, and they do not address the problem of "rational irrationality"—voters' bias in the evaluation of information. For example, effective retrospective voting requires understanding what issues particular incumbents are responsible for, and what impact they have had on them. If voters are ignorant on these points, they could easily end up rewarding and punishing incumbents for events they did not cause, while overlooking those they do have an impact on.

Sadly, that is exactly what happens in most elections. Voters routinely reelect or defeat incumbents based on short-term economic trends the latter have little if any control over.[80] Electorates also reward and punish incumbents for a wide range of other events outside their control, including shark attacks, droughts, and even local sports team victories.[81] Similarly, voters also often fail to understand which office-holders are responsible for which issues, and thereby attribute responsibility to the wrong officials.[82]

The effectiveness of retrospective voting is also often undermined by bias in the evaluation of information. The theory implicitly assumes that voters objective consider the state of the world and then judge incumbent politicians by what they see. But, in reality, the reverse is often true. Partisan and other biases often skew perceptions of underlying reality, causing voters to believe that conditions are better than they really are when their preferred party is in power, and worse than they are when the opposing party is.[83] For example, Republicans tend to believe that inflation and unemployment are higher than is actually the case when a Democrat is in the White House, while Democratic voters have the opposite bias.[84]

When voters reward and punish incumbents for things they did not do or act on highly biased perceptions of reality, retrospective voting not only fails to offset voter ignorance. It may even make the situation worse than before. Similar problems beset other information shortcuts.[85] They too often require information that most voters do not know, and they too routinely fall prey to biases exacerbated by rational irrationality.

The amount of preexisting knowledge needed to use shortcuts effectively is exacerbated by the enormous size, scope, and complexity of modern government. That makes it much harder to find a few simple rules of thumb that suffice to address the full range of issues at stake in modern elections.[86]

The flaws of shortcuts cannot be overcome if voters simply make choices based on their "values" while leaving the details of policy to others. Many important political disagreements come down to differences over how to achieve widely shared values, such as economic prosperity, national security, crime reduction, and environmental protection. Deciding between the competing options requires factual knowledge, not just moral principles.[87]

In addition, to the extent that values are important to political choice, it is unlikely that rationally ignorant and biased voters will do any better in assessing competing values than in assessing competing policies intended to achieve a shared goal. Unless we are pure moral relativists, we must admit the possibility that voters might sometimes make choices based on wrong values, such as racism, sexism, or militarism. If, on the other hand, we deny that any set of values can be superior to another, we also have no basis for preferring liberal democracy to any other type of political regime, such as monarchy, theocracy, or a totalitarian state.[88] There would then be no basis for preferring the values of one regime to another.

Shortcuts are by no means completely useless. In some situations, they can help voters make good decisions. For example, retrospective voting can be effective in cases where incumbents have failed in large and obvious ways, such as by losing a war or deliberately causing a famine.[89] But most government policies are more complicated than this and require greater knowledge to properly understand and assess.[90]

Miracles of Aggregation?

Even if most individual voters are generally ignorant, the electorate as a whole could potentially make well-informed decisions. One possible mechanism by which this could happen is that poorly informed voters could cancel each other out, thereby enabling the well-informed minority to control electoral outcomes.[91]

Assume, for example, that an electorate of 10 million voters is choosing between a Democratic candidate and a Republican one, and that 90 percent of them are poorly informed, and make decisions based on ignorance. If their ignorance-driven errors are randomly distributed, then almost exactly half of the ignorant group (45 percent) will choose the Democratic candidate based on their flawed reasoning, and a very similar number will choose the Republican. Poorly informed votes for the Democrats will be offset by poorly informed votes for Republicans, leaving the true outcome to be determined by the knowledgeable minority of 10 percent, who—by assumption—have a far better understanding of the issues at stake.

Another way in which the collective electorate might make good decisions despite the ignorance of individual voters is by taking advantage of its superior aggregate knowledge.[92] A large group with a low average level of knowledge might nonetheless have a high level of total knowledge, perhaps greater than that of a smaller group in which each individual knows far more than the average member of the larger group. For example, a group of 100 voters, each of whom knows one unit of information, has a higher total level of knowledge than a group of 10 people, each of whom knows 5 units. Although the average member of the smaller group knows 5 times more than the average member of the larger one, the latter group still has twice as much total knowledge (100 units) as the former (50 units). In this way, "diversity trumps ability"—a large, diverse group, can know more than a smaller, more expert one.[93]

Unfortunately, neither of these versions of miracle-of-aggregation theory even comes close to accurately describing real-world electorates. The errors-cancel-out version fails because real-world errors caused by ignorance rarely cancel each other out, for the simple reason that they are rarely randomly distributed. Errors in one direction tend to be more common than those in the other. And in a large group, if one type of error is even slightly more common than the other, it will almost certainly be decisive in determining the outcome.[94]

In addition, the knowledgeable minority that supposedly determines the outcome when effects of ignorance are indeed random is often highly unrepresentative of the larger electorate. In the United States, for example, its members tend to be wealthier, and more likely to be white and male than the American electorate as a whole.[95]

The diversity-trumps-ability version of aggregation theory also turns out to be overly optimistic. Among other flaws, it assumes that voters have enough basic general knowledge of the political system to be able to properly assess the ways in which their more specific individual knowledge applies to the issues at stake in an election. As Helene Landemore, a leading academic advocate of the theory, puts it, diversity is only likely to trump individual knowledge if the participants in the diverse group are "relatively smart (or not too dumb)."[96]

In addition, the theory also assumes that individual voters make their decisions objectively and independently based on their own private knowledge, as opposed to being influenced by the views of others and by cognitive biases of the sort incentivized by rational irrationality.[97] Neither assumption holds true in most real-world situations. Voters are routinely influenced by misconceptions widespread in society, and their evaluation of political information is often highly biased.[98] Even relatively small biases of this kind can easily unsettle the "diversity trumps ability theory" and cause a large group with low average levels of information to make serious systematic errors.[99]

Deliberation and Political Participation "Beyond Voting"

Ballot box voting is not the only way citizens can influence government policy in a democratic political system. They can also do so by engaging in political speech, activism, demonstrations, lobbying, campaign contributions, and other such activities. Does the availability of such options mitigate the shortcomings of ballot box voting as a mechanism of political freedom? If so, it could reduce or even completely eliminate the advantages of foot voting. Unfortunately, such a happy scenario is both empirically dubious and, in some ways, impossible even in theory. The same goes for efforts to mitigate political ignorance and enhance political freedom by increasing opportunities for deliberation.

Political Participation "Beyond Voting"

In some cases, participation beyond voting surely does enable individual citizens to increase their influence over policy. Prominent activists, intellectuals, campaign donors, and others surely have influence far greater than that of the average voter. Nonetheless, participation beyond voting does not and cannot overcome the difficulties inherent in the insignificance of any one vote to electoral outcomes.

One problem is that participation beyond voting is very unequally distributed. A recent study found that only about 25 percent of Americans engage in such activities at all.[100] Those who participate in this way differ from the rest of the population in terms of both policy preferences and background characteristics, such as income, race, and gender.[101]

If political participation beyond voting is unequally distributed and largely confined to a relatively small minority of the population, its effect is to increase the political leverage of some people only by reducing that of others. A simple example illustrates the point: imagine an electorate that consists of 1 million citizens. Initially, the only way any of them can influence electoral outcomes is by casting votes at the ballot box. But due to a technological change or an increase in her capabilities, one member of the electorate, Jane Smith, manages to increase her influence by a factor of 1,000. She now has as much electoral clout as 1,000 conventional voters previously did. This greatly increases her odds of affecting electoral outcomes. But it also proportionately reduces the leverage of everyone else, which is diminished to the exact same degree as Smith's influence is increased.

The same point applies if Smith's increased influence takes the form of affecting policymaking by pathways other than influencing electoral results. The more influence she has over policy, the less is available to everyone else.

Given enormous differences in capabilities, opportunities, and interest in politics, it is difficult to see how inequality in participation beyond voting can be eliminated, or even reduced to a low level. To the contrary, it seems likely to persist in any society where there are substantial inequalities in wealth, ability, acquired skills, and interest in politics.

But even in a quasi-utopian world where participation beyond voting was completely equalized, the problem of the insignificance of individual voters' influence would still persist. If each person had exactly the same ability to exercise influence by using methods other than voting, then each individual's influence beyond voting would be insignificant for much the same reasons as each individual vote currently is. In a society where an individual vote has only a 1 in 60 million chance of influencing electoral outcomes,[102] each person's participation beyond voting would have exactly the same odds of determining the result, if such participation were equalized to the same degree as voting is. The same goes for opportunities to influence policy by means other than affecting election results, so long as those opportunities are also equally distributed.

The fundamental problem is that political influence is a zero-sum game. If some people gain more of it, it can only be by reducing the influence of others. In a dictatorship or oligarchy, the rulers have enormous political influence, but only by denying access to power to all or most of the rest of the population. The same is true, albeit to a less extreme degree, in a democracy where some citizens wield far greater influence than others.

In a hypothetical society where political influence is equally distributed, such equality can only be guaranteed (if at all) by simultaneously ensuring that the leverage of each individual is infinitesimally small. The only exception might be a society with an extremely small population, where each individual vote is likely to have greater significance. But such tiny micropolities probably cannot handle many of the larger-scale issues that arise in modern societies.[103]

If participation beyond voting does not eliminate the insignificance of any single vote, it also cannot mitigate the problem of rational ignorance. Currently, people who participate beyond voting have somewhat higher levels of political knowledge than the rest of the population.[104] But this is unlikely to hold true in a society where such participation is equally distributed. In that world, each person's influence beyond voting would be just as infinitesimal as their influence at the ballot box. Neither would provide much incentive to achieve more than minimal levels of political knowledge.

Moreover, those most interested in politics—the people most likely to engage in political participation beyond voting—also tend to be the most biased in their evaluation of the information they do know.[105] By engaging emotions such as partisan bias and hatred of political opponents, participation beyond voting may actually lead to more poorly informed decision making, even if those involved in the process know more facts.

Increasing Knowledge through Deliberation

In recent years, a number of scholars have argued that we can greatly mitigate the problem of political ignorance by increasing opportunities for deliberation.[106] Such proposals come in two general types. Some try to get the entire population to engage in greater deliberation, and thereby increase their understanding of the issues they vote on. For example, Bruce Ackerman and James Fishkin's "Deliberation Day" proposal would establish a national day during which voters across the nation would be incentivized to hear presentations about the issues at stake in an upcoming election, and deliberate together about them.[107] More commonly, proposals to increase deliberation rely on "sortition": randomly selecting a small, representative fraction of the population to make decisions on behalf of the rest. Because each of the voters in the small group chosen by sortition would carry far greater weight than a vote in a conventional election, the participants would have incentives to seek out more information and consider it more carefully.

Some sortition proposals would rely on the small groups to make policy decisions across the board, or to select political leaders in place of the broader, conventional electorate.[108] Others would give each small group of sortition-selected voters a different, more narrowly defined task, such as deliberating over one particular area of policy.[109]

In previous work, I have criticized different variants of these proposals in some detail.[110] Here, I emphasize a few key points that are especially relevant to the issue of political freedom.

First, even if these proposals for increasing deliberation work exactly as advertised, they still would not change the fact that almost all voters have only an infinitesimal chance of influencing policy outcomes. Where the deliberation in question is conducted by the entire voting population, each individual's likelihood of influencing the outcome would be about the same as before, even if they ended up casting their votes in a better-informed manner.

Where the deliberation is conducted by a small group selected through sortition, those selected might potentially have very great influence. But those not selected by the sortition process would have even less ability to influence policy than before. Here, as elsewhere, increasing the political influence of one part of the population reduces the influence of others.[111]

The second problem is that deliberation proposals are unlikely to result in the sorts of improvements in political knowledge that advocates claim. There are several massive obstacles to such success. One is that the enormous size and scope of modern government make it difficult for participants to become informed on more than a fraction of the relevant issues.[112] The deliberators can only do so if they serve as members of the "sorted" group for a very long time, thereby becoming a kind of quasi-professional political class of the type that sortition is intended to avoid in the first place.

The experience of juries in the legal system indicates that lay jurors have great difficulty dealing with complex scientific evidence and large-scale policy issues that come up in some cases.[113] This suggests they are likely to have similar or greater difficulty in dealing with public policy issues in settings where they have broader responsibilities than on a jury.

These problems can, to some degree, be mitigated by giving each group selected through sortition only a narrow area of responsibility. But that in turn creates serious difficulties in ensuring that the different groups do not work at cross-purposes and in weighing resource trade-offs between the issues handled by different groups.[114]

Whether they rely on sortition or on deliberation by the entire community of voters, deliberative democracy proposals are also highly vulnerable to manipulation by politicians and interest groups. Someone has to decide what issues will be on the agenda, which groups will handle which questions, and who will get to submit information or make presentations to the deliberators. For obvious reasons, each of these choices is ripe for abuse, and real-world interest groups and political leaders are likely to exploit them.[115]

For reasons covered in my book *Democracy and Political Ignorance*, I am also skeptical that voter knowledge and the quality of deliberation can be greatly improved by more conventional means, such as greater investment in education and reform of media coverage of politics.[116] At the very least, optimism on this score must be tempered by the painful reality that voter knowledge has not increased substantially in recent decades despite large increases in educational attainment (measured in terms of years of schooling), increased per pupil spending, and massive increases in the availability of information through online and other media.[117]

To the extent that deliberative democrats seek to promote decision making that is well-informed, they would be well advised to reconsider at least some of their traditional skepticism of foot-voting mechanisms. The latter incentivizes well-informed decision-making without requiring reliance on some small segment of the population or opening the door to agenda manipulation by powerful interest groups. It also enables a wide range of people to make choices that are individually decisive.

Foot voting probably cannot realize all the aspirations of deliberative democracy, especially in its more demanding forms, which require a high degree of sophisticated thinking. But it is at least likely to result in better-informed and more thoughtful decision making than ballot box voting.[118]

Is Foot Voting Truly "Political"?

Despite its advantages over ballot box voting, many might be tempted to dismiss the efficacy of foot voting as a mechanism for political freedom because the motivations of most foot voters are not sufficiently "political." Critics point out that the goals of many foot voters are actually primarily economic: seeking better jobs and housing, for example.[119] Thus, perhaps foot voting cannot be considered a form of political choice in any meaningful sense.

Such criticism ignores the fact that economic opportunities are often closely tied to public policy decisions: for example, job opportunities are often determined in large part by government policy decisions on labor markets, while housing costs are in large part the product of zoning decisions.[120] In the case of international migration, migrants' choice of destination country is often heavily influenced by the extent to which the government's policies protect economic freedom, which influences the availability of job opportunities for new arrivals.[121] Seemingly "economic" choices are usually at least in significant part "political."

The same is true of foot-voting decisions made in the private sector, at least with respect to issues that might otherwise be controlled by the government. Choices between private planned communities, for example, are often based on considerations of quality and cost similar to those that influence foot-voting decisions between local governments.[122]

If foot-voting decisions based on "economic" considerations do not qualify as exercises of political freedom, the same applies to many ballot box voting decisions. The biggest determinant of most electoral outcomes is the recent performance of the economy, often based on exercises of crude "retrospective voting" that gives little or no consideration to the extent to which incumbents are truly responsible for current economic conditions.[123]

In many cases, moreover, foot voters are not motivated solely or even primarily by narrowly "economic" considerations. The most obvious examples are migrants and refugees fleeing war or oppressive regimes of various kinds. Many internal migrants also fit that description, such as unpopular minorities moving to more tolerant jurisdictions.

Closely related to the claim that foot-voting decisions are "economic" rather than "political" is the idea that they cannot be truly political because they are generally motivated by narrow self-interest rather than the public interest.[124] Whether ballot-box voting decisions are motivated more by public-spirited considerations than self-interest is actually a disputed point among experts.[125] But even if, as I believe to be the case,[126] ballot-box voters are on average less self-interested than foot voters, it does not follow that the decisions of the latter are not meaningfully "political." After all, few would say that of ballot-box voters who, for example, choose which candidate to support based primarily on how it would affect their income, or their and their family's social status.

It is also a mistake to assume that self-interested political decision-making is necessarily worse than that based on calculations of societal interest. To the contrary, the latter may actually be far more dangerous than the former, especially if based on ignorance, bad values, harmful ideologies such as fascism or communism, or some combination of all three.[127]

It is also possible to argue that foot voting does not qualify as a meaningful endorsement of the political system chosen by migrants, because the latter are often fleeing terrible conditions out of desperation. Some move because "anything is better" than the awful status quo where they currently reside.

But if terrible initial circumstances undermine the validity of foot-voting decisions, the same is often true of ballot box voting decisions. Elections often turn on voters' rejection of what they see as a badly flawed status quo. The point is not that foot voting is ideal in this respect, but that it outperforms ballot box voting by enabling individuals to make more decisive choices, and by giving them better incentives to become informed.

Moreover, even if the initial impulse to move is a result of terrible conditions, a foot voter can still exercise meaningful choice if he or she has a wide range of options. That can occur in a federal system with a variety of jurisdictions, through international migration (if there is a wide range of nations open to migrants), or in the private sector (again, assuming there is a range of options). In such a situation, a foot voter's choice among multiple possible destinations does carry an element of endorsement, even if initially she decided to consider moving primarily to escape terrible circumstances.

Availability of a wide range of options can also mitigate the potential danger that migration will massively increase heterogeneity of preferences in a jurisdiction, thereby making it more difficult to satisfy a large proportion of them simultaneously. If there is a wide range of options available to potential movers, they can choose those where the existing package of policies set by current residents fits their needs well. In that scenario, many individual jurisdictions will be relatively homogenous in the preferences of their residents, but the existence of extensive "second order diversity" *between* jurisdictions creates a broad range of choice for foot voters.[128]

Finally, foot voting might not be properly "political" because it may not communicate any clear message as to why the movers chose one jurisdiction over another. If I move from Jurisdiction to A to Jurisdiction B, it might be difficult for government officials and others to figure out which policy differences were factors in my choice.

Fortunately, the effectiveness of foot voting as a mechanism of political choice does not depend on effective communication of this type. Even if no one else knows why any given set of foot voters acted as they did, they themselves presumably know, and still were able to choose which policies they wish to live under. If I move because my new jurisdiction has lower taxes, a cleaner environment, or better schools, I can enjoy the benefits of those policies even if no one else knows that was my motivation.

Another, related, constraint is that the attractiveness of a jurisdiction to foot voters may, in part, be the product of past government policies rather than present ones. For example, past policies might have established conditions that create employment and housing opportunities, but those policies are no longer in force, or no longer have the same beneficial effects. When foot voters make choices based on the effects of past policies, that makes it even more difficult to discern the "message" sent by their decisions.

This same problem, however, also bedevils ballot box voting, where retrospective voting—evaluating incumbents based on current conditions that may have been caused by policies they did not create, or that may not even be in force anymore—is a ubiquitous factor in most elections.[129] Foot voters, at least have stronger incentives than ballot box voters to try to determine whether current beneficial conditions (which may be the result of past policies), will endure in the future.

To the extent that clear communication is necessary, it can be partially achieved through studying patterns of foot-voting choices. For example, data indicate that American movers tend to seek out areas with relatively lower taxes, greater job opportunities, and relatively inexpensive housing.[130] Local and regional governments seeking to attract migrants can take account of these preferences and plan accordingly.

Such communication is necessarily imperfect. But the same is true to an even greater extent of ballot box voting, where it is often difficult or impossible to tell whether the winner of an election truly has a "mandate" for his or her policies and—if so—which ones.[131]

Are Foot Voting and Ballot Box Voting Complements or Substitutes?

Despite its significant advantages, foot voting probably cannot completely displace ballot box voting. So long as *some* government exists, there will be government policies that are not determined by foot voting alone. For that reason, foot voting cannot totally displace ballot box voting.

In some situations, the two institutions are not substitutes, but complements—each can enhance the effectiveness of the other. Forks and knives are useful even in the absence of the other, and sometimes serve as substitutes for each other; each can be used to pick up or cut certain types of food. But, much of the time, they are more effective together and increase each other's value. The same is true of foot voting and ballot box voting, which have value independent of the other, often serve as substitutes, but can also be mutually reinforcing.

While some libertarian anarchists argue that government can be completely replaced by voluntary private institutions,[132] I am skeptical they are correct and in any case do not try to defend that position here. Even if it is theoretically possible, it is unlikely that the complete abolition of government in any sizable area will be politically feasible in the foreseeable future.

To the extent this is true, foot voting cannot completely replace ballot box voting. Moreover, when foot voting takes place between jurisdictions controlled by governments—such as in federal systems and through international migration—it is to a large extent dependent on the existence of political institutions, including democratic ones.[133] Thus, it might not mitigate the problem of political ignorance, since foot voters will not have good choices unless ballot box voters are knowledgeable enough to incentivize good policies in at least some substantial number of jurisdictions—in which case the problem of ignorance may not be so significant to begin with. If ballot box voters indeed suffer from ignorance, they could easily end up killing off the policies that attracted foot voters in the first place—or not enact attractive policies to begin with.[134]

This is indeed a danger. But it is not as great a risk as critics claim.[135] Even if ballot-box voters are generally ignorant or do not care about attracting foot voters, some jurisdictions are likely to enact relatively good policies, if only through random variation. Once established, there is still a great deal of inertia in government, especially when it comes to changing long-established policy. Interest groups, bureaucracies, and others who have become habituated to the status quo will not easily accept change. If a policy has been in place for a long time, that is some evidence that it is unlikely to be radically altered in the short to medium term future.[136]

Moreover, at least in a system where subnational governments must raise a large proportion of their own funding,[137] they do in fact have strong incentives to adopt policies that attract foot voting taxpayers and businesses. Otherwise, they risk losing valuable tax revenue that can be spent on projects they value, or on efforts to help keep them in power.

Additional tax revenue is valuable to officials even if voters remain poorly informed and do not directly reward them for it. If nothing else, it can be useful in enriching the officials themselves and their political allies. Thus, competition can incentivize local and regional governments to cater to the needs of foot voters, even in the absence of electoral pressure to do so.[138]

Nonetheless, effective foot voting requires at least some minimum competence in political institutions in order to provide options for the foot voters to take advantage of. Foot voting, by itself, cannot ensure the availability of those options. But it can certainly help on the margin. By stimulating competition for foot voters, it can provide incentives for government officials to improve their performance.

Even if foot voting does not improve institutional quality, it can enable more people to live in areas with relatively good institutions, thus ensuring that more of the population live under relatively high-quality policies, even if the land area over which those policies apply does not increase. In some instances, competition for foot voters can even incentivize jurisdictions to expand the range of people who are offered ballot box voting rights, as in the notable case of western states in the nineteenth-century United States, which extended the ballot to women in order to entice more women to move there.[139]

The purpose of institutional development, like economic development, is to improve the quality of governance for people, not territories. Foot voting can do much to improve the former, even when it does little for the latter.[140]

Ballot box voting could, potentially, be completely dispensed with if it is replaced by some combination of foot voting and nondemocratic political institutions. Foot voters could then choose between jurisdictions run by different types of dictatorships and oligarchies. But I do not deny the strong evidence that democracy generally performs better than nondemocratic government.[141] So I see little justification for replacing democracy with dictatorship or oligarchy, as opposed to constraining it for purposes of enhancing foot voting opportunities.

Ultimately, this book does not provide a comprehensive theory of how government should be structured, or a complete account of the extent to which foot voting can displace ballot box voting, as opposed to complementing it. It does, however, explain ways in which giving greater scope to foot voting can enhance political freedom on many dimensions and address a wide range of objections to moving in that direction.

Conclusion

Foot voting has two major advantages over traditional ballot box voting that often make it a more effective tool for expanding political freedom. It cannot completely displace the ballot box as a mechanism of political choice. But expanding its domain can nonetheless have great value.

2

Foot Voting and Federalism

Choosing between regional and local governments in a federal system is perhaps the most common type of foot voting in many countries, and certainly the one that most readily comes to mind in discussions of the subject. As of 2012, Census Bureau data indicated there were over 89,000 local governments in the United States, in addition—of course—to the fifty states.[1] That provides a wide variety of options for foot voters seeking to exercise political freedom. Other federal systems also often have a range of alternatives for foot voters.[2]

This chapter explains how foot voting within federal systems enhances political freedom in a number of ways. It also addresses several potential downsides and limitations of this type of foot voting, including moving costs, the danger of races to the bottom, potential oppression of local minorities, the problem of immobile people and assets, and the difficulties arising from problems that are too large-scale to be addressed by subnational jurisdictions. These are genuine issues. But they are not as severe as is often claimed. Federal systems can be structured in ways that mitigate such problems.

As Charles Tiebout explained in a classic 1956 article on mobility and jurisdictional choice, foot voting can provide a wide range of options to potential movers even if jurisdictions make no special effort to compete.[3] Jurisdictions that, at least initially, cater solely to the preferences of current residents, can nonetheless provide valuable opportunities to foot voters, as well. The policies that appeal to the former can also attract at least some of the latter. And if the preferences of current residents differ across jurisdictions in ways that are reflected in public policy, that can create a variety of options for foot voters.

Many options can arise simply because local and regional governments try to meet the diverse preferences of their preexisting residents. But competition provides incentives for localities to offer still better alternatives that meet the needs of foot voters more fully.[4] While Tiebout focused on ways in which interjurisdictional mobility can enhance efficiency and human welfare in an environment with no interjurisdictional competition, this chapter explains how it can also expand political freedom and how competition can contribute to that outcome.

I do not attempt to provide anything approaching a comprehensive theory of the appropriate distribution of powers between different levels of government in a federal system. Foot voting is obviously far from the only consideration relevant to such analysis. But this chapter explains how political decentralization can create foot-voting opportunities and thereby enhance political freedom.

How Interjurisdictional Foot Voting Enhances Political Freedom

Throughout American history, foot voting between states and localities has done much to enhance freedom of choice and human welfare. The same has occurred in many other countries with multiple jurisdictions. Internal foot voting has often been a particularly massive boon for the poor and disadvantaged minorities.

By making it possible for people to choose between a wide range of options, foot voting under federalism increases the consensuality of government, for reasons covered in Chapter 1. It also helps increase negative freedom—the ability to escape unwanted government coercion. The same is true of nondomination. The more foot voters enjoy exit rights against local and regional governments, the less the latter can exercise domination over them.[5]

Foot voting within federal systems can also increase positive freedom. Historically, it has enabled many to migrate to areas where they are more productive and can increase their capabilities. It has also opened up numerous opportunities for the poor and for unpopular minorities.[6]

Many options can arise simply because local and regional governments try to meet the diverse preferences of their preexisting residents. But competition provides incentives for localities to offer still better options that meet the needs of foot voters more fully. Foot voting can be enhanced by political institutions that promote "competitive" federalism. If regional and local governments are required to raise all or most of their own funds by taxing their own residents, they will have stronger incentives to adopt policies that offer attractive options to potential migrants, in order to increase revenue.[7]

Foot Voting and Federalism in American History

American history dramatically illustrates how foot voting within federal systems can help enhance political freedom. The most famous example of successful foot voting in American history is, of course, westward migration to the frontier in the nineteenth century, in which millions moved west to settle the vast territories acquired in the 1803 Louisiana Purchase, the Mexican War of 1846–47, and other land acquisitions. Westward settlement provided expanded opportunity for millions of people, many of them poor by the standards of the time.[8]

But the United States also has an extensive history of other forms of internal foot voting, most notably that by ethnic and religious minorities seeking more tolerant jurisdictions. The best-known case is, of course, the migration of African Americans from the South to other parts of the country from the late nineteenth century on through the middle of the twentieth.

Between approximately 1880 and 1920, over 1 million southern-born African Americans migrated to the North or the West.[9] By 1920, such migrants accounted for some 10 percent of the total black population of the United States, which then stood at 10.4 million.[10] There was an even larger black migration from South to North in the years immediately following World War II.[11] A 1917 publication of the National Association for the Advancement of Colored People (NAACP) explained that migration to the North was "the most effective protest against Southern lynching, lawlessness, and general deviltry."[12]

African-American migration to the North is just one of a number of examples of oppressed minority groups using foot voting to better their lot. Other cases include the movement of the Mormons to Utah, fleeing persecution in the eastern states, and—in more modern times—the movement of gays and lesbians to cities and states with more tolerant policies.[13]

Much internal migration is driven by economic factors, such as the search for job opportunities and affordable housing. But economic migration is also often a form of political foot voting. State and local government policies on such issues as zoning, labor market regulation, and taxation has a major impact on the economic factors that incentivize internal migration.[14]

This was even to an important degree true of westward migration during the "frontier" era. In addition to free or cheap land and other narrowly "economic" opportunities, western territories also often offered new forms of governance that were more flexible and tolerant than those in the East. Contrary to the mythology of the "Wild West," these institutions often kept order and provided public goods better than their eastern counterparts.[15] Many western territorial and state governments also offered greater tolerance and a measure of equality to groups that were marginalized or excluded elsewhere. In order to attract more female settlers, for example, western governments were the first to give women the right to vote, starting with the Wyoming territory in 1869.[16] Freedom of movement combined with interjurisdictional competition also incentivized many states to adopted laws allowing married women to own and control property independent of their husbands, reversing the previous common law rule under which the husband controlled all of his wife's property.[17]

Foot voting in developing nations also generates large gains for the poor and disadvantaged. Increased development is often driven in large part by the migration of rural people to cities, where there are greater job opportunities. In China—the most dramatic recent example of this phenomenon— some 260 million people migrated from rural to urban areas between 1978 and 2012, usually in search of economic opportunity.[18] Much of the migration flow was toward special economic zones with better institutions.[19] This massive migration has been an important factor in the country's rapid economic development, accounting for somewhere between 20 and 33 percent of the stupendous economic growth China experienced from the late 1970s to the present.[20]

Foot voting can also generate major gains for poor people in affluent Western nations, including the United States. Recent research indicates that moving to an area with lower poverty rates can have particularly large benefits for the life prospects of poor children under the age of thirteen at the time of the move: substantially increasing their incomes and college attendance rates, while reducing the likelihood of them becoming single parents.[21]

Potential Limitations of Foot Voting Under Federalism

While foot voting under federalism can do much to enhance political freedom, it does have a number of downsides and limitations. These are genuine problems. But they are not as severe as often claimed, and much can be done to mitigate them.

Moving Costs

The most obvious shortcoming of foot voting under federalism is moving costs. Charles Tiebout's classic stylized model of jurisdictional choice assumes zero moving costs, and also that would-be movers have perfect information about the characteristics of different communities.[22] That model is valuable for theoretical analysis. But, in reality, of course, most migrants must at least pay the direct costs of moving themselves and their possessions. Often, these direct moving costs are less significant than much greater indirect costs, such as the cost of parting with employment opportunities, family members who stay behind, and social networks. Where moving costs are high, the choices potentially created by foot voting may remain out of reach for many who might otherwise use them.

Moving costs can indeed undermine the freedom of choice of potential foot voters. But they are not as prohibitively high as is sometimes supposed. Modern technology has made it cheaper and easier to move from one jurisdiction to another than ever before. And, in a relatively large federal system such as the United States or Canada, the existence of numerous different jurisdictions with a wide range of job opportunities reduces the extent to which people in most professions are limited to just one part of the country.

Interstate and other moves are actually extremely common, which suggests that moving costs are often quite manageable. A 2008 Pew Research Center study showed that 63 percent of Americans have moved at least once in their lives, and 43 percent have made at least one interstate move.[23]

Contrary to claims that foot voting is usually a realistic option only for the relatively affluent, census data indicate that the poorest households—those with an income under $5,000 per year—are actually twice as likely to make interstate moves as the population as a whole.[24] The poor often actually face lower effective moving costs than more affluent households because they own much less in the way of immobile assets, such as property in land.

Moving costs can often be further reduced by devolving authority to the local level rather than to regional authorities, such as American state governments. It is generally easier and cheaper to move from one nearby city or town to another, than to move to a different region. Devolution of this kind can also potentially increase the range of options available to foot voters, as there are many more local governments than regional ones.

Some types of decentralized federalism can even enable people to choose between governments without physically moving at all. This is true of choice of law clauses in many types of contracts, and of proposals for "overlapping" competitive jurisdictions, advanced by economist Bruno Frey and others.[25] With choice of law clauses, parties to a contract can choose to have their contracts governed by the law of a jurisdiction in which they are not physically present.[26] Similarly, overlapping jurisdictions could allow people to get some public services from a different jurisdiction than they would get others.[27] Law and economics scholar Gillian Hadfield contends that similar arrangements could be used to allow private firms to offer competitive voluntary regulatory frameworks to businesses, consumers, and others, though she believes such markets would require substantial government regulation.[28]

Such arrangements enable foot voters to subject some transactions to the laws of a jurisdiction in which they do not physically reside, thereby largely eliminating the moving costs. Frey's more radical ideas suggest that we can often have "overlapping" jurisdictions that enable competition and choice across a wide range of government services, without requiring any physical movement.[29] For example, a given family might choose to get garbage removal services from one government agency and education from another without necessarily having both answerable to a common local authority.

Overlapping jurisdictions do have a potential downside that may make foot voting more difficult: they potentially increase the information costs faced by those choosing between them. Foot voters would now have to make multiple jurisdictional choices, instead of just one or two. The latter is the more typical scenario currently, where movers need only choose between regional governments and then local governments within that region.

Overlapping jurisdictions can also potentially exacerbate the effects of ballot box voters' political ignorance, by making it harder to tell which of several such jurisdictions to blame for fiscal problems, as all impose burdens on the same tax base.[30] This could create situations in which each jurisdiction has an incentive to free ride on others' possible efforts to address the problem. They may be tempted to let other entities suffer the political backlash caused by difficult decisions to reduce spending or increase taxes. This sort of challenge, however, must be weighed against the difficulties created by having one jurisdiction manage a wide range of different policy areas. Such a system increases the range of issues voters must pay attention to in elections for that jurisdiction, and making it more likely that some will be overlooked.[31]

Moreover, to the extent that individuals have an opportunity to make foot-voting choices about jurisdictions, they have stronger incentives than ballot box voters to consider potential fiscal problems, especially if those problems are likely to lead to higher taxes or user fees in the future. Both foot voters and ballot box voters surely make mistakes on such matters. But the former are more likely to avoid them.

Overlapping jurisdictions cannot displace all territorially constrained government services. Some may be impossible to arrange in this way because of the danger of conflict between multiple government entities within the same territory, or because it is too difficult to coordinate in situations where the entities must address common problems. Here, as elsewhere, political freedom and choice are not the only factors that must be taken into account. But the more we can expand such options, the more we also expand political freedom in a way that carries minimal moving costs.

A special kind of moving cost is created by "agglomeration," the tendency of people in many professions to be more productive when located in the same area as other enterprises, particularly those in the same or related fields.[32] For example, professionals in the high-tech industry are often more productive if located in the Silicon Valley region of California or one of the other areas where there is a large concentration of high-tech enterprises.

Agglomeration effects can impose significant limitations on the foot-voting options of people who work in industries where it is essential to reside in an area where participants in the same industry are clustered.[33] Even workers in other, seemingly unrelated fields, can be more productive if located in areas with large agglomeration effects, since they might provide needed goods or services to industries that directly benefit from agglomeration.

Agglomeration effects necessarily increase moving costs associated with foot voting. But these can be mitigated in various ways. First, areas with agglomeration effects can still have multiple regional or local governments located within them. For example, Silicon Valley contains numerous local jurisdictions. Foot voters can choose among these without leaving the agglomeration area. The more authority is devolved to multiple local jurisdictions within a given agglomeration zone, the more foot voters can choose between a variety of options without foregoing the advantages of agglomeration.

Second, there is often more than one area with agglomerations of a given industry. For example, Silicon Valley is rivaled by similar concentrations in the Route 128 area near Boston, Massachusetts, and the Research Triangle in North Carolina.[34] Other areas have begun to compete in this domain as well.[35] The existence of multiple similar agglomerations can further increase opportunities for foot voters.

In recent years, regulatory barriers have increased moving costs and thereby made foot voting more difficult for many Americans, particularly the poor.[36] Restrictive zoning in major cities such as New York and San Francisco has artificially inflated the cost of housing and locked millions of the poor and disadvantaged out of areas where they could otherwise find valuable job opportunities.[37] State-based occupational licensing has also become a major barrier to movement, cutting off potential movers from important job opportunities.[38]

Realizing the full potential of foot voting under federalism will require reductions in these barriers to foot voting, including by constraining or eliminating zoning and licensing restrictions. Cutting back zoning in some of the most restrictive jurisdictions in the United States to the level prevalent in the median American city could open up housing and job opportunities for millions of people and potentially increase gross domestic product by some 9.5 percent.[39] That would enhance political freedom in multiple different ways. From the standpoint of negative freedom, it would remove government interference that stands in the way of foot-voting choices. It would thereby also increase the consensuality of government. The added income, housing, and employment opportunities would do much to enhance positive freedom, specially for the poor, who often stand to reap the greatest benefits from effective foot-voting opportunities.

It is neither possible nor desirable to eliminate all regional or local policies that might make moving more difficult. Some such policies are actually necessary contributions to the interjurisdictional diversity that increases the range of possible options for foot voters. Having some jurisdictions that mainly appeal to those with a specific set of preferences might make those jurisdictions relatively homogenous, but would also increase the overall diversity of options in the system as a whole.[40]

For understandable reasons, policies that repel some potential movers are actually attractive to others. However, there is a strong case for curbing policies, such as restrictive zoning, that literally and directly make it impossible for millions of people to live in the jurisdictions of their choice.

Immobility and Inequality

Even if moving costs are substantially reduced by a variety of means, it will be difficult or impossible to achieve a situation where the ability to move is equally distributed, or even close to it. Unless moving costs are literally reduced to zero, some will always find it too costly to move. Others might own immobile assets that they cannot take with them, most notably property in land.

In most situations, immobile assets are less likely to be an obstacle for movement by the poorest and most oppressed parts of the population. Almost by definition, the poor and disadvantaged rarely own major immobile assets, such as valuable land. If they did, they would not be poor.

Nonetheless, some potential movers are indeed constrained by immobile assets. There are potential strategies for mitigating this problem. As already noted,[41] it is possible to make some issues subject to foot voting without the need for physical mobility.

In cases where the person in question is moving for reasons unrelated to threats to the immobile property itself, he or she can often offset all or most of the costs by selling the immobile asset in question. If, for example, you own a house in City A and have no objection to that city's regulatory regime for residential property, but prefer the policies of City B on other issues, you can sell your house in A and use the proceeds to acquire a new home in B. On the other hand, if the problem with City A is a matter of excessive restrictions on the use of the residential land itself, moving is less likely to fix the issue, as you cannot take the land with you. Selling it also would be less likely to solve it, since the harmful policies are likely to be capitalized into the price soon after adoption, since potential buyers are likely to consider the effects of restrictions on land use in determining how much they are willing to pay.[42]

For that reason, exit rights work better for countering threats that do not target immobile property, than those that do.[43] Regardless, in many situations, the benefits of foot voting may be great enough to justify some sacrifice of immobile property.

At the same time, however, there is little doubt that moving costs and immobile assets can often block some otherwise desirable efforts at foot voting. Even if the asset in question can be sold for its full market value, this might still not be enough to offset the additional "subjective value" many people have in their homes, businesses, or other immobile property.[44] By its very nature, subjective value includes value over and above the market price of the asset, and therefore is unlikely to be recouped by the owner in a sale.

A different kind of immobility is experienced by people who cannot make autonomous decisions on whether to move. This is often true of people with families who can move only if spouses, parents, siblings, or other family members agree. It is, of course, even more true for children, who usually move only if their parents or guardians decide to do so.

These are indeed genuine constraints on foot voting. But people with families still generally have greater leverage over foot-voting decisions than voters do on ballot box decisions. With rare exceptions, you have more chance of influencing a spouse's or relative's decision-making about where to live than you do of affecting the outcome of an election or a government's decision on a public policy issue.

Children, of course, generally have less ability to influence family decisions than adults do. But they are also almost completely excluded from ballot box voting, usually barred from doing so until the age of eighteen. Some jurisdictions have lowered the voting age to sixteen,[45] and a few scholars advocate allowing even younger children to vote, at least in some circumstances.[46] But even if more minors get the ballot, they will—like adult voters—still have only an infinitesimal chance of influencing government policy.

Because of the existence of moving costs, immobile people, and immobile assets, foot voting cannot be effective for everyone. The challenge posed by moving costs and immobility can be mitigated, but not completely eliminated. But the expansion of foot-voting options can still increase political freedom for millions of people in the United States and elsewhere.

The ineradicable nature of some aspects of immobility does raise the question of whether foot voting is a flawed form of political participation because it is unavoidably unequal: some can use it more effectively than others. To the extent that political choice must be equal to be just, that could be a substantial negative.[47]

In assessing this question, it is important to avoid comparisons between imperfect foot voting and an idealized model of ballot box voting where all citizens have genuinely equal influence. In reality, ballot box voting is far from equal, especially when we consider major inequalities in political knowledge, under which some people have a much better understanding of what the consequences of a victory for one side are likely to be than others.[48] Inequality of influence in ballot box voting systems is even greater once we consider the many ways in which people can exercise leverage in ways that go beyond casting votes at the ballot box.[49]

These are even more unavoidably unequal, given that the ability to engage in lobbying, persuasive speech, campaign contributions, activism, and other such efforts is highly unequal to the point where only a minority of the population actually participates in such activities at all.[50] And such ine-quality of influence is not limited to, or even primarily caused by, inequalities in the ability to make financial campaign contributions. In the United States, for example, studies find that wealthy voters wielded disproportionate influ-ence even during periods when contributions were strictly limited.[51]

In a well-known article, the late philosopher G. A. Cohen argued that even if some members of a group are able to escape a condition in which their freedom is constrained, the group in question nonetheless suffers from "col-lective unfreedom" if it is not possible for *all* members of the group to do so.[52] His theory is meant to show that members of the "proletarian" class are not free to avoid selling their labor to survive, even if some individual workers can "exit" and become members of a different social class.[53] But, arguably, the same reasoning applies to potential foot voters, not all of whom can leave a given jurisdiction they would prefer to avoid, even if some can.

Even if it is impossible to "liberate" all members of a given group, there are still major gains to be had from liberating most, or even some. And those who are freed still exercise meaningful political choice, even if the option is not available to others. Here, as elsewhere, the best should not be the enemy of the good.

Moreover, the shortcomings of foot voting in this respect must be weighed against the much greater similar limitations of conventional political par-ticipation. The former can give meaningful political freedom to a very wide range of people, whereas the latter gives only a tiny minority the opportunity to make decisive choices about the public policies they wish to live under.[54]

At least for the foreseeable future, there is likely to be a substantial degree of inequality with respect to both foot voting and ballot box voting. Foot voting, however, has the advantage that it enables a wide range of people to make individually decisive choices. Millions of ordinary people, including many who are poor, can and do achieve major changes in the policies they live under by voting with their feet. With ballot box voting, by contrast, only a small elite has a more than infinitesimal chance of exercising meaningful influence over the government policies they live under. In that respect, foot voting is actually far *more* egalitarian than ballot box voting is ever likely to be.

Inequality in the ability to move can potentially be reduced through redis-tributive programs that increase the income of the poor and perhaps other groups that face unusually high moving costs. As already noted, in some cases the poor actually face lower moving costs than more affluent citizens who face higher costs precisely because they own valuable immobile assets.

But those costs are still severe in some cases, and can potentially be reduced further.

A redistributive program that sought to equalize moving costs might potentially have to give extra grants to the upper middle class, or even some of the wealthy. This could be a reason to either accept a degree of inequality in moving costs, or at least only redistribute to the point where as many people as possible have a minimally sufficient ability to move, not an equal one.

In this book, I do not take a position on the extent to which governments should redistribute income and wealth to the poor or other groups. That issue is sufficiently complicated that it cannot be covered here without overshadowing the actual topic of the book.[55]

Here, it is enough to make the more limited point that even a relatively high degree of redistribution is compatible with decentralization of numerous functions of government to the regional or local level. The central government can use taxation and spending to supplement the incomes of the poor (or other groups) while leaving most other policy issues in the hands of local and regional governments. Some scholars argue that concentration of redistributive functions in the central government and many other policies at the subnational level is actually the most efficient approach for federal systems.[56] A high degree of foot-voting opportunities is compatible with a wide range of views on the appropriate level of redistribution in a just society.

Races to the Bottom

In some situations, there is a danger that competition will result in a "race to the bottom" in which jurisdictions try to attract business investment in ways that harm ordinary citizens by, for example, damaging the environment.[57] However, race to the bottom concerns are greatly overstated on both conceptual and empirical grounds. Theoretically, there is no good reason to suppose that subnational governments will overvalue the needs of business interests relative to those of other foot voters, or that preferences of the former will be uniformly harmful to the latter.[58] Workers and families also vote with their feet, as do businesses that benefit from a healthy environment. Localities have incentives to cater to their needs, as well as those of business interests that may prefer laxer pollution controls. Empirical data suggest that subnational governments have often pioneered various forms of environmental protection and have not simply catered to the needs of mobile businesses to the detriment of the general public.[59]

This is not to suggest that subnational governments are immune from "capture" by business interests that might lobby for excessive pollution or other policies that enable them to benefit at the expense of the general population. Far from it.[60] But there is no inherent reason why such capture is more of a danger at the local and regional level than with central governments. The possibility of foot voting also puts constraints on such favoritism, as jurisdictions especially prone to it are likely to lose investors and taxpayers over time.

Recent research also casts doubt on earlier concerns that decentralization of political power will lead to "race to the bottom" effects that undercut redistributive programs that serve the poor.[61] To the extent such effects nonetheless occur and are considered undesirable, they can be countered by centralizing some degree of redistribution, which is compatible with decentralization of most other areas of public policy.[62]

Oppression of Unpopular Minorities

Foot voting in federal systems depends on the devolution of power to local and regional governments. But the political decentralization that facilitates foot voting could end up harming vulnerable minorities if it empowers subnational governments to oppress them. For such groups, the benefits of foot voting might turn out to be illusory, or even actively pernicious.

In the United States, there is in fact a historic association between federalism oppression of racial and ethnic minorities. For a long time, conventional wisdom held that federalism was largely a disaster for African-Americans and other minorities, which was mitigated only by the growth of federal government power.[63] As political scientist William Riker famously put it in 1964, "[t]he main beneficiary [of federalism] throughout American history has been the Southern Whites, who have been given the freedom to oppress Negroes. . . . [I]f in the United States one approves of Southern white racists, then one should approve of American federalism."[64]

There is no doubt that American state and local governments have in fact oppressed minority groups on many occasions, and that federal intervention sometimes played a key role in diminishing that oppression. The abolition of slavery in 1865 and racial segregation in the 1960s are the most famous examples. But the traditional conventional wisdom on the relationship between federalism and minority rights is nonetheless in need of serious qualification.

Although state and local governments often oppressed African Americans and other minorities, the same can be said of the federal government throughout much of American history. And in many cases, oppressed minorities would have been even worse off with a unitary state than they were under federalism.

During much of American history, a unified national policy on racial issues might well have led to greater oppression for minorities rather than less. At the time the Constitution was drafted in 1787, all but one state (Massachusetts) still had slavery, though a few others had enacted gradual emancipation laws.[65] A unitary policy on slavery at that time might well have resulted in nationwide protection for that institution.

During much of the era before the Civil War, Congress and the presidency were controlled by pro-slavery forces, which succeeded in enacting such measures as the Fugitive Slave Acts of 1793 and 1850, which tried to force free states to return escaped slaves.[66] During this period, too, a unitary state might well have had a more pro-slavery policy than that which existed under federalism. The antebellum federal government flexed its muscles in support of slavery much more often than against it.[67]

After the end of Reconstruction in the 1870s, there was a long period when the white South was far more committed to maintaining segregation than most white northerners were to eliminating it. During this era, too, it is quite likely that a unitary national policy would have been more repressive than that of the northern states, even if not as much so as that of the South. Institutions under the complete control of the federal government, during this period, tended to be highly segregated, as in the cases of the armed forces and the federal civil service.[68]

In addition to its role in promoting slavery and racial segregation for much of American history, the federal government also took the lead in a number of other notorious episodes of persecution of minority groups. For example, it interned over 100,000 Japanese Americans in concentration camps during World War II, and extensively persecuted the Mormon religious minority during the nineteenth century.[69]

Foot voting between states played a key role in preventing the plight of African-Americans and other minorities from being even worse than it was during the late nineteenth and early twentieth centuries. Between 1880 and

1920, some 1 million blacks left the South for less oppressive states in the North and West. This greatly improved the lives of the migrants themselves, and to a lesser extent even some of those blacks who stayed in the South.[70] Without variation in policies created by federalism, things would likely have been worse for minority groups than they were. In more recent years, other unpopular minorities—notably gays and lesbians—have also benefited from foot voting and federalism.

In a democracy where public opinion was as much contaminated by racial and ethnic prejudice as it was in the nineteenth- and early twentieth-century United States, minorities were likely to experience extensive oppression regardless of whether the government was federal or unitary. Foot voting was far from a panacea for this tragic state of affairs. But, for a long time, it made the situation substantially less bad than it might have been without it.

Foot voting under federalism can also be of great benefit to minorities in a situation where some local or state governments are controlled by the minority group in question, or at least substantially influenced by it. In such a scenario, pro-minority jurisdictions can serve as a valuable exit option for minority group members facing adverse policies elsewhere; such jurisdictions are also likely to be more favorable to the minority group than is the majority-dominated central government. This is widely recognized in federal systems outside the United States, where the existence of national minorities that are regional majorities is one of the main justifications for the establishment of a federal system in the first place.[71]

None of this shows that federalism is always a net positive for minority groups. In situations where the national majority strongly supports protection for a minority group, while a regional majority supports discrimination against them, concentration of power in the central government may well be the most advantageous political structure for the minority in question. This, of course, is exactly what happened in the case of African-Americans during the civil rights revolution of the 1960s. But such a configuration of opinion is far from a universal rule. It is risky to design a political system on the assumption that this unusual configuration of political forces will be the norm.

Where feasible, it will often be best for oppressed groups to have their suffering alleviated without having to move. But just as obviously, it is also often not feasible; and greater centralization of political power can as easily expand the domain of oppression as diminish it. My argument in this chapter does not depend on any claim that foot voting is always the best way to address the problems that might lead people to leave. Rather, the key point is that foot voting can expand political freedom, including for minority groups, whom it often benefits as much or more than the majority.

The Curley Effect

The Curley Effect, named after early twentieth-century Boston Mayor James Michael Curley, is a special case of local or regional government oppression of minorities. In this scenario, the government not only oppresses a minority group but actively seeks to force out its members, so as to reduce the number of voters who might oppose the ruling political party in future elections.[72] Thus, Curley, the leader of a primarily Irish-American political machine, sought to push out Anglo-Saxon "Yankee" voters.[73]

The Curley Effect potentially undermines the utility of foot voting, since group members' ability to exit actually incentivizes political leaders to push them out. If they have nowhere to go (or if moving costs are extremely high), Curley-like policies would be less attractive to political leaders.

However, as economists Edward Glaeser and Andrei Shleifer note in their pioneering analysis of this issue, Curley Effect policies are generally attractive only to leaders who expect to serve in office for a long time, as all but the most extreme brutal tactics (such as physical violence) will take a long time to reshape the electorate by selectively incentivizing departures.[74] This may explain why deliberate efforts to force out minorities for the purpose of altering the composition of the electorate are actually rare in the history of American state and local government, though other oppressive policies are far less so. Moreover, to the extent that the minority in question is productive, forcing them out can undermine the tax base and damage the local economy, thereby harming even the leader's own supporters (and perhaps incentivizing some of *them* to leave).

The Curley Effect is, in some circumstances, a genuine threat. But it is likely to occur only in unusual circumstances where political leaders expect to serve long enough to benefit from it, but also hope to structure the policy in such a way that the expulsion of electoral opponents outweighs the negative effects (for their own political fortunes) of diminishing the tax base and damaging the local economy.

Moreover, to the extent that there are jurisdictions where the ruling party is so hostile to a given group that it seeks to pressure members to leave, the latter stand to benefit from having as many good foot-voting options as possible. Admittedly, the lack of options might reduce the incentive to use pressure tactics for the specific purpose of forcing them out. But if the ruling coalition is that hostile to the group in question, it is nonetheless likely to target them for other reasons. At the very least, such a ruling party is likely to neglect the rights and interests of the disfavored minority, and sacrifice them whenever they conflict with other priorities.

Foot Voting in Ethnically Divided Federal Systems

Unlike in the United States, where major nationwide minorities also tend to be minorities within states, many federal systems are structured in ways that give national minorities majority control within specific regional governments. For example, French Canadians are a minority in the nation as a whole, but a majority in Quebec.

Foot voting may have less to offer minority groups in systems where they control one region but are unpopular elsewhere. Many federal systems were established for the specific purpose of giving regionally concentrated national minorities a jurisdiction of their own, thereby ensuring peace.[75] In such situations, it might be difficult or even impossible for individuals to move to a region dominated by another ethnic group.

For example, an Iraqi Kurd moving into a majority Arab province might reasonably fear violence or at least discrimination. Even in the absence of overt hostility, such minority groups might face painful cultural and linguistic adjustments if they move out of their home areas. A French Canadian who moves from Quebec to an overwhelmingly Anglophone province such as Alberta is unlikely to face ethnic violence or perhaps even much in the way of discrimination. But moving to an Anglophone province might still be a difficult transition, with substantial moving costs entailed by adjusting to a different language and culture.

Foot voting is, nonetheless, still potentially useful in such conditions. The federal system in question can and often should include multiple majority-minority districts.[76] For example, the French-speaking minority in Switzerland can choose between multiple majority-French cantons. Similarly, Iraq has three majority-Kurdish provinces, albeit partially unified under the Kurdistan Regional Government.[77] French Canadians would enjoy a broader array of foot-voting options if Quebec were divided into several smaller provinces rather than one big one.

I do not suggest that any particular majority-minority jurisdiction must necessarily be broken up in order to facilitate foot voting. Other considerations would have to be weighed as well before reaching that conclusion in any given case. But the foot-voting benefits of such partitions should not be neglected.

The Problem of Scale

Some issues may be too large-scale for any local or regional jurisdiction to deal with effectively. Obvious examples include the dangers of global climate change and nuclear proliferation, which can be dealt with only through national-level—or even international—policies. When such issues arise, foot voting will often be ineffective as a mechanism of choice when it comes to such issues.

It is impossible to deny that at least some policy issues can only be addressed by national governments, or sometimes even only through international cooperation. There are also likely to be other policy questions, which—though not completely intractable for smaller jurisdictions— probably have to be addressed by larger ones due to "economies of scale." In such situations, a given public service can be produced at lower per-person cost by an entity that produces a larger quantity of it. For example, it may cost less, on a per student basis, to educate 1,000 students than to educate 100. At the same time, however, a wide range of issues currently handled by large national governments can potentially be addressed by regional or local ones.

Research indicates that the quality of public policy in smaller democracies is, at the very least, no worse than that in larger ones.[78] Many of the world's most successful democratic states are very small, including countries such as Denmark, New Zealand, Norway, Switzerland, and even tiny Luxembourg and Liechtenstein.[79] Switzerland even decentralizes many functions of government to its cantons, which enjoy at least as much autonomy as American states.[80] There is little, if any, indication that these countries are losing out on significant economies of scale in the provision of public services.

If these small countries can operate effective health care, education, and pension policies, among others, there is no reason—at least no reason related to scale—why American states or Canadian provinces of comparable size cannot do the same. In the case of several of these countries, effective handling of these policies is combined with freedom of movement for numerous migrants to and from the nations of the European Union.[81] Handling a wide range of policy issues in relatively small jurisdictions is compatible with freedom of movement and is not undermined by problems of scale.

Scale is a genuine constraint on the scope of foot voting. In this chapter, I cannot evaluate the full range of issues to which it may be relevant. But it is unlikely that problems of scale preclude greater decentralization of a wide range of government policies.

Conclusion

Internal migration within federal systems is the type of foot voting most familiar to scholars and many laypeople. But its enormous potential for expanding political freedom has not been fully appreciated. Historically, it has done much to expand liberty and opportunity in the United States and elsewhere. We should not overlook its genuine limitations and downsides. But there is much to be done that can reduce those constraints and make internal foot voting more effective and more widely available than ever before.

3

Foot Voting and International Migration

The potential gains from foot voting through international migration are even greater than those possible through foot voting within a single country. The possible increases in political freedom are truly enormous. At the same time, the obstacles to effective international foot voting are also often substantially greater than those facing internal migrants. In particular, moving costs of various kinds can be extremely high.

This chapter summarizes the enormous potential increases in political freedom from reducing barriers to international migration. It also addresses the problem of moving costs and the objection that the utility of international foot voting is undermined by its inherently unequal nature. Some scholars argue, therefore, that wealthy nations can best assist the poor and oppressed by increasing foreign aid. I suggest that such claims fail even on their own terms, because they overlook the far greater relative effectiveness of immigration as a tool for reducing global inequality.

The final part of the chapter briefly explains how immigration restrictions undermine the political freedom of natives as well as those of would-be immigrants. This is because the measures necessary to enforce laws against illegal migration also impose substantial constraints on natives, up to and including even detention and deportation of thousands of American citizens. This chapter does not consider objections to international foot voting based on concerns that it will undermine the self-determination of receiving countries or otherwise harm native-born citizens. Such issues are covered in Chapters 5 and 6.

How International Foot Voting Promotes
Political Freedom

The variation in policy and quality of government between nations dwarfs that between subnational jurisdictions within any one nation. No American state, for example, is as poor or corrupt as Mexico, to say nothing of far worse-off developing nations. A Mexican who migrates to the United States stands to increase his or her wages by two- to six-fold, and migrants from other poor nations make similar wage gains.[1] A migrant from a repressive authoritarian state to a liberal democracy enjoys a massive increase in individual freedom, greater than any that is likely to be achieved through internal migration alone. Many of the gains go far beyond the narrowly "economic." Consider those accruing to refugees fleeing authoritarian societies; members of persecuted racial, ethnic, and religious groups; and others facing terrible conditions.

These gains translate into major enhancements of political freedom, defined in any of the ways considered in Chapter 1. From the standpoint of making government more consensual, they make a big difference by enabling migrants to exercise far greater freedom of choice than would be possible otherwise. When it comes to negative freedom, emigration enables migrants to escape a wide range of severe government-imposed restrictions on its exercise. Likewise, there are few if any better ways to promote the nondomination: international migration can allow many people to escape the domination of particularly brutal and oppressive regimes.[2] Such governments exercise arbitrary authority over their subjects far more extensively than is the case for almost any residents of Western liberal democracies.

Finally, the increases in income and opportunity migrants stand to gain are also obvious improvements from the standpoint of positive liberty, defined as enhancing human capacity.[3] In addition to the constraints imposed by poverty caused by flawed government policies, migrants can also escape those inflicted by government-aided oppression of specific social groups. Consider such cases as religious and ethnic minorities fleeing persecution, women fleeing sexist patriarchal societies, and political dissenters fleeing repression.

Even the most casual observation of migration flows confirms that international migration is often driven by the relative quality of government policy in the destination nation compared to the migrants' country of origin. Migrants typically move away from areas where government policy leads to violence, oppression, and poverty (or fails to alleviate these problems), and toward those where public policy functions better, or at least causes less harm. In that sense, international migration is often an exercise of political choice. The worst and most oppressive governments often use force to keep their citizens from leaving, not keep potential migrants out. Well-known examples include such cases as Cuba, North Korea, and the former Soviet bloc nations of Eastern Europe.

More systematic studies also show that variations in public policy have a major impact on political choice. Migrants tend to choose nations with greater economic freedom because relatively lower levels of economic regulation offer greater employment opportunities for immigrants.[4] Many migrants also tend to choose destination countries with greater political freedom (defined in terms of democracy, freedom of speech, and other rights relevant to political participation).[5] Conversely, migrants are more likely to leave nations where democratic institutions are performing poorly.[6] For many female migrants, the extent to which a government protects women's rights is also an important determinant of their choice of destination.[7]

For much of the world's population, international migration is virtually their only chance of exercising any meaningful political freedom at all. Some 2.7 billion people (more than a third of the world's population) live in the 49 countries designated as "not free" in Freedom House's most recent annual survey of political freedom.[8] In "not free" states, the government is undemocratic and there is little or no protection for civil liberties.[9] Another 1.8 billion people live in the 58 "partly free" countries, where political rights and democracy are still very limited.[10]

For the vast majority of people living in "not free" societies and many of those in "partly free" ones, international migration is probably the only way for them to have any say in deciding what kind of government they wish to live under, short of violent revolution or some other radical transformation of the political system in their home countries. That greatly differentiates their condition from that of internal migrants within a federal system in liberal democracies and makes their need all the more pressing.

To take just one dramatic example, virtually all currently living Cubans who have ever exercised any meaningful political choice have done so through emigration.[11] Almost the only exceptions may be members of the Communist Party political elite who have influence over government policy, and even many of them probably lack the power to make truly fundamental changes to policy. Much the same can be said for people born into many other societies that have had nondemocratic governments throughout their lives, with little prospect for change.

Potential Gains from Reducing Migration Restrictions

Unfortunately, most citizens of poor and oppressive nations are severely limited in their emigration options because advanced liberal democracies greatly restrict entry. Even for refugees from highly oppressive governments, gaining admission to advanced democratic states is often difficult or impossible.[12] In 2018, the United States Department of Justice Bureau of Immigration Appeals even ruled that refugees who had been forced to work as slave laborers by insurgent groups do not qualify for asylum because their slave labor is considered to be "material support" for terrorism.[13] As a result of such restrictive policies, hundreds of millions are denied their only possible opportunity for political freedom as well as their best chance of escaping other forms of oppression and rising out of poverty.

For these reasons, there is a strong political freedom case for liberalizing immigration law in liberal democracies, especially for migrants from authoritarian states where the population lacks even minimal political rights. If political freedom is ever a morally significant concern in public policy, it should be here.

In a recent book defending "liberal nationalism," prominent political theorist Yael Tamir largely dismisses migration as a mechanism of political freedom because, thanks to migration restrictions and moving costs, "true voluntarism is enjoyed by only a fortunate few," thereby ensuring that for most people, the choice of which government to live under is more a matter of "destiny than choice."[14] Even the most liberal immigration regimes, she writes, "take closure as a given and determine a set of exceptions to the rule."[15]

That may well be true for most of the world's people today. But it does not have to be that way. Instead of "taking closure as a given," migration policy can instead adopt a presumption of freedom of movement, with exclusion being the exceptional case—just as it generally is in the case of internal migration. Even if policy reform stops short of going that far, it can still greatly reduce the extent of closure and therefore open up "voluntarism" to many more people than is presently the case.

Even in the best possible circumstances, international migration will often be more difficult than internal movement. But it can be made far easier than is currently the case for all too many potential migrants.

The United Nations estimates that there are currently 258 million migrants living outside their countries of origin, some 3.4 percent of the world's population.[16] But many more would be able to move to freer societies if immigration restrictions were eliminated or reduced. Recent survey data indicate that 750 million people worldwide say they would migrate to a different country if they could.[17] This figure probably greatly overstates the true number who would move if migration restrictions were abolished. But, while distance and transportation costs prevent many cases of what might otherwise be benefi-cial migration, by far the biggest barriers to international migration are legal restrictions imposed by national governments.[18]

It is impossible to determine exactly how many might move if barriers were eliminated or greatly lowered. But standard economic estimates suggest it could be many millions of people—potentially enough to approximately double world GDP.[19]

The main driver of such gains is the "place premium": the fact that workers can be as much as several times more productive in societies with greater re-sources and better political and economic institutions—even if the workers' own skill levels do not increase.[20] The gains can be even greater if the workers do improve their job skills and other "human capital" in their new homes, as is likely to happen in many cases. In addition to its purely "economic" value, this extra production represents an enormous amount of increase in positive freedom, as reflected in enhancement of human capabilities.

It is worth emphasizing that these gains cannot be achieved simply by instituting free trade between the nations in question.[21] Most of the place premium consists of increased productivity arising from the superior capital, resources, and institutions of destination countries relative to the migrants' countries of origin. Thus, in most cases, they cannot achieve the same pro-ductivity increases by staying in their countries of origin and producing goods for sale in the destination countries—even if the latter impose no trade barriers. If, for example, a Salvadoran would be twice as productive in the United States as she currently is in El Salvador,[22] she could not get a com-parable increase in productivity by staying in El Salvador and attempting to produce the same goods and services there as she could work on in the United States.

Critics argue that free migration cannot actually achieve such large eco-nomic gains. One concern is that doubling of world GDP would require im-plausibly large migration flows from poor nations to wealthy ones, on the order of as many as 2.6 billion workers moving.[23] Even in the absence of legal barriers, migration is far from costless. It seems highly unlikely that so many people would actually move, especially in the near future. Thus, it may be that not enough people will move to realize the potentially huge economic gains of lowering barriers to migration.

The other major line of criticism—in some tension with the first—is that *too many* people would move if restrictions were lifted. If so, they might potentially bring with them their possibly dysfunctional cultures and undermine the institutions on which the relatively high productivity of currently wealthy nations depends.[24]

It is indeed true that the full potential economic gains of free migration are highly unlikely to be realized quickly. On the other hand, history shows that substantial outmigration can occur relatively fast when previously existing barriers to migration are relaxed, as in the case of Russian Jews, who became free to migrate to Israel in the years leading up to the fall of the Soviet Union, which led to half or more of that group departing within a few years.[25]

Moreover, even if increases in migration are gradual rather than sudden—as is likely to be the case—they can gradually accelerate over time, leading to large gains over a period of decades.[26] This slows down the rate of economic gain but also creates time for institutions and markets to adjust to a larger and more diverse population.[27]

It is also important to recognize that the increased economic benefits of migration arise not just from those who literally move but also from others who—in the absence of migration restrictions—would be consigned to live out their lives in areas where they are likely to be far less productive. For example, if a Cuban moves to the United States and has children there, those children will not themselves count as immigrants and might never make any international move in their lives. But, had immigration restrictions barred their parents from moving, they would either not have existed at all or have had to live their lives in poverty and oppression back in Cuba.

Once we understand that much of the movement will be gradual rather than sudden, and that many of the people whose productivity increases will not be the initial immigrants themselves but their children and grandchildren born in destination countries, the estimate of 2.6 billion workers ending up in more productive locations than where they would be otherwise seems much more plausible.

The 36 million people who moved to the United States between 1820 and 1924—if combined with their American-born descendants, accounted for the overwhelming bulk of the tenfold increase in US population during that period. The population increased from 9.6 million in 1820 to 106 million in 1920.[28] In an age where transportation and communications are cheaper and faster than in the nineteenth century, comparably large migration trends could likely occur faster, though of course still far from immediately.

Some of the economic gains of free migration accrue not just to workers who move, and their children, but also to their countries of origin, which benefit from remittances they send to family members back home, and from increasing interchange of ideas with freer and more economically advanced societies, which help generate economic innovation. The latter can also speed up the pace of liberalization and democratization of the migrants' home societies.[29] This can in turn generate economic progress even among those who do not move,[30] thereby reducing the number of people who must migrate to achieve a given level of increased economic growth.

Even if the doubling world GDP estimate is indeed overly optimistic, as critics claim, an effect half or a quarter that size would still be a gigantic boon to positive freedom, including for many of the world's poorest and most oppressed people. Indeed, even a 5 percent or 10 percent increase in global GDP arising from reductions in migration restrictions would be enough to lift millions out of poverty and otherwise transform their lives. One leading academic critic of the "doubling world GDP" argument estimates that world GDP would still increase by 17 percent even if only 10 percent of the potential movers actually do move to more advanced nations in the global North.[31] Thus, even relatively conservative estimates of the potential economic gains from free migration would far outweigh any other policy change economists have been able to measure the effects of, such as liberalizing international trade or expanding foreign aid.[32]

The opposite concern—that migration might undermine the institutions that enable greater productivity—is more weighty. Such effects could occur because immigrants have harmful cultural values, because their political influence leads to a degradation in the quality of government policy, or because a massive influx of migrants ends up "swamping" existing institutions. Each of these scenarios is considered in some detail in Chapter 6.

Immigration and Foot Voting in American History

Even more than in the case of internal foot voting, American history dramatically demonstrates how foot voting through immigration can enhance political freedom along multiple dimensions.

As noted earlier in this chapter, between 1820 and 1924, some 36 million immigrants arrived in the United States.[33] The vast bulk of the American population consists of their descendants. Under federal law, immigration from around the world was almost completely unconstrained until the Chinese Exclusion Act of 1882, and immigration from Europe remained so until the 1920s.[34] The Immigration Act of 1924, driven by rising nativist sentiment, greatly curtailed immigration for the next forty years by adopting strict national quotas favoring Northern and Western European nations.[35] But the Immigration Act of 1965 once again greatly liberalized immigration, if not to the near-"open borders" extent of the pre-1924 era.[36] The result has been another major expansion of immigration from many parts of the world. All told, some 100 million immigrants have come to the United States since the end of the Revolutionary War in 1783.[37] Today, over 13 percent of the American population consists of foreign-born immigrants, up from about 5 percent in 1960.[38]

The reasons so many immigrants have come to the United States over the last two centuries vary greatly. But foot voting in favor of a better political system with more favorable government policies has been a major factor. Many of the nineteenth-century immigrants came to the United States in search of religious and ethnic toleration, as in the case of Jews fleeing czarist Russia, Irish Catholics fleeing Britain, and many others. Other nineteenth-century migrants were political dissenters, including many who fled in the aftermath of the suppression of liberal revolutions in European, in 1848.

The same, of course, is true of numerous modern immigrants, who also include many fleeing ethnic and religious persecution, or political repression. Refugees from Nazism, Cubans, Soviet Jews, Vietnamese "boat people," and—most recently—Syrian refugees fleeing oppression by the so-called Islamic State of Iraq and Syria (ISIS) and the regime of Bashar Assad, are obvious examples.

Even many "economic" migrants were, at least in large part, choosing the United States for policy-related reasons. Economic opportunity is to a large extent the product of government policy, and the relative lack of opportunity in many immigrants' homelands was heavily determined by the policies of the regimes in power there. This is true of both nineteenth- and early twentieth-century immigrants, and those of today.

What is true for the migration to the United States is also often true for migration to other nations that have taken in large numbers of immigrants since the nineteenth century, including Canada, Australia, the United Kingdom, and France, among others. They too have taken in numerous migrants fleeing oppressive and undemocratic regimes. And "economic" migrants seeking refuge there have often in fact been victims of their home government's public policies.

The Problem of Moving Costs

As already noted, moving costs for international migration are a far more severe problem than in the case of internal foot voting within a federal system. The problem is not just that transportation costs are often higher. On average, these are indeed likely higher than those of internal foot voting. But they will vary depending on the distance between the migrant's home country and destination. Cubans, Mexicans, and Haitians, for example, live close enough to the United States that the distance they must travel is smaller than that which must be covered by many internal migrants in the United States.

The really great moving costs of international migration are those of cultural and linguistic adjustment. Moving to a nation with a different language and culture from the one you have lived in for all or most of your life can be a difficult and wrenching process. Failures of adjustment are a major cause of "return migration" back to the migrants' countries of origin.[39]

As a result of these sorts of issues, international migration often does not occur on the scale that would be predicted by economic variables alone. For example, within the European Union and several associated states, there has been nearly full open migration since 2004 (though in some cases introduced only gradually).[40] Yet, despite very large wage differentials between member states within the EU, migration between EU states averaged only about 0.29 percent of the population per year in 2009–15, though some 10 percent of high-skilled workers within the European Union now live outside their home countries.[41] As of 2015, only about 3.27 percent of EU citizens live in countries other than their country of origin.[42]

However, some of the constraints are due to restrictive labor regulations in destination countries, and the percentage of emigrants from poor EU nations is much higher.[43] Moreover, differences between EU nations, while large, are not as great as those between advanced nations and many of the world's poorest and most oppressed societies. Bigger differences in freedom and economic welfare could stimulate greater migration, as is dramatically illustrated by the transformation of post-apartheid South Africa, where the end of racially restrictive constraints on migration enabled millions of black South Africans to move, and played a key role increasing their average income by over 60 percent between 1993 and 2008.[44]

There is no way to fully overcome the relatively high moving costs of international migration. But some measures can help mitigate it. First, the more relatively affluent nations are open to immigration, the greater the odds that potential migrants will be able to find a country that is relatively congenial in terms of culture and other adjustment costs. For example, French-speaking migrants can more easily adjust to a French-speaking country, migrants from a given cultural background can more easily adjust to a new country with an at least somewhat similar culture, and so on.

Second, integration into the labor market greatly facilitates cultural adaptation,[45] and governments can reduce regulatory barriers that prevent immigrants from seeking and holding jobs. Increasing employment prospects of immigrants both makes integration easier for them and increases their productivity to the benefit of immigrants and natives alike.[46]

In sum, moving costs are a serious and—at least for the foreseeable future—unavoidable constraint on international foot voting. But reducing barriers to it can still create valuable foot-voting opportunities for many millions of people. And for those who take advantage of them, the gains are truly enormous—far outstripping not only those of internal foot voting, but those of almost any other policy reform that can plausibly be imagined.

The Inequality Objection and the Foreign Aid Alternative

Despite the enormous gains from international foot voting that can occur even without major reductions in moving costs, some argue that expanding this type of foot voting is problematic because access to it will still be unequal. Even if moving costs are reduced, they will still be prohibitive for many, including many of the world's poorest and most oppressed people. Thus, the inequality objection to international foot voting is potentially more potent than the similar objection to relying on the domestic variant, discussed in Chapter 2.

Instead of allowing residents of poor and oppressed nations to go where the money and freedom are, perhaps we should instead export wealth and liberty to them, in the form of foreign aid. This would potentially benefit those unable to move to a greater extent than emigration could. For example, political philosopher Thomas Pogge claims that those who can emigrate from poor nations to advanced ones are likely to be the "more privileged" members of their societies; he therefore contends that financial assistance to poor nations is the more just and egalitarian way to assist the worst-off people in the world.[47]

In theory, Western nations can alleviate all or most of the poverty in the world simply by making massive transfers of wealth to underdeveloped nations.[48] Even Joseph Carens, probably the leading academic advocate of open borders, suggests that because of the problem of moving costs, reducing barriers to immigration is only of "secondary importance for the task of reducing international inequalities."[49]

The extent to which affluent nations have a duty to redistribute wealth to poor ones depends in large part on the status of theories of distributive justice, an issue I cannot address in any detail in this book. But even if a duty of this sort exists, reducing barriers to migration is a better way of discharging it than foreign aid, for the simple reason that despite its shortcomings, it is likely to be more effective.

Studies on the impact of foreign aid indicate that its effectiveness in alleviating poverty is, at best, extremely limited.[50] As economists Daron Acemoglu and James Robinson explain in their much-acclaimed book *Why Nations Fail,* "the idea that rich Western countries should provide large amounts of 'development aid' in order to solve the problem of poverty [in poor nations] . . . is based on an incorrect understanding of what causes poverty," which is largely the result of flawed institutions in the poor nations themselves under which those nations lack effective property rights and the rule of law, and local elites have a stranglehold "over political and economic life."[51] They point out that "[t]he same institutional problems mean that foreign aid will be ineffective, as it will be plundered and is unlikely to be delivered where it is supposed to go."[52] In some cases, "it could even prop up the regimes that are at the very root of the problems of these societies."[53]

A possible alternative to either migration or providing aid to the existing governments of poor nations is setting up "charter cities," jurisdictions located in the developing world that will be largely independent of the governments of their host countries and operated with Western-style political and economic institutions.[54] Some argue that charter cities or less ambitious "special economic zones" could be an alternative refuge for migrants and refugees, thereby obviating the need for international migration.[55]

Charter cities and other similar ideas are promising reforms that could create new opportunities for foot voters. But getting corrupt and oppressive governments to agree to their establishment within their borders—and to make a credible commitment to respecting their autonomy—is likely to be difficult, at best. Even when established, it will take years or even decades for new cities to become viable and to provide potential employment and refuge for more than a small number of people. For these reasons, charter cities and similar reforms are unlikely to be adequate substitutes for reducing migration restrictions.

By contrast, reductions in migration restrictions enable many victims of corrupt and oppressive governments to immediately escape their reach. They can thereby exercise meaningful political choice and control over their own fate.

Recent proposals to consign refugees to closed camps in Western nations are similarly problematic.[56] Their only advantage over charter cities is that Western governments can probably establish such camps relatively quickly.

Closed camps may be better than barring the refugees in question from these nations entirely. But they deny their inmates any meaningful opportunity to integrate with the larger economy and society of the destination country and thus largely deny meaningful political choice. The refugees cannot choose to live under the political and economic institutions of the host nations if they are confined to closed camps deliberately isolated from the rest of society.

In sum, measures such as foreign aid, charter cities, and closed refugee camps are no substitute for migration rights. Migration provides far more in the way of genuine political freedom.

Migration can also help alleviate the poverty even of people who stay behind in the migrants' home countries. Remittances sent by migrants to relatives can greatly increase their families' resources and—indirectly— those of their nations as a whole.[57] Unlike foreign aid channeled through national governments, remittance payments are far less likely to be squandered or siphoned off to corrupt local elites.

Even if foreign aid turns out to be effective and is successful in alleviating poverty, it is still not a complete substitute for foot voting through international migration. Effective development assistance can make residents of poor nations wealthier. But it still does not offer them political freedom in the form of the ability to make decisive choices about the kinds of government policies they would prefer to live under. Particularly in undemocratic nations, foot-voting opportunities would still be the best way to address that problem.

Charter cities could potentially offer some genuine political choice. But, again, it is unlikely that they could do so for more than a small number of people, at least not for a long time to come. Initiatives such as charter cities may be worth pursuing. But, if so, it should be as a complement to expanding migration rights, not an alternative to it.

Even with the additional leverage provided by remittances, international migration cannot help all of the global poor, or—most likely—even come close to doing so. But it can greatly increase wealth by a process that also greatly reduces inequality, by enabling many of the poor and oppressed to exercise greater political freedom and live vastly better lives.

How Migration Restrictions Reduce the
Political Freedom of Natives

This chapter focuses primarily on how reductions in restrictions on international migration can enhance the political freedom of would-be immigrants, the group is that the primary victim of status-quo policies. But it is worth considering how such reductions can also enhance the political freedom of native-born citizens of migrants' destination countries.

The reason this should be so is that restrictions on migrants necessarily also impact those natives who choose to interact with them. They can even affect those natives who do not interact with migrants but merely look (at least in the eyes of the authorities) as if they might be illegal migrants themselves. As political theorist Chandran Kukathas explains, it is impossible to impose constraints on migrants without also constraining natives, as well:

> Regulating immigration is not just about how people arrive, but about what they do once they have entered a country. It is about controlling how long people stay, where they travel, and what they do. Most of all, it means controlling whether or not and for whom they work (paid or unpaid), what they accept in financial remuneration, and what they must do to remain in employment, for as long as that is permitted. Yet this is not possible without controlling citizens and existing residents, who must be regulated, monitored and policed to make sure that *they* comply with immigration laws. . . .
>
> Immigrants are not readily discernible from citizens, or from residents with 'Indefinite Leave to Remain', especially in a multi-ethnic and multi-cultural society. So any effort to identify and exclude or penalize immigrants will generally require stopping or searching or questioning *anyone*. . . .
>
> Immigration controls are controls on people, and it is difficult to control some people without also controlling others.[58]

As Kukathas emphasizes, immigration restrictions undermine the freedom of natives for many of the same reasons that apartheid in South Africa (and, we might add, racial segregation in the United States) violated the liberties of whites as well as blacks. Both involve large-scale efforts to separate groups when many of their members want to interact with each other in ways forbidden by the state. Racial segregation in the United States and South Africa required extensive government regulation of members of both races, even if the burden fell far more heavily on blacks. Similarly, restrictions on immigration cannot be effectively enforced without also imposing serious restrictions on the activities of natives.

Perhaps the most dramatic example is the painful reality that efforts to deport undocumented immigrants have also led to the deportation of numerous American citizens. In the 1930s, the US government deported some 600,000 citizens to Mexico, most of them Mexican-Americans whom the authorities mistook for aliens.[59] Such problems persist on a much smaller but still substantial scale, even today.

Political scientist Jacqueline Stevens estimates that the federal government detained or deported some 4,000 American citizens in 2010 alone, with a total of 20,000 between 2003 and 2010.[60] Virtually any law enforcement system occasionally makes mistakes that harm the innocent. But this is an extremely high error rate that has resulted in serious harm to many thousands of people. Some 1 to 2 percent of the people detained for deportation by US immigration enforcement agencies are estimated to be US citizens.[61]

Other mechanisms of deportation enforcement impose smaller but still-substantial burdens on natives as well. For example, federal law enforcement agencies are permitted to engage in racial profiling for purposes of immigration enforcement in "border" and coastal areas that include regions where some two-thirds of Americans live[62]—a form of racial discrimination that necessarily impacts large numbers of native-born citizens who belong to the same ethnic or racial groups as immigrants, or look as if they might.

More generally, immigration restrictions necessarily bar natives from voluntarily interacting with would-be migrants in a variety of economic and social relationships. That includes connections as employers, employees, participants in religious and civil society organizations, and many other endeavors.

Much of this imposes constraints on political freedom as well as on other aspects of liberty. Most obviously, natives who are detained or deported are by virtue of that fact denied any opportunity to vote with their feet for so long as that status persists, which sometimes can be for many months or even years.[63] But even less severe burdens imposed by enforcement impact natives' foot-voting opportunities, as well. For example, constraints on interactions with immigrant workers and entrepreneurs can diminish natives' opportunities to vote with their feet in the private sector.

Thus immigration restrictions necessarily impact both the negative and positive freedom of natives. Negative liberty is undermined by restrictions on natives' ability to form commercial and personal connections with migrants; positive liberty is adversely affected by the destruction of the additional wealth and opportunity immigrants create, much of which would accrue to natives who employ immigrants, use the products they make, and otherwise benefit from their presence.

In the case of natives subjected to detention, deportation, and racial profiling as a result of immigration restrictions, nondomination is also undermined, along with negative and positive freedom. There are few clearer instances of domination of individuals by the government than involuntary detention and deportation. Racial profiling by law enforcement can also be considered a form of domination, insofar as it exposes both natives and migrants to arbitrary coercion by law enforcement officials, based merely on aspects of their appearance that victims of these policies cannot control.[64]

In principle, immigration enforcement efforts can be restructured in ways that greatly reduce such impositions on natives. For example, stronger safeguards could be instituted to reduce deportation and detention of natives wrongly suspected of being aliens.[65] But such increased protections for civil liberties necessarily make it harder to deport illegal migrants to begin with, which is one of the reasons they are often resisted by authorities. Thus, there is an unavoidable trade-off between the two goals, often a very severe one.

Moreover, even the most humane and error-free enforcement mechanisms still necessarily constrain natives' freedom to interact with migrants, thus also constraining a variety of foot-voting opportunities that could otherwise enhance political freedom.

Conclusion

Overall, foot voting through international migration is a tremendously important mechanism for exercising political freedom and increasing human freedom and welfare more generally. It does have significant limitations, most notably relatively high moving costs. For that reason, it cannot help as many people as we would ideally want. It is also subject to a variety of objections that will be considered in more detail in Chapters 5 and 6. Nonetheless, we should not let the currently unattainable best blind us to the merits of this enormous good. For many people around the world, international foot voting can literally make the difference between life and death, prosperity and poverty, or freedom and slavery.

4

Foot Voting in the Private Sector

At first glance, foot voting in the private sector may not seem like foot voting at all. Or at least it may not seem like a form of political choice. In fact, however, private sector decision-making can often enhance political freedom. In some respects, it can do so even more than foot voting in federal systems or through international migration.

The most obvious form of foot voting in the private sector occurs when people choose among private organizations that offer services similar to those provided by local or regional governments, most notably private planned communities. But, as we shall see, private sector foot voting can also take place in situations where the private sector can offer a substitute for services provided by the state, even though the structure of those services often differs greatly from that of those provided by government. This latter type of foot voting is not as clearly "political" as the former. But it still enhances political freedom in the sense that it provides an *alternative* to the government.

Ultimately, private sector foot voting has many of the same advantages as domestic and international migration between government jurisdictions. If deployed in tandem, the three types of foot voting are mutually reinforcing, helping to expand political freedom more than any one could by itself. In many situations, expanding opportunities for one type of foot voting also helps expand the others. The three types can also sometimes help offset each other's shortcomings.

This chapter also considers two common objections to private sector foot voting: that it fosters unjust inequality, and that it is not sufficiently "political" to be considered a true alternative to public sector decision-making. In addition, as with, foot voting under federalism, private sector foot voting may not be applicable to some issues that require solutions too large for the organizations in question to handle.

Decentralization of power to local governments is sometimes described as "federalism all the way down," in Heather Gerken's phrase, since it seemingly devolves authority to the lowest level possible.[1] But devolution to the private sector takes decentralization even further,[2] often devolving power to still lower levels. Instead of empowering local governments, it empowers private sector individuals and organizations. In many situations, a territory that contains only one or a few local governments can include a much larger number of private individuals and private sector organizations. This reduces moving costs and offers would-be foot voters a far greater range of options.

Private Planned Communities

The clearest example of private sector foot voting in advanced modern society is represented by private planned communities. Approximately 69 million people live in private communities in the United States.[3] That amounts to some 21 percent of the population of the United States.[4] The number of people living in private communities has risen from a mere 2.1 million in 1970 to 29.6 million in 1990, to today's total of 69 million.[5]

This increasing popularity is a notable testament to the success of this form of "private government," as it is often called.[6] Similar institutions have become common in many other countries around the world, both advanced liberal democracies and many developing nations.[7]

In the United States, private communities generally take one of three forms: condominiums (about 42–45 percent of the total), homeowners associations (51–55 percent), and cooperatives (3–4 percent).[8] Each has somewhat different governance structures.[9] Private communities can also be structured as land trusts, in which a trust has title to the land[10] and the buildings are owned by members who pay ground rent to the trust, and sometimes as private mobile home parks, in which park owners create governance structures for mobile homes owned by individual residents or families.[11] Such organizations perform many functions similar to those traditionally associated with local government. These include the provision of land use planning, waste removal, management of common spaces, recreational facilities, and security, among others.[12]

Private communities expand foot-voting options for political freedom in several ways. First, and most obviously, they fit the consent model of political freedom well. Unlike regional and local governments, they exercise authority only over those property owners who voluntarily join them. The establishment of such a community requires unanimous consent by the owners of the land in question.[13]

There is one notable caveat to the otherwise consensual nature of private planned communities. In some areas, local governments require all new housing developments to compel residents to join a private community, thereby potentially reducing the fiscal burden on the local government.[14] While potential residents still have the option of choosing to live in a different area, this imposition does reduce the consensuality of the system. Political freedom would be better promoted if it were abolished.[15]

Private planned communities also enhance negative freedom. To the extent that control over land use passes from a relatively nonconsensual organization to a relatively more voluntary one, there is less interference with the negative liberty and property rights of residents.

Private communities similarly improve on conventional local governments from the standpoint of nondomination. The requirement of consent minimizes potential residents' subjection to the arbitrary will of others. In addition, the fact that large numbers of private communities can exist in a relatively small geographic space increases the options available to potential residents and thus reduces the extent to which any one community can impose onerous terms as a condition of joining.

Currently, there are over 340,000 private planned communities in the United States, as compared to only about 89,000 local governments.[16] Overall, the former offer far more options than the latter, and it is likely possible to create many more of them. The variety of organizational forms for private communities provides a range of options for potential foot voters to choose from, and reduces the risk that any one type will dominate the market, leaving potential residents with few or no alternatives.

Finally, by providing higher quality and more differentiated services than local governments, private planned communities can also enhance political freedom in the sense of positive liberty.[17] Data indicate that properties located within private planned communities are some 5 percent more valuable than otherwise similar properties in the same area, located outside them.[18] This is a substantial premium and an indication of the value of services provided by private communities. The difference might be even higher were it not for the problem of double taxation, discussed later in this chapter. Having to pay fees for the same services to both the government and a private community necessarily reduces the relative attractiveness of private communities, relative to more conventional public ones.

The Inequality Objection

Perhaps the most obvious criticism of private planned communities is that "they foster a separation of wealthy people in gated communities, apart from the rest of the population, especially the poor."[19] Perhaps they represent the "secession of the successful," in the famous phrase of former US Secretary of Labor Robert B. Reich.[20] The wealthy can use them to keep out ordinary people and create a system of community amenities that they alone have access to. If private planned communities are just a mechanism by which the wealthy wall themselves off from the rest of society, they cannot be considered a viable foot-voting option for the rest of the population, particularly the poor.

The fact that almost 70 million Americans now reside in private communities undercuts the notion that they exist to serve only a small wealthy elite. Unfortunately, we do not, as yet, have systematic data on the income distribution of private community residents in the United States. But many contractual communities already include lower-income tenants, and the city of St. Louis, for example, has privatized neighborhoods in predominantly African American lower-income areas.[21] Overall, it is likely that private communities include people in a wide range of income classes but also that access is generally more difficult for the poor than others.[22]

Various reforms can make private planned communities a more accessible option for the less affluent. One of the main obstacles to participation in private communities is the cost imposed by double taxation: residents pay fees to the private community for the same kinds of services for which they also pay taxes to local government, even if they make little or no use of the latter.[23] The fact that many are willing to pay additional fees for the same services they already—in theory—get from the government is a strong indication of the value of the services provided by private communities. But this kind of double taxation also increases the cost of joining a private community.

Fred Foldvary proposes that private community residents be able to deduct from public taxes the costs of those services they pay to be provided by the private community.[24] This would increase the accessibility of such institutions to the poor and lower middle class. The point of this reform is not to forestall redistribution but rather to prevent participants from having to pay twice for the provision of the same service to both the government and the private sector. Taxation intended to defray the cost of public services provided to the taxpayer himself is distinct from taxation for purposes of redistributing wealth to others. Where redistributive taxation is justified in order to aid the poor, it can be imposed irrespective of whether an individual lives in a private community or not and the proceeds transferred directly to the poor recipients in question. In some cases, it may be optimal for redistributive taxation to be conducted by the central government rather than by local governments that provide the types of services also produced by private communities.[25]

Another reform that could expand the availability of private planned communities is loosening zoning restrictions on new construction, a policy that could also help promote foot voting between traditional state and local governments.[26] The cheaper and easier it is to build new housing, the easier it will be to start new private planned communities where prices are comparatively low.

The late Robert Nelson, a leading academic expert on private local governments, proposed that residents of neighborhoods where they do not currently exist should be permitted to band together and establish new ones.[27] He argued that such organizations could help revitalize distressed urban neighborhoods and provide better security and other services.[28] Nelson's proposal would allow the establishment of a private neighborhood association in any area where advocates followed certain procedural requirements and secured supermajority support in a vote of local property owners (perhaps 80 percent).[29] This would reduce the consensuality of private planned communities, since dissenting minorities might be forced into one without their consent. But it is plausible that Nelson's proposal would still be an improvement over the status quo in many areas, where the preexisting extent of consent to traditional local government is likely to be far lower. Nelson's policy would create options for both current residents of communities and foot voters from elsewhere considering moving there.

If state and local governments reduce zoning and adopt Foldvary's and Nelson's proposals, private planned communities could be made available to a substantially wider range of people. This in turn would help increase foot-voting options.

Nonetheless, it will still be the case that private planned communities will not be a feasible option for everyone. The cost will still be prohibitive for some, and others will be unable either to move to an area that has one or establish a new one where they currently live.

That is a genuine constraint of private planned communities as a foot-voting option. But it is not a decisive objection, for much the same reasons as similar concerns about moving costs and inequality should not lead us to reject foot voting between regional and local governments.[30]

Both represent foot-voting opportunities that can give many millions of people—including many who are poor and disadvantaged—the opportunity to make decisive choices about the sort of governance structure they prefer to live under. And both spread that opportunity far more widely than the traditional political process, under which only a small elite is likely to ever have similar opportunities by means of voting or other mechanisms of influencing government policy.

To the extent that a group is "collectively unfree" if not all of its members have access to a given mechanism of choice,[31] private sector foot voting reduces the degree of such constraint as compared to traditional ballot box voting. Especially when combined with interjurisdictional foot voting in the public sector, it greatly reduces the number of people who lack access to the opportunity to make a decisive choice about the political arrangements they prefer to live under.

Here, as in Chapter 2, I do not attempt to resolve the question of the appropriate level of redistribution a liberal democratic society should provide to the poor. I would, however, emphasize that a high degree of private sector foot voting, like that between regional and local governments, is compatible with extensive centralized income redistribution.[32]

The US federal government, for example, can increase income subsidies to the poor, such as those currently provided through the earned income tax credit,[33] while simultaneously giving extensive autonomy to state and local governments and leaving wide scope for private planned communities, as well. Increasing the incomes of the poor in this way would, of course, potentially increase their ability to vote with their feet in various ways, including by joining existing private planned communities or establishing new ones.

Is Private Sector Foot Voting Truly "Political"?

As a tool for exercising political freedom, private sector foot voting is potentially subject to the objection that it is not truly a form of political choice at all. After all, by definition the organizations foot voters are choosing among are private entities. In most cases, both current community residents and potential new entrants are likely motivated by seemingly mundane considerations about cost and quality of life rather than moral or ideological principles.

But the points made on this issue in Chapter 1 nonetheless apply to private planned communities in much the same way as to foot-voting choices between conventional public governments.[34] As discussed there, the fact that individuals' motives for choosing a given community are not explicitly "political" does not mean they aren't affected by public policy (or in this case the policies of private planned communities). In addition, ballot box voters are also sometimes motivated by economic or other self-interested considerations.[35]

In this case, admittedly, the organization chosen by foot voters is private rather than public. But it is also one that is an alternative to standard public services, such as land-use management, public recreational facilities, security, and others. Those who choose the private community's version of those services are—at least implicitly—rejecting the alternative offered by government.

Finally, it is worth noting that private planned communities generally have a quasi-democratic governance structure in some ways similar to that of local governments, with an elected board of directors, and some decisions taken through a form of direct democracy.[36] The voting systems differ from those of traditional public sector governments, insofar as they are often based on property ownership rather than a "one person, one vote model"; thus, owners of multiple properties may have multiple votes.[37] But choosing between private communities nonetheless involves choosing between competing models of governance, as is also the case with choosing between traditional public local governments.

This, perhaps, is another example of how foot voting and ballot box voting can be complements as well as substitutes.[38] Foot voters deciding between rival planned communities may do so in part based on how well each community's governance system works. But it is also the case that the prospect of competition increases communities' incentive to organize their internal "political" systems well.

Ultimately, not much hinges on the question of whether opting for a private community is itself a "political" choice or whether it is instead a search for an alternative to political institutions. In either case, it enables the decision-maker to make a decisive choice about an issue that would otherwise be within the ambit of the government. In the latter scenario, the choice is one to avoid government services, at least in part. In the former, it is a preference for one "governmental" structure over another.

The Problem of Scale

Like local and regional governments, private planned communities are constrained by the problem of scale. Some issues are sufficiently large that they cannot be effectively handled by these sorts of institutions. As a result, foot voting between private communities will often not be an effective mechanism of choice with respect to the handling of these questions.

Because private communities are generally smaller than local governments—to say nothing of regional and national governments—the problem of scale is likely to constrain them even more. For this reason, private sector foot voting cannot be the exclusive mode used handle all possible issues.

But it is important to recognize that planned communities can function on a much larger scale than is often thought. For example, Celebration, Florida, a private city built by the Walt Disney Company, provides effective governance for a community with over 10,000 residents.[39] The quality of those services compares favorably with those offered by conventional local governments, in large part because Disney had strong incentives to make the city attractive to potential residents, else it would not be able to profit from the enterprise.[40]

Even larger private communities than this are feasible. The Indian cities of Gurgaon and Jamshedpur are largely run by private organizations, and each has a far bigger population than Celebration.[41] Their record in providing public services is very mixed, but is often equal to or superior to that of traditional state-run city governments in India.[42] There are also large contractual communities among new developments in China.[43]

The idea of "bottom-up federation" offers a potentially more complete solution to the problem of scale.[44] A set of local private communities can federate, creating a higher-level association to handle issues that have significant economies of scale. The governing councils of the second-level federation could be selected by the leaders of the smaller initial private communities, thereby ensuring accountability to the former, but avoiding reliance on a large electorate in which there are strong incentives for rational voter ignorance.[45] The second-level associations can in turn federate into still-larger units, if necessary to address even bigger common problems.

The larger the second, third, and higher-level associations become, the higher the costs of exiting them will be, and the more opportunities for foot voting might be reduced. A federation of private communities large enough to handle problems that currently require the intervention of a regional or national government will probably be as hard to exit as the latter. In addition, for areas with a very large number of private planned communities, there may be a danger of free-riding, with some communities refusing to join the larger association in order to profit from the public goods it provides without paying for them.

Thus, it is unlikely that bottom-up federation can fully overcome the problem of scale—at least not without raising some of the same problems as traditional political centralization. But it is nonetheless an idea worthy of serious consideration. Even if all it can achieve is "merely" doubling the scale at which private communities can currently address issues, that would still be an important advance. It would significantly mitigate the problem of scale, even if it would fall far short of completely solving it.

Other Types of Private Sector Foot Voting

Private planned communities are just the most expansive private alternative to public sector foot voting. In principle, any private sector service organization that allows consumer choice can be a form of foot voting. And any service that is an alternative to state provision can potentially help expand political freedom.[46]

Private sector foot voting need not be limited to for-profit or commercial organizations. Nonprofit and charitable institutions, and other civil-society organizations can also foster foot voting. For example, competing religious institutions are an alternative to state-funded churches and often offer superior services to community members, thanks in part to competitive incentives.[47] Even such seemingly core public services as security against crime are often privately provided. In most nations, including such advanced democracies as the United States, Germany, Canada, and the United Kingdom, there are actually many more private security guards than public police officers.[48]

These types of private services usually do not have the elaborate governance structure of private communities and do not have the "look and feel" of governments. But they are nonetheless often meaningful alternatives to them. Moreover, they often have the advantage that an individual can switch service providers without having to physically migrate at all. In that respect, they largely avoid the sorts of moving costs that often inhibit foot voting between both governments and private communities.

In this book, I cannot assess the strengths and weaknesses of all such organizations relative to conventional public alternatives. In deciding how much scope to give them, foot-voting opportunities are just one of multiple issues that need to be considered. But the role of these options in enhancing political freedom is an important issue that must be accounted for more fully than is often the case in debates about the proper scope of private provision of traditionally public services.

How Private Sector Foot Voting Augments Public Sector Foot Voting—and Vice Versa

Private sector foot voting is not just valuable in itself. It is also a useful adjunct to foot voting in the public sector: both internal foot voting in federal systems and foot voting through international migration. The three types of foot voting are, in crucial, respects, mutually reinforcing.

The greater the extent of available foot-voting opportunities through internal or international migration, the more migrants can potentially avail themselves of any private sector opportunities available in the regional or national jurisdictions they have access to. Conversely, the more private sector foot-voting opportunities there are in a given jurisdiction, the more options residents have even without moving outside it.

Where possible, competition for residents between public sector jurisdictions can incentivize them to foster a supportive environment for private sector foot-voting options within their respective areas. A public jurisdiction with numerous successful private communities within its territory can generate extra tax revenue for government programs, as a result. In this way, public sector foot voting can reinforce private sector foot-voting opportunities.

The availability of multiple levels of foot-voting opportunities also enables one type to at least partially offset the limitations of the other. For example, problems of scale may prevent some issues from being subject to private sector foot voting, because private organizations are too small to handle them. But those issues might still be subject to interjurisdictional foot voting between governments. On smaller-scale issues, by contrast, private associations can offer a much wider range of options than is available from public entities alone.

Obviously, not all shortcomings of particular modes of foot voting can be offset in this way. And, as is evident from many issues addressed in this book, regional and national governments can also do much to impede foot voting, for example, by imposing migration restrictions or other impediments to mobility.[49] Nonetheless, multiple overlapping levels of foot voting can help expand political freedom in ways that would not be possible through any one level alone.

Conclusion

Private sector foot voting cannot fully replace political decision-making. But it can greatly increase foot-voting opportunities beyond what is available through government-controlled institutions alone. There is much that can be done to make private sector foot voting feasible for more people, especially the poor and disadvantaged. Where private sector foot voting is available, it can be part of a mutually reinforcing network that includes public foot-voting options alongside private ones.

5

Foot Voting and Self-Determination

Even if foot voting can enhance the political freedom of migrants, it does not follow that it increases political freedom overall. Perhaps the political freedom of foot-voting migrants is at odds with that of ballot-box voting natives. One of the most common objections to free migration across international—and sometimes even regional—boundaries is that the existing population within those jurisdictions has a right of self-determination that entitles it to keep migrants out.

Some self-determination arguments of this type are based on individual rights theories that analogize states to private individuals or private groups that have a right to exclude. They assert that national governments' right to exclude is similar to the way members of a club can exclude new applicants for membership, or property owners can exclude those who wish to trespass on their land.[1] Others rely on group rights notions, holding that the right to exclude newcomers from a given territory rests with a particular ethnic or cultural group. Additional group right justifications for the power to exclude hold that it is simply inherent in the notion of national sovereignty, or in democratic citizens' collective right of self-determination.

In addition, some claim that migration rights can be restricted to benefit not the receiving society but that which migrants seek to leave behind. Perhaps they have a duty stay home and "fix their own countries" or prevent them from suffering "brain drain." By depriving their homeland of valuable labor that it is supposedly entitled to control, migrants' departure could potentially impede the self-determination of their countries of origin, not just their new ones.

In this chapter, I assess and largely reject both collective rights and individual rights theories of self-determination that justify exclusion. I also criticize claims that migration can justifiably be restricted because the migrants' home societies have a right to force them to stay. The last part of the chapter explains why self-determination arguments often deployed as justifications for restricting international migration would actually justify extensive constraints on internal migration as well. Those who advocate restricting the former type of migration, but not the latter, cannot logically defend their position on the basis of reasoning that would actually justify both.

This chapter does not consider the related, but distinct, argument that migration can be restricted in order to prevent migrants from creating "political externalities": influencing their new jurisdiction's government policies in harmful ways. Political externality criticisms of foot voting will be addressed in Chapter 6.

Group Rights Claims

Ethnic and Cultural Self-Determination

Perhaps the most common type of group right claim for a power to restrict immigration is based on the rights of distinct ethnic, racial, or cultural groups to self-determination.[2] As Michael Walzer puts it in a well-known defense of this theory, nations must maintain a "community of character" dependent on culture, and "[t]he distinctiveness of cultures and groups depends upon closure and, without it, cannot be conceived as a stable feature of human life."[3] Otherwise, he fears, people will become "radically deracinated."[4] The right of "peoples" to "self-determination" is even enshrined in international law through the International Covenant on Civil and Political Rights (ICCPR), which goes on to say that "[b]y virtue of that right they freely determine their political status and freely pursue their economic, social and cultural development,"[5] though it does not spell out the possible implications of "self-determination" for immigration policy.

Arguments for restrictions on migration based on group membership founder on the flaws inherent in claims that there is a right to live in a polity that privileges a particular culture or ethnic group. Among other shortcomings, such a right would imply the power to coerce even currently existing residents to keep them from changing their cultural practices. To adopt Walzer's terminology, that may be the only way to truly guarantee "closure."[6]

After all, a culture can be transformed through internal change no less than through immigration. Older generations often complain about the cultural changes created by the choices of the young. Over time, the latter often end up radically changing the manners, morals, and social norms they inherited. Yet few argue that their elders have a right to use force to prevent it, much less to expel anyone who fails to conform to the previously dominant cultural patterns.[7]

Indeed, virtually any significant social change can potentially undermine an existing culture or "way of life," sometimes radically so. As Michael Clemens and Lant Pritchett point out, "if migration barriers are deemed necessary to preserve a 'way of life' of inherent value, it would need to be clarified why similar reasoning would not have obstructed the Industrial Revolution, the entry of women into the labor force, and the abolition of serfdom—all of which greatly altered an existing 'way of life.' "[8]

David Miller points out that internal cultural change is usually smaller than that which might be brought about by immigrants because "normal processes of education and socialization" will ensure "a good deal of continuity" between parents and their children.[9] But this is a difference of degree rather than kind. If members of a dominant cultural group have the right to use the power of government to forestall unwanted cultural change, why does that authority only apply to rapid change, and not the slower kind? Some cultural conservatives may have strong objections to the latter almost as much as the former.

In addition, sometimes internal cultural change can be very rapid, as in the dramatic shift toward greater acceptance of gays and lesbians in many Western societies over the last twenty to thirty years. Many social conservatives deeply resented both the speed and direction of that transformation.

Theories like Miller's and Walzer's also imply a much higher degree of cultural consensus within the native population of a country than is actually likely to be the case. Far from having a unitary "community of character,"[10] most societies actually have considerable disagreement over cultural issues, often even among people who belong to the same ethnic and linguistic groups. Some natives may fear the cultural impact of immigrants, while others either actively welcome it or at least do not object to it. It is not clear why restrictionists' values should be treated as if they exemplify the society's true "character," as opposed to those who favor greater openness.[11] International law on the definition of the "peoples" who have a right to "self-determination" is similarly vague, and does not offer a clear indication of who, if anyone, has the right to define those "peoples' " cultural values.[12]

Anna Stilz suggests that such difficulties can be avoided if the right to exclude migrants for purposes of protecting natives' culture is limited to states with "a largely culturally homogenous population" in which "almost all constituents" share the dominant culture.[13] In such cases, states can exclude migrants on cultural grounds without thereby biasing the state's institutional framework "in favor of some cultural preferences over others."[14]

Unless the terms "largely" and "almost all" are given very loose definitions, this approach would deny the right to cultural exclusion to all or nearly all existing states. Certainly, the United States, Canada, the nations of Western Europe, and other countries to which most potential migrants seek to move are nowhere near "homogenous" and do not have a single dominant culture to which "almost all" current residents subscribe.

But, even in the case of a genuinely homogenous nation, Stilz's argument does not avoid the problems that bedevil other justifications for a right to exclude based on culture. If the government of a society with a "homogenous" culture has a right to use coercion to preserve that culture from change, it presumably does so against internal transformations, as well as those that might be caused by immigrants.

Even in relatively homogenous nations, internal forces can also cause cultural change over time, unless suppressed. Thus, the Stilz approach still ends up providing a justification for internal cultural repression in any society for which it could justify immigration restrictions.

Another problem with the cultural self-determination argument is that only a small fraction of the world's ethnic or cultural groups have a state of their own. There are currently some 190 nations in the world. At the same time there are also thousands of ethnic, religious, and cultural groups who lack a nation of their own, or even a province within a larger nation where they are the majority.

Few argue that the principle of self-determination entitles each such group to sovereignty over a territory from which they can exclude others. And it seems clear that many such groups do maintain a functioning culture that persists over time, even if not in a completely unchanging fashion. Certainly, most members of such groups have not become "radically deracinated."[15] If this is true of currently stateless groups, it is difficult see why it is not equally true of those who—often through conquest or historical accident—happen to have a majority in an existing nation-state.

Perhaps things are different in the case of an ethnic or cultural group that has acquired previously unoccupied territory and then developed it. It could be argued that such a group then has exclusive rights to the territory that cannot be claimed by ethnic groups that coexist with others or acquired "their" land by conquest.[16] But, if so, virtually no actual government can claim such a right, as nearly all are the products of repeated conquest or coercion, and most rule territories occupied by multiple cultural or ethnic groups, not just one. As Jacob Levy points out, "[i]t is unlikely that the current possessor of any piece of land on earth acquired it peacefully and legitimately from someone who acquired it peacefully and legitimately from someone who acquired it peacefully and legitimately from someone, and so on until original acquisition. . . . [M]any of the forceful dispossessions and acquisitions have been ethnic or nationalistic" in nature.[17] Because of this history of conquest and dispossession, "most or all land is subject to more than one claim of past possession by some ethnic or national group."[18]

This is undeniably true of the Western democracies of Europe, North America, Australia, and New Zealand, the countries to which the largest number of potential migrants seek access. Nations such as the United States, Britain, Germany, France, and others, are all the products of a long history of aggression and coercion, and all rule over populations that are far from being ethnically or culturally homogenous.

In the case of the United States, for example, the nation was established in the Revolutionary War, despite the opposition of a large minority of Loyalists who preferred continued British rule.[19] Later, the United States acquired much additional territory through conquest and coercion, in wars with Mexico and various Native American peoples. Other advanced nations that are popular destination countries for immigrants have comparable histories of conquest and coercive acquisition of territory.

That does not prove that these governments have no right to exist or that they are necessarily worse than those of other states. It certainly does not prove that the establishment of the United States or any other nation was necessarily unjust, relative to the available alternatives at the time.[20] But it does foreclose claims to a right to restrict migration based on exclusive development of their territory by a particular ethnic or cultural group.[21]

The same goes for the notion of an exclusive historic attachment to the territory that no other group can lay claim to. Given the multiethnic nature of nearly all modern nations—particularly those advanced societies that most migrants seek to enter—it will rarely, if ever, be true that members of only one group have a historical connection to the area in question.

Similar flaws bedevil nationalistic theories that ground the right to exclusive control of territory on the basis of a group's "family-like bonds of mutual loyalty that persist among them," as Yoram Hazony does in a prominent recent defense of nationalism.[22] Hazony contends that such states can justly be formed when "a permanent peace has been formed among a number of competing tribes that share a common language or religion and an earlier history of banding together for the sake of common efforts"[23]

In reality, however, virtually all governments rule over large numbers of people who do not feel anything approaching "family-like bonds" with many of their compatriots, and virtually all were formed in large part by conquest, not voluntary agreement among "tribes."[24] Elsewhere in his book, Hazony recognizes that his conception of nationalism in fact requires "a majority nation whose dominance is plain and unquestioned, and against which resistance appears to be futile."[25] If so, his approach is little different from more traditional justifications for the domination of majority ethnic or cultural groups over others.

The Injustice of Discrimination Based on Parentage and Place of Birth

Ethnic and cultural group–based claims for a right to exclude are particularly problematic for liberal democrats committed to principles of nondiscrimination on the basis of race and ethnicity. The standard defense of racial and ethnic nondiscrimination is that race and ethnicity are morally irrelevant characteristics that people have no control over.[26]

Whether a person is black, Asian, white, or Hispanic says nothing about her moral worth, or what rights she should have. Most liberal democrats recoil at the idea that we should restrict people's freedom because they chose the wrong parents.

What is true of race and ethnicity is also true of place of birth. Whether a person was born in the United States, Mexico, or China is also a morally arbitrary characteristic that she has no control over, and which should not determine how much freedom she is entitled to. To adapt a famous quote from Martin Luther King Jr., place of birth is no more indicative of "the content of your character" than race of birth.[27]

In principle, immigration restrictions based on culture might not be based on either place of birth or parentage and thus might be different from racial and ethnic discrimination. A person not born in France or in an ethnically French family might still become familiar with French culture and choose a life that follows French cultural mores as completely as any native of France. In practice, however, virtually all efforts to discriminate on the basis of culture in immigration policy *do* rely on place of birth, parentage, or some combination of the two. These characteristics are used as proxies for culture, in much the same way that domestic racial and ethnic classifications were historically often used as proxies for a variety of traits.

Outside the context of immigration, legal and political theorists who argue for racial and ethnic preferences generally do so on a strictly limited basis, usually in order to compensate for large-scale historic injustices through, for example, race-based affirmative action programs or reparations payments.[28] Some also argue that racial and ethnic discrimination is defensible in cases where it is the only way to avoid a great evil, such as a massive terrorist attack.[29]

Whatever the merits of such arguments, they clearly cannot justify systematic discrimination against migrants based on place of birth—discrimination that often targets groups who are themselves the victims of massive injustices at the hands of the rulers of the nations they seek to leave. And, as we shall see in Chapter 6, few migration restrictions are the only means to avoid a still greater evil.[30]

In addition to their similarity to racial and ethnic discrimination, migration restrictions based on parentage or place of birth also have troubling similarities to medieval feudalism. As Joseph Carens puts it, "[t]o be born a citizen of a poor country . . . is like being born into the peasantry in the Middle Ages. . . . Like feudal birthright privileges, contemporary social arrangements not only grant great advantages on the basis of birth but also entrench those advantages by restricting mobility, making it extremely difficult for those born into a socially disadvantaged position to overcome that disadvantage, no matter how talented they are or how hard they work."[31]

For most people, citizenship status determines where they are allowed to live and work, which in turn largely determines not only their economic fate but often whether they will have protection for even very minimal human rights. And citizenship itself is largely determined by birth—much like membership in old-time aristocracies. If you were not born a US citizen or a close relative of one, there is very little chance you will ever be allowed to emigrate to the United States. For most others, the so-called "line" they must join to enter the United States is either nonexistent or likely to be decades or centuries long.[32] The same point applies to your chances of emigrating to other advanced liberal democracies, if you were neither born there nor are the child of a current citizen.

Some countries have established a "right of return" for members of the majority ethnic group within that nation, such as Germany for ethnic Germans, and Israel for Jews.[33] This, too, however, is a kind of hereditary privilege, albeit based on race or ethnicity rather than family connections to current citizens.

Like many traditional aristocracies, the modern aristocracy of citizenship is not a totally hermetically sealed class. Just as a commoner could sometimes join the nobility by marrying an aristocrat, so a foreigner can become eligible for American citizenship by marrying a current citizen. And just as kings and emperors would sometimes elevate to the nobility those commoners they considered especially deserving (or especially useful), so modern governments sometimes grant residency rights (and the opportunity for eventual citizenship) to particular classes of migrants without family connections to current citizens, such as workers in certain professions. These exceptions to the rule of hereditary privilege are important. But they are still exceptions to a general rule that keeps the vast majority "in their place."

Today, we reject traditional hereditary aristocracy, and especially the notion that nobles had a right to use mobility restrictions to keep the serfs tied to the region where they were born. And we reject it despite the fact that nobles and their defenders could plausibly have argued that aristocrats had a distinct culture that might be imperiled by allowing peasants to move about freely.

Place of birth may sometimes correlate with morally relevant characteristics, even though it does not cause them. People born in one nation may, among other things, be more likely to become criminals or terrorists than those born in another.

But the same is true of different racial and ethnic groups. In the United States, African-Americans, on average, have higher crime rates than members of many other ethnic groups.[34] White males are disproportionately likely to become domestic terrorists.[35] It does not follow, however, that we would be justified in imposing severe restrictions on the freedom of either blacks or white males as a group.

In both cases, it would be unjust to restrict people's freedom merely because they happen to be members of the same racial or ethnic group as others who have committed various crimes and misdeeds. The same point applies to potential immigrant groups singled out for exclusion merely because others born in the same place have a disproportionate propensity to engage in some form of wrongdoing.

Defenders of migration restrictions might argue that the ideal of self-determination allows current residents to impose ethnic-, cultural-, and parentage-based restrictions on immigrants that would not be permissible in the case of natives. But this argument is circular. It assumes the validity of the very point that must be proven: that governments have a special right to exclude potential immigrants, based on culture, that does not apply to otherwise similar natives.

Ethnic, racial, or cultural characteristics of immigrants cannot justify uniquely negative treatment for them. That is because many natives also have similar characteristics, yet it is not considered permissible to impose discriminatory treatment on *them*.

The Sovereignty Argument

Another variant of the group rights justification for exclusion holds that governments can exclude migrants not because of the special claims of any particular racial or ethnic population but because the right to bar migrants is intrinsic to the very nature of sovereignty: an independent nation must have it if it is to continue to exist. This argument has little support from political theorists. But it often occurs in public discourse. For example, President Donald Trump claimed during the 2016 presidential campaign that "A nation without borders is not a nation" and therefore "[t]here must be a wall across the southern border" of the United States.[36] When, in 1889, the United States Supreme Court belatedly ruled that the federal government had the power to exclude migrants, despite the lack of any explicit statement to that effect in the Constitution, it was based on the theory that the power to "exclude aliens from its territory . . . is an incident of every independent nation" and therefore must be an "incident of sovereignty belonging to the government of the United States."[37]

It may well be true that nations must have borders of some kind in order to exist. Perhaps each government must have some form of authority bounded by territorial limits. But even if we assume that a nation cannot exist without borders, it does not follow that the maintenance of borders requires immigration restrictions.

In reality, borders have a wide range of other functions besides regulating immigration. For example, they define the territory within which a given government's laws are binding and also the land area within which it may deploy its armed forces without obtaining permission from other governments.

If all immigration restrictions were abolished tomorrow, borders could readily continue to facilitate these and other purposes. A nation that does not exclude peaceful migrants can still bar invading armies. And its government can still exercise territorially defined authority from which the authority of other governments is excluded.

Empirically, it is unquestionably the case that sovereign nations existed for centuries without exercising a general power to bar peaceful migrants. As Joseph Carens points out, most states began to make significant efforts to restrict entry and exit only in the late nineteenth century, and passport systems were not introduced until after World War I.[38]

Perhaps the sovereignty argument rests not on the idea that states simply cannot exist without immigration restrictions but rather that the power to impose them is a traditionally accepted attribute of sovereignty. Under current international law, it arguably is, though there are some limitations based on obligations to admit certain categories of refugees.[39]

But the fact that current practices hold that a given power is an attribute of sovereignty does not mean that such a power is morally justified. Historically, state practice and dominant public and elite opinion also held that sovereignty included such powers as the authority to suppress political speech and the practice of religions considered inimical to the ruler's interests. For example, the influential 1555 Peace of Augsburg was based on the principle of *cuius regio, eius religio* ("Whose realm, his religion") which insured that rulers could promote their preferred official religion and suppress rival faiths.[40]

The governments of that era agreed that they had the right to suppress religion and censor speech, and these principles were enshrined in international law, as it was then understood. But that did not make them right and just. Similarly, we should not assume that current state practices, including those supported by the current system of international law, are necessarily just.

In both earlier centuries and today, governments often have an interest in claiming powers to which they may not have any just entitlement. And international law is heavily influenced by the preferences of such governments, including even the most deeply unjust ones.[41] Thus, we should not assume that any power considered a standard attribute of sovereignty in current international law is therefore defensible. Like any other government power, its existence requires an independent normative justification.

Democratic Self-Determination

Sarah Song offers a collective rights justification for immigration restrictions specifically linked to the ideals of democracy. She contends that democracy necessarily requires that citizens have the ability to participate in political decision-making and that ability entails a right to collective "self-determination." That, in turn, require states to have the power to restrict "admission" into the society, because that is the only way in which we can respect "the right of individuals to be regarded as equal participants in significant political decisions by which they are bound."[42] New entrants could potentially dilute the participation rights of existing citizens and reduce their influence over public policy.

It is worth noting that Song's argument applies to nondemocratic governments as well as democracies. As she puts it, the "conditions for collective self-determination . . . can also be met through nondemocratic institutions that secure basic protections for the security and liberty of persons and provide ways for people to form and express public opinion."[43] Depending on how stringently we interpret these conditions, it may be that a wide range of nondemocratic states can meet them, so long as they protect "security and liberty," at least to some extent, and provide at least some mechanisms for the formation and expression of public opinion. But, in fairness, democratic governments constitute the overwhelming majority of those states to which a significant number of migrants seek access.

Even if it is otherwise valid, Song's argument seems to justify not restrictions on immigration but merely restrictions on access to political participation. As Song puts it, "[t]he right to control immigration derives from the right of the demos to rule itself" under conditions where "all members have an equal right to participate in shaping collective life."[44] An entrant who does not have the right to participate in political decision-making does not diminish existing citizens' ability to influence public policy.[45]

The political participation in question here is the use of the franchise, or other methods of influencing government policy through "voice."[46] Influence through voice is necessarily a zero-sum game in which increasing the influence of some participants necessarily means diminishing that of others.[47] This is not the case with foot voting, in which the ability of some to choose which policies they wish to live under does not in and of itself reduce the ability of others to participate in the formation of policy. Indeed, if a person eligible for the franchise departs a jurisdiction, that may slightly increase the leverage of those voters who remain behind in a smaller electorate where each of their votes has a marginally higher chance of determining electoral outcomes.

Moreover, even if we agree that citizens must be able to participate as equals, it does not follow that they are entitled to restrict participation in the political process to a particular set of people. They can still participate equally even if the number of citizens is increased, though the leverage of each individual participant is reduced whenever the number of citizens eligible to vote increases.[48]

There is, also, an even deeper limitation of the appeal to democratic self-determination. Before the democratic electorate in question has a right to self-determination, there must be a prior determination of who is eligible to be part of the electorate in the first place. As Arash Abizadeh puts it, "the appeal to self-determination here begs the question of who the relevant collective 'self' rightly is."[49]

Democracy may be "rule by the people." But there is no democratic way to determine who qualifies as a member of the people to begin with. Before any democratic procedures can even start to function, there must be a prior decision on who gets to participate. Thus, democracy cannot be democratic all the way down. Given the coercive history of virtually all existing states, it is likely impossible to identify a non-arbitrary point at which the existing inhabitants of a territory become the "people" who have a right to exclude future newcomers.

In the case of the United States, for example, was it when the ancestors of Native Americans first settled North America, when European colonists first established governments under the aegis of their homelands' monarchs, or when the United States was established as an independent state in 1776? Should it matter that none of these regimes were anywhere close to being democratic, or that the United States arguably falls short of various democratic ideals even today?

Song herself suggests that a group can gain the status of a "people" presumptively entitled to exclude migrants from a particular territory if they aim at "collective self-rule" and have "a history of political participation and contestation."[50] If this criterion requires all or most adult members of the group to have such a history, few if any existing states can meet its requirements, since virtually all have a long history of excluding women, some minority groups, and others from meaningful political participation.

While many formerly excluded groups have eventually obtained the right to participate in politics, that right exists within institutions that structure and constrain it—institutions that are often hard to change and were established during the period when women and other such groups were not allowed to participate. Thus, it is questionable that the resulting state really is "authorized by the people," in Song's terms, as opposed to a mere subset thereof.[51]

If the "history" in question must be that of the group as a whole, it is unlikely that existing states can meet this test. If, on the other hand, it is enough that some subset of the group—perhaps even a small minority—has a history of participation and contestation, then that suggests that small elites can rightfully exercise the power to exclude (and perhaps other government powers), regardless of the preferences of the rest of the population, so long as there is some appropriate sense in which the elite and the masses are part of the same "people."

If Song's argument does justify restrictions on mere entry into the territory of a state, and not merely restrictions on eligibility for the franchise or other access to political power, it can just as easily be used to legitimize coercive restrictions on fertility as on immigration. After all, a baby born within the territory of a state also thereby "enters" the society and also may eventually vote and otherwise participate in politics, thereby reducing the influence of current citizens. In Song's terminology, the power to restrict fertility is essential to a self-determining community because "part of what it means for a political community to be self-determining is that it controls whom to admit as new members."[52]

It follows, therefore, that existing citizens of a democracy (acting through their governments) should have the right to forbid births, or—alternatively—deport infants unwanted by the government (or, perhaps by a political majority) beyond the nation's borders.[53] This implication might be avoided if the needs of self-determination might be satisfied by giving existing citizens the power to deny children the right to vote when they come of age. But, if so, the same can be said of the power to restrict migration, which also becomes unnecessary, insofar as restrictions on the franchise are an adequate substitute.

In sum, Song's argument is insufficient to justify immigration restrictions, as opposed to restrictions on political participation. It also has morally unacceptable implications that few, if any, advocates of liberal democracy would embrace.

Individual Rights Claims

In addition to group rights claims for states' authority to exclude migrants, there are also individual rights theories, which analogize the nation-state to a private house or club.[54] As one leading advocate of this theory puts it, "groups, even political states, can have rights to autonomy analogous to those enjoyed by individuals."[55]

More individualistic versions of the right to exclude migrants suffer from serious flaws, as grave as those of group rights theories. The most significant is that real-world states are not voluntary organizations but coercive ones.[56] Unlike club members, residents of nation-states are born into their polities and not allowed to choose freely whether to live under the authority of the government.

The House Analogy

The analogy between nations and private homes is ubiquitous in debates over immigration. It is commonly deployed by both laypeople and professional political theorists. But despite its popularity, it has serious shortcomings.

The house analogy appeals to the notion of property rights. But it actually ends up undermining private property rights rather than upholding them. Far from protecting property rights, immigration restrictions actually abrogate the rights of property owners who want to rent their property to the excluded migrants, associate with them, or employ them on their land. In this way, the house analogy justifies policies that actually restrict the property rights of true owners of private property.

Perhaps, however, the government is a kind of super-owner that has the right to supersede the decisions of private owners whenever it passes a law that does so. On that view, the state has all the same rights over land within its jurisdiction as a private owner has over his house. And when the two types of property rights conflict, the state's claims prevail over those of the private owner.

Restated in this way, the house analogy could indeed potentially justify almost any immigration restrictions a government might choose to set up. But it can also justify a variety of repressive government policies that target natives, as well. If a state has the same powers over land within the national territory as a homeowner has over her house, then the state has broad power to suppress speech and religion the rulers disapprove of.

After all, a homeowner has every right to mandate that only Muslim prayer will be permitted in his house, or that the only political speech permitted within its walls is that which supports the Republican Party. The same logic would justify all kinds of other illiberal and oppressive policies as well, so long as a homeowner could adopt the same rules within her house. [57]

Ironically, the house analogy argument for immigration restrictions—most often advanced by those on the political right—has the same kinds of dangerous implications for individual freedom as the traditional left-of-center argument that government can override and restructure property rights as it wishes because it supposedly created them in the first place by virtue of enacting laws that define their scope and institutions that protect them against trespass.[58] If this latter argument is correct, it would also justify governmental restructuring of a variety of personal liberties that the government can be said to "create" by virtue of establishing rules related to their scope and protection.[59] The house analogy deployed by many immigration restrictionists has similar dangerous implications.

In a democratic society, the extent of the resulting oppression might well be less than in a dictatorship. Still, the house analogy would justify suppression of religion, speech, association, and other behavior that the political majority disapproves of.

Perhaps a democracy could prevent some of the illiberal consequences by establishing constitutional rights against them. But if the house analogy is valid, such guarantees are not morally required. They can be granted or withheld at the discretion of the government of the day, or whoever controls the constitutional amendment process. If, for example, the United States were to enact a constitutional amendment abolishing freedom of speech and religion and instead require all residents (on pain of expulsion) to become members of the ruling party and the newly established official church, dissenters would have no basis for complaint.

As a homeowner, I can choose to let people who disagree with my political views enter my house, or host religious services for faiths I disapprove of. I could even promulgate rules guaranteeing freedom of speech and religion on my land. But I have no moral duty to do so. A government entitled to the same rights as a homeowner could exercise such powers as well.

The Club Analogy

The club analogy has many of the same flaws as the house analogy. It too would justify a variety of illiberal and oppressive policies. After all, private clubs can and do restrict membership on the basis of speech, religion, and other similar criteria. Michael Huemer points out that a private club could potentially require members to "refrain from expressing political opinions, refrain from voting if they are female, and so on."[60]

Like the house analogy, the club analogy ends up justifying policies that trample on the liberties of actual private organizations. It restricts the ability of natives to freely associate with immigrants whom they want to hire for jobs, rent property to, or even form genuine private clubs with.

In addition, there are crucial differences between a government and a private club. The latter includes only members who join voluntarily and agree to follow all of the club's rules. If members wish to leave the club, they can do so while retaining all of their preexisting property and other rights. The justification for the club's broad power to set membership criteria and expel violators is that it is a consensual organization. No one has to join it unless they have consented to do so.[61]

Anna Stilz points out that "a state is not an intimate, face-to-face association, a fact which may have consequences for its right to exclude."[62] As she notes, antidiscrimination law often forbids discrimination on the basis of race, ethnicity, or national origin by large private organizations.[63] To the extent such antidiscrimination norms are justified for large private organizations, they should also be applied to states that are meaningfully analogous to them, which would mean forbidding immigration restrictions based on ancestry or place of birth, which is how most immigration restrictions currently classify people. [64] As explained earlier in this chapter, such discrimination is closely analogous to discrimination based on race and ethnicity.

Libertarian critics of anti-discrimination laws contend that most such restrictions on private organizations are unjust or at least unnecessary.[65] But most libertarians also argue that there must be much tighter constraints on government powers than those of private organizations, and that the former are legitimately subject to severe restrictions on discrimination on the base of race, ethnicity, and similar characteristics.[66] Consistent libertarians should be the last to accept any argument implying that governments should have the same sort of authority over their territory as private property owners have over their houses or clubs. Any such theory would authorize the state to trample all the rights libertarians hold dear.

Democratic governments are more consensual than authoritarian states but not nearly as much so as the club analogy assumes. Unlike genuine private clubs, every real-world democratic state was initially established in large part by coercion. For example, the American Revolution that established the United States prevailed only because the revolutionaries successfully coerced the substantial minority of Loyalist supporters of the British Empire into accepting the new government or, in many cases, fleeing.[67] Black slaves, of course, had even less opportunity to meaningfully consent than white loyalists. That does not necessarily mean that the Revolution was unjustified or that the United States should not exist. It *does* suggest that the US government is not meaningfully analogous to a genuinely consensual private club. The same is true of every other actually existing government in the world.

Most people would take a dim view of a private club that proclaims everyone within a 100-mile radius has to be a member whether they want to be or not and is therefore subject to all club rules. If such a mandatory club should be allowed to exist at all, it at the very least should not be given the broad powers permitted a voluntary organization. Governments are much more like mandatory clubs than voluntary ones.[68] When a genuinely consensual private club asks you to join, it has to take "no" for an answer. The state, by contrast, usually treats "no" as if it were just another way of saying "yes."[69]

Political theorists and libertarian activists have sometimes imagined governments established through genuinely consensual processes more akin to those by which clubs are formed.[70] Perhaps such a government really would be analogous to a private club and be entitled to exercise all the same rights. But there are no such club-like governments in the real world and we are unlikely to see one established anytime soon.

Other Freedom of Association Arguments

In addition to the club and house analogies, political theorists have offered a number of other freedom of association rationales for a right to exclude migrants. These theories all have flaws similar to those of the club and house arguments.

Political philosopher A. John Simmons argues that a state may be justified in restricting immigration if it consists of "a substantial group of persons who willingly create (or join) a group committed to persisting as a viable, governed territorial polity."[71] In that event, the resulting government would have the right to "fence, control, and exclude in the same ways that an individual landowner" does.[72] But virtually no actually existing government meets these criteria. None rule over only persons who "willingly" created or joined the polity in question. To the contrary, every actual government in the world was created at least in part through violence and coercion, and it exercises power over anyone who enters or is born within its claimed domain, regardless of whether those individuals voluntarily agree to its authority or not.

Simmons recognizes that real-world governments rule over "many unwilling persons and groups."[73] But he suggests that they might still have a broad power to exclude migrants so long as they are "honestly working towards full rectification" of this and other similar injustices.[74] However, it is difficult to show that *any* existing states are in fact working toward anything approaching "full rectification" of their involuntary nature, and it may not even be possible for them to do so without ceasing to exist as effective governments.

Christopher Wellman argues that the right of states to make treaties implies that they also have a right to exclude migrants.[75] The power to make (or refuse to make) treaties indicates that states have a right of freedom of association. But freedom of association in turn also implies a right to exclude migrants with whom the government chooses not to associate.

But the power to make treaties does not necessarily imply a general right of "freedom of association" that includes the power to exclude migrants. Rather, a treaty is simply a contract between governments. As John Jay put it in *Federalist* 64, "a treaty is only another name for a bargain."[76]

Governments, like other entities, have the right to make bargains only on matters that are legitimately within their control. For example, I can sign a contract under which I have an obligation to teach classes at my university. But I cannot sign a contract requiring Bob to teach those classes in my place, unless he has voluntarily authorized me to do so. Similarly, the power to make treaties only authorizes governments to make agreements on whatever subjects are otherwise within their legitimate authority. It does not, in and of itself, create a power to impose whatever restrictions they wish on either current residents of their territory or potential migrants.

The fact that governments are coercive rather than voluntary does not prove they should not exist, or by itself determine what powers they can legitimately exercise. But it does indicate that those powers cannot be justified by analogies to the powers of private homeowners or club organizers, or by reference to theories of freedom of association, more generally.

The Right to Avoid Unwanted Political Obligations

Michael Blake argues that restricting migration is necessary for individual members of a society to be able to avoid the imposition of "unwanted obligations."[77] He contends that states have a responsibility to provide "legal protection" of the "basic rights" of people living within its territory.[78] Blake does not fully spell out exactly what is meant by basic rights; but he means such things as providing "physical security," procedural protections extended to people accused of crimes, and the protection of criminal and civil law that applies to all persons within the state's territory.[79] If governments are not allowed to keep out migrants, their presence could impose unwanted obligations to protect rights on the existing citizens of the state in question.

To the extent that avoiding unwanted obligations is an important element of liberty and autonomy, immigration restrictions may be essential to ensuring its protection.[80] The only way that existing citizens of the state can avoid unwanted obligations would be to prevent migrants from entering, though Blake is careful to emphasize that this right to avoid unwanted obligations does not necessarily "trump" all competing considerations, such as the needs of people fleeing severe oppression.[81]

Blake's argument is an interesting and original approach to justifying immigration restrictions. But, even if we grant the contestable assumption that avoiding unwanted obligations really is an important human right, it has a number of significant limitations. The most serious arises from the fact that immigration restrictions themselves impose unwanted obligations. Most obviously, they impose obligations on those potential migrants who are required to avoid entering the nation in question. In many cases, that imposition might be very severe, since it could consign the person in question to a life of poverty and deprivation.[82]

Migration restrictions also impose unwanted obligations on natives, who are required to cooperate with deportation efforts and often must face the risk of racial and ethnic profiling, civil liberties violations, and even deportation as a result of bureaucratic error in cases where the authorities confuse them with illegal migrants.[83] Migration restrictions also, of course, impose the obligation to refrain from commercial and cultural relationships with migrants that require the physical presence of the latter.

On balance, migration restrictions are likely to impose far more severe unwanted obligations than those that Blake argues can be avoided by means of immigration restrictions. Protection of basic rights will, in most cases, impose only a modest increase in marginal tax rates for necessary government services, an increase that could be offset by the extra wealth created by migration itself.[84] By contrast, the unwanted obligations imposed by immigration restrictions are often far more severe, for both would-be migrants and many natives.

Imposition of unwanted obligations is a potential downside of almost any enforceable legal duty. In many cases, it is surely outweighed by the considerations justifying the imposition in the first place. But a legal duty that is itself justified by the need to avoid unwanted obligations is uniquely vulnerable to the objection that it actually imposes unwanted obligations more severe than those it prevents.

Like Sarah Song's argument,[85] Blake's theory also potentially justifies restrictions on fertility as well as migration. After all, the birth of a child creates unwanted obligations to protect its basic rights similar to those created by the arrival of a migrant.

To his credit, Blake recognizes this, but suggests that the creation of an unwanted obligation might be outweighed by the harm and injustice inflicted by fertility restrictions.[86] But if so, the same can be said any time exclusion of a migrant causes harm comparable in magnitude to a restriction on fertility. For many millions of people, being consigned to a life of poverty—or worse—in their nation of origin is, plausibly, at least as severe an imposition as having to have one less child than they would otherwise. This is especially true if the restrictions on fertility imposed by the state do not ban families from having children entirely, but "only" limit the number they are allowed to have, perhaps along the lines of China's notorious "one child" policy.[87]

Finally, it is worth emphasizing that the obligation to protect basic rights can often be fulfilled through expenditures that a state already undertakes on law enforcement institutions simply to provide that protection for natives. In other cases, it can be carried out by utilizing resources raised from the extra wealth created by migration itself. As such, the "extra" burden this obligation creates will often be minimal or even nonexistent. Blake's "unwanted obligation" argument is distinguishable from the related, but distinct, concern that immigration might harm natives by overburdening the welfare state or increasing crime. These issues are discussed in Chapter 6.

At least in the vast majority of situations, we can protect the legitimate political freedom of natives without denying it to foot-voting immigrants. Unconstrained foot-voting rights may not be feasible in all cases. But it should be possible to expand them far beyond their current level without endangering legitimate rights of self-determination or creating dangerous political externalities.

Do Migrants Have a Duty to Stay Home and "Fix Their Own Countries"?

Even if migration does not undermine the self-determination of the receiving nation, perhaps it violates the rights of the migrants' nation of origin. The latter might have a right to compel the migrants to stay and contribute to the improvement of their homeland rather than departing for greener pastures elsewhere. If their government is unjust, corrupt, or oppressive, perhaps that makes the duty even stronger. In common parlance, this is the idea that would-be migrants have a duty to "stay and fix their own countries." In a related vein, President Donald Trump suggested in a speech to the United Nations that potential migrants should "build more hopeful futures in their home countries" and "make their countries great again."[88]

Even if not everyone has an obligation to work to "fix their own countries," perhaps such an obligation does apply to people with skills that might be especially useful to poor nations where they were born, such as health care professionals or engineers. Some political theorists argue that such people have a special duty to stay and work for the betterment of their home nations, either as a general principle or in order to repay their home society for the "investment" it has made in their education and training.[89] Such "brain drain" concerns might justify forcing people to stay in their home countries, either by directly barring them from leaving or by achieving the same result through denying them the right to move to other societies with greater opportunities.[90]

The "fix their own countries" theory has several serious weaknesses. Consider the following paraphrase of an exchange I had with a questioner who came up to me after I participated in a public debate on immigration policy in 2017:[91]

QUESTIONER: Why do Middle Eastern refugees have to come here? They should fix their own governments instead.
ME: Do you happen to know where your ancestors came from?
QUESTIONER: They were Jews who emigrated from czarist Russia.
ME: Do you think they should have stayed in Russia and worked to fix the czar?

I do not blame the questioner for failing to come up with a good answer on the fly. Anyone can fall short when put on the spot, myself definitely included. Still, the fact remains that the "fix your own country" argument implies that the ancestors of most Americans (and also many Canadians, Australians, and others) were wrong to emigrate. The Russians should have tried to fix the czar and (later) the communists; the Irish should have stayed home and worked to fix the British Empire. President Donald Trump's grandfather should have stayed in Bavaria and worked to fix imperial Germany.[92] And so on.

The fact that the "fix your own country" argument implies that the ancestors of most Americans were wrong to come does not by itself disprove it. We should not automatically assume that every longstanding American practice was necessarily right. Past generations of Americans erred in committing such injustices as slavery and segregation. Perhaps they were also wrong to come to the United States in the first place. I suspect, however, that most people are not willing to bite this particular bullet. And they would be right not to.

The claim that immigrants fleeing poverty or oppression have a duty to stay home and "fix" their countries is wrong for reasons that go beyond intuitions about American history. Most fundamentally, it treats people as the property of their home societies and suggests they have a moral duty to perform labor for them. If they can be forced to forego emigration in order to help their home society, why not also require them to perform forced labor? Otherwise, they might potentially choose to remain unemployed or work at a job less useful to "fixing" the society than the one that might be chosen by the state.

In most cases, potential migrants have little or no responsibility for the injustice and poverty they are fleeing. Russian Jews like the questioner's ancestors were not responsible for the many injustices of the czarist regime.

Likewise, today's refugees from Venezuela, Syria, and other unjust and corrupt governments generally had no meaningful role in creating the awful conditions there. It is therefore wrong to claim they must risk lifelong privation in order to "fix" the unjust regimes in their home countries. That point applies with extra force in cases where efforts to fix the regime are likely to result in imprisonment or death at the hands of the state. We rightly honor brave dissidents who risk life and limb to oppose injustice. But such sacrifices are not morally obligatory, and no blame attaches to those who forgo them—especially if they have family members to protect, as well as themselves.

In addition, most migrants have little if any chance of succeeding in "fixing" their home governments, even if they did stay to try to do so. In most such societies, the injustice and oppression is deeply embedded in the political system, and most would-be migrants lack the clout to fix it. Had the questioner's ancestors stayed in Russia, it is nearly certain they would not have succeeded in reforming the czarist regime, no matter how hard they tried. The same goes for most migrants and refugees today. At least as a general rule, there is no moral duty to take great risks to attempt the nearly impossible.

This point is especially strong when it comes to authoritarian states, where ordinary people have little or no influence on government policy. But the constraint also applies, though with lesser force, to many dysfunctional countries that are democratic. Even in advanced democracies such as the United States, Canada, and the nations of Western Europe, many harmful and unjust government policies persist because of widespread voter ignorance and bias.[93] The same is true (often to a much greater extent) in the corrupt and dysfunctional democratic governments many migrants flee from. In most cases, potential migrants have little or no chance of reversing this dynamic anytime soon.

Occasionally, an unjust political system comes to a turning point where change is more feasible than is usually the case. But such situations are difficult to foresee, and it is wrong to demand that people (often literally) bet their lives on the hope that such an opportunity is going to come up soon.

Even when an opportunity for transformative change does arise, it is still far from clear that the average would-be migrant could make a real difference to the outcome. In addition, there is the very real possibility that a revolution could result in a worse government rather than a better one. Had the questioner's ancestors stayed in Russia long enough to witness the fall of the czarist regime, they would have seen exactly that scenario play itself out, when the communists won the resulting civil war and proceeded to engage in oppression and mass murder on a vastly greater scale than the czars ever did.[94]

The "brain drain" theory has similar flaws to those of the more general "fix your own country" theory. It is, at the very least, questionable whether forcing skilled workers and professionals to stay in their own countries would really improve conditions there. Even if it would, it is no less wrong to treat highly skilled workers as forced laborers. They too have a right to own their own labor, and—in most cases—they too played little or no role in causing their home societies to have unjust governments and poorly developed economies. The brains in question do not belong to the government of their home state or to its other residents. They belong to the people to whom they are attached. As Philippe Legrain puts it, "[p]oor countries have no automatic right to their citizens' labor—or indeed their allegiance."[95]

The argument that skilled workers have a duty to "repay" their home country's investment is equally unavailing. It too implies a right to impose forced labor on the person in question. If a Zimbabwean trained as a doctor at state expense chooses to stay home, but work as a painter, the government's "investment" in her medical education is no less "lost" than if she migrates abroad. If it is unjust to forbid the former choice, it is not clear why it isn't also wrong to forbid the latter.[96]

Moreover, any obligation the worker might have to "repay" the state for assisting her education is surely at least in part vitiated by the fact that the state's policies are also often responsible for the relatively poor quality of the opportunities available in her home country as compared to others. This problem is accentuated if the state's flaws are not limited to poor economic opportunities, but also extend to various forms of political and social oppression. If there is some sort of "account" to be balanced between the state and workers who get training at public expense, the latter should get "credit" for the poor quality of the opportunities provided by the state and for exposure to various forms of oppression.[97]

Things may be different in cases where the worker has voluntarily signed a contract to provide X years of service in exchange for subsidized education or training. Assuming the contract is genuinely voluntary and not obtained by means of coercion or some other form of unjust pressure, the individual in question may indeed have a duty to carry out his or her end of the bargain.[98] But there is no general obligation for a skilled worker to stay in his home country merely because he has received some form of subsidized education or training.

In sum, at least in the vast majority of cases, would-be migrants have no moral obligation to stay and "fix" their own countries. Are there exceptions to that generalization? Perhaps a few.

Consider the case of the Shah of Iran, who fled his country after his regime was overthrown in 1979. The corruption and repression of the Shah's government played an important role in stimulating the rise of the even more oppressive regime that replaced him.[99] Quite possibly, the Shah had an obligation to stay in Iran and work to fix the horrible mess he himself had played a major role in creating. Perhaps he even had an obligation to do so despite the fact that staying in Iran could well have led to his execution by the new government. Similar reasoning arguably applies to other powerful government officials in unjust regimes.

Of course, this admonition applies only in situations where staying behind to remedy the wrongs you yourself caused has a real chance of succeeding. Arguably, even a leader as blameworthy as the Shah did not have an obligation to remain in Iran if doing so would accomplish nothing. But one could also plausibly argue that he had a duty to stay so long as doing so had even a small chance of mitigating the harm he had caused—regardless of the risk to his personal safety.

Whatever we ultimately conclude about cases like that of the Shah, the vast majority of potential migrants are neither morally responsible for the injustices in their homelands nor in a position to do much about them. In many cases, they can actually do more to help their compatriots by leaving, earning higher wages abroad, and sending remittances to relatives who remain at home. It is therefore wrong to claim they have a duty to stay.

Often, people who migrate away from poor countries actually benefit their homelands rather than harm them. Emigrants often send remittances back to family members who remained in their countries of origin. For some developing countries, remittances account for a high proportion of their GDP, including 29 percent for Haiti and over 17 percent for El Salvador.[100] One study finds that a 10 percent increase in the proportion of a nation's population that emigrates leads to a 2 percent decline in the proportion of people living on less than $1 per day, and a 10 percent increase in remittances is sufficient to reduce the poverty rate by 3.5 percent.[101]

Evidence on the political effects of remittances is more mixed, with studies concluding that it may increase participation in civil society groups and strengthen electoral competition, but also that it may modestly reduce voter turnout.[102] The latter effect is not necessarily negative, as in some cases reduced turnout may actually modestly decrease the negative effects of political ignorance.[103] But such incremental political effects are likely to be small compared to the much larger positive economic impact of remittances on poor societies.

In addition to the benefits of remittances, emigration can increase growth in home countries in other ways. These include stimulating investment in education, promoting innovation through increased flow of ideas, and even increasing the likelihood of democratization through greater contact with freer societies.[104] Migrants to freer and more liberal societies can have a significant effect on political attitudes in their countries of origin,[105] which in turn can help promote liberalization there.

Applications to Internal Migration

Nearly all of the self-determination arguments for restricting migration considered in this chapter can be used to justify constraining internal migration, no less than that across international boundaries.[106] Yet, strikingly, this is rarely done.[107] Those who support free internal mobility but use these sorts of claims to advocate constraints on international migration have a serious contradiction in their positions.

The existence of this contradiction does not prove there can never be any justifiable restrictions on freedom of movement. Some restrictions can potentially be justified if applied equally to internal and external migrants. For example, a quarantine may be the only way to protect innocent life against the spread of a deadly disease, and that quarantine could be applied to all known carriers of it, regardless of their country of origin. But those who seek to justify selective restrictions imposed on one type of migration, but not the other, cannot do so based on reasoning that actually applies to both.

Self-Determination Arguments for Restricting International Migration Also Justify Restricting Internal Migration

Consider the house and club analogies. At least as a general rule, the owner of a private house can choose to give people access to some rooms within it but not others; for example, he can let them into the living room but not the bedroom or the basement. Similarly, he might choose to give different access rights to different visitors—allowing some full access to all parts of the house while others are permitted to enter only designated areas. As anyone who has lived in an apartment building or condominium knows, such variations in access are not unusual.

If a government has the same rights to restrict access to its territory as a private homeowner, it follows that it can forcibly confine some residents to a particular part of its territory and forbid them to move elsewhere. For example, the US government might permit some people to live only in Virginia but not in other states, or only on the East Coast, but not the West Coast. Christopher Wellman, a leading advocate of the house and club analogies, actually concedes that his theory would allow governments to impose significant restrictions on internal migration, so long as those restricted in this way could still live somewhere sufficient to maintain a "minimally decent life."[108]

The club analogy has much the same implications. Like a homeowner, club members can restrict access to parts of the club's property. Even members of the club might face some restrictions. The club could have a multi-tier membership structure, with "first class" members given full access to all club properties, while others are restricted to only specific parts of it. The implications for restrictions on internal mobility are fairly obvious, and similar to those of the house analogy.

Arguments that migrants from troubled societies have a duty to stay home and "fix their own countries" can also be readily applied to residents of subnational jurisdictions seeking to move elsewhere in the same country. This logic suggests that residents of relatively impoverished American states, such as Mississippi and West Virginia, or those with comparatively corrupt and badly run state and local governments, such as the city of Detroit throughout much of the last fifty years, have a duty to stay there and work to improve their policies and governance.

From the 1950s to the present, Detroit lost many hundreds of thousands of people to out-migration, in large part as a result of its poor governance,[109] going from being the fourth largest city in the United States in 1940 to merely the twenty-first largest as of 2016.[110] Perhaps some or all of those people instead had a moral obligation to stay and "fix" the Motor City.

The "brain drain" argument suggests that this duty is particularly strong in the case of skilled professionals and those whose education was subsidized by the state government in some way. That category might, for example, include students who benefited from favorable in-state tuition rates at state universities, which give students from within a state a steep discount compared to the rates paid by out-of-state students.

J. D. Vance, author of *Hillbilly Elegy*, whose story is discussed in the Introduction, recently advanced an argument of this type—though significantly he does not advocate actually forcing people to stay in their home regions. In 2017, Vance returned to his home state of Ohio, feeling an obligation to contribute to his community by doing so.[111] "Many people," he wrote, "should leave struggling places in search of economic opportunity, and many of them won't be able to return. . . . But those of us who are lucky enough to choose where we live would do well to ask ourselves, as part of that calculation, whether the choices we make for ourselves are necessarily the best for our home communities—and for the country."[112]

Vance's concern for disadvantaged communities is admirable. But the advice he offers civic-minded successful people may not be the best way for them to help. In most cases, they can best serve society by living wherever they can be most productive. If an engineer or a computer programmer can produce more and better innovations in Silicon Valley than in her hometown in Appalachia, she might well benefit society more by moving than by staying put or returning "home" after a stint in another part of the country. The ideas and products she develops will help not only people in Silicon Valley but also those back in Appalachia, as well. Over time, even people who stay put benefit greatly from the achievements of those who move in search of opportunity.

It is notable that Vance himself did not actually move back to the depressed community where he grew up, but to Columbus, a thriving city whose economy has done very well in recent years.[113] He likely concluded that he and his family would be happier, more productive, and better able to serve society there than in a less successful part of the state. This, of course in some ways mirrors the situation of migrants from poor countries who can often better serve their homes and families by moving to more productive areas.[114]

Michael Blake's argument from "unwanted obligations" also implies that internal migration can be restricted, a point Blake himself concedes.[115] If a US citizen moves from one state to another, for example, authorities in the migrant's new home will now have a duty to protect her "basic rights," one which the existing inhabitants of that state might prefer to avoid.

David Miller argues that restrictions on internal migration are less justifiable than those on international migration because governments can adjust policies to reduce the differences in relative attractiveness between regions within their own countries, and because constraints on internal migration might enable a government to impose discriminatory restrictions on vulnerable minorities.[116]

These distinctions are much less impressive than they may at first seem. While governments can *potentially* manage interregional differences in the way Miller suggests, in reality major differences in economic and social conditions often persist for decades. Consider the long-lasting differences between the American South and many northern states, or those between northern and southern Italy.[117] Such differences may be the result of deeply entrenched institutions or political culture that take a long time to eliminate, assuming it is even possible to do so.

The problem of discriminatory targeting of vulnerable minorities arises with international migration, as well. Governments can and often do impose discriminatory immigration restrictions on minorities who have little or no ability to find refuge elsewhere, thanks to immigration restrictions imposed by other nations. Historically, those restrictions themselves have often been, in large part, motivated by racial or ethnic prejudice,[118] as in the case of Australia's long-standing "White Australia" policy, or various US laws motivated by prejudice against Asian and Southern and Eastern European immigrants.[119]

Miller notes that discriminatory barriers to entry imposed by one country may not prevent oppressed groups from seeking to migrate to other nations.[120] For example, Syrian or Venezuelan refugees barred from the United States might still be able to escape to Canada, or vice versa. Thus, they may still have a way to escape injustice and are not "trapped" in the way that discriminated-against internal minorities are. For that reason, the United States can bar them as long as Canada or some other refuge remains open.

But one could offer the same defense for a system in which minority groups are forbidden to move to some regions within a given country but permitted to settle in others. For example, the United States could potentially have adopted a policy under which African Americans fleeing the Jim Crow-era South were permitted to move to some northern states but not others. So long as they still had the right to move to at least one (relatively) discrimination-free jurisdiction, on Miller's logic they would still have access to a location where they can "exercise their human rights."[121]

Miller could, perhaps, respond by arguing that governments can eliminate invidious racial and ethnic discrimination from immigration policy while still maintaining a broad power to exclude on other grounds. For example, exclusion based on race and ethnicity might be forbidden but would still be permitted on the basis of education, occupation, and various other non-ethnic and non-racial classification.

But, of course, the same can be said for internal migration restrictions: the state can, at least in theory, bar those internal migration restrictions that discriminate against particular types of minorities, while maintaining broad power to impose other constraints on movement.[122] For example, an American state could be forbidden to exclude African-Americans who seek to migrate from elsewhere in the United States, but permitted to exclude those who lack a college degree.

In sum, Miller's effort to distinguish internal migration restrictions from international ones fails no less than other attempts have, and for very similar reasons. The logical price of accepting standard rationales for restricting international migration is acceptance of the use of similar justifications for restricting domestic freedom of movement.

Conclusion

A wide variety of self-determination arguments have been made to justify restrictions on international migration and—to a lesser extent—even internal migration. But they suffer from serious flaws. In many cases, accepting them would have deeply illiberal implications for native-born citizens, not just migrants. At least in the vast majority of situations, the migrants' freedom to vote with their feet does not undermine any defensible conception of political freedom for natives.

6

Problems and Keyhole Solutions

The self-determination rights of natives are not the only possible objections to expanding opportunities for foot voting. Many others have been advanced against it, especially in the case of international migration rights. These include fears that it will increase crime and terrorism, reduce the wages of natives,[1] overburden the welfare state, destroy the environment, lead to the spread of harmful cultural values,[2] and potentially even "swamp" natives, thereby overwhelming institutions. No one book can comprehensively address all possible objections. But it is possible to sketch out a general framework for dealing with them, which the purpose of this chapter.

At least as a general rule, we should apply a three-stage approach. First, we should ask whether the supposed problem is real, and if so how serious it is. Many of the standard objections to free migration are significantly overblown. If there is little or no problem to begin with, we should not be willing to make any significant sacrifices to "solve" it.

Second, where migration creates genuine problems or negative side effects, it is often possible to deal with the issue by means of "keyhole solutions" that minimize the risk without barring large numbers of people.[3] Instead of applying a meat cleaver that undermines political freedom and inflicts great harm on migrants, it is better—where possible—to apply a scalpel. Often, negative side effects of migration can be mitigated by means less draconian and less costly than exclusion.

Finally, where other keyhole solutions might be inadequate, policymakers should also consider tapping the vast wealth created by expanded migration to mitigate negative side effects that cannot be addressed in other ways. It is often both more humane and more efficient to tap newfound wealth to address possible harm than to bar people from moving in the first place.

I do not claim that this three-prong approach can solve all conceivable problems potentially caused by foot voting. There are likely to be extreme cases where migration restrictions really are the lesser evil compared to any other feasible alternative.[4] But this framework can be effectively applied to a wide range of issues that are often seen as strong justifications for imposing severe restrictions on migration.

This chapter examines several such cases. They include the danger of migrants wielding harmful influence on government policy (creating what are called negative "political externalities"), burdens on the welfare state, increased risks of crime and terrorism, displacement of native workers by immigrants, environmental degradation supposedly caused by migration, the potential spread of harmful cultural values, and the danger of immigrants "swamping" natives to such an extent that the receiving country's institutions suffer severe damage.

I also consider two objections that are usually raised against internal rather than international foot voting: Albert Hirschman's classic argument that exit rights will destroy incentives to invest in "voice" mechanisms that can improve institutions in the would-be migrant's home jurisdiction, and concerns that excessive foot voting will lead to a "Big Sort" under which society is becomes increasingly polarized into ideologically homogenous enclaves.

The last part of the chapter explains many of the considerations traditionally used to justify restrictions on international migration can often just as easily be used to justify restrictions on internal migration. Historically, they in fact sometimes have been used that way. Those who believe that these sorts of risks can justify excluding immigrants from abroad, but not constraining domestic migration, cannot easily defend that position.

The analysis in this chapter is not intended to prove that restrictions on freedom of movement can never be justified. In a range of situations, they can be imposed because the justification for the restriction applies irrespective of whether the persons in question are engaged in international or internal movement, and irrespective of their citizenship status. But, at least as a general rule, we cannot justify selective restrictions on international migration on the basis of reasoning that, if applied consistently, would also justify constraints on internal freedom of movement.

Readers interested in possible harms caused by foot voting that are not specifically covered here should at least consider whether the three-stage framework I outline could be used to address them as well. No one can foresee all possible contingencies. But the framework is flexible enough to apply to a wide variety of potential negative side effects of migration.

Political Externalities

Some critics of immigration who do not necessarily endorse strong theories of self-determination nevertheless worry that free migration might undermine the freedom of natives, or otherwise lead to harmful public policies. For example, migrants from an illiberal culture might vote in a government that oppresses the natives. Such negative effects on public policy are known as "political externalities" of immigration.[5]

Political externalities can potentially inflict severe costs on natives and earlier immigrants. In the extreme case, they could even "kill the goose that produces the golden eggs" and destroy those features of their new society that made it attractive to migrants in the first place.

The risk of political externalities is often overblown. Studies repeatedly show that recent immigrants actually have relatively little political influence, compared to longtime residents: even those who do have the franchise vote at lower rates, and their political influence in other respects trails that of natives even more.[6] Data from the United States suggest the political views immigrants and their children strongly converge with those of natives strongly converge over time, especially in the second and third generations.[7].

In some cases, nonetheless, political externality concerns are legitimate. But, fortunately, there are often ways to deal with them short of forbidding migration itself.

The most obvious keyhole strategy for controlling political externalities is to deny the franchise to migrants until they become sufficiently assimilated and supportive of liberal values that they no longer pose a threat to the natives. In the United States, for example, immigrants cannot become citizens unless they have lived in the country for five years, demonstrate knowledge of the English language, and pass a civics exam that many native-born citizens would fail.[8] A recent study found that only 36 percent of adult Americans could pass the multiple-choice civics test required of immigrants applying for citizenship.[9] When and if necessary, such standards could potentially be made more stringent, tests could become tougher, naturalization periods can be extended, and so on. Many European nations require candidates for naturalization to pass more difficult tests than the United States does.[10]

Long-term exclusion from citizenship or the franchise may be unjust to immigrants. It either makes them second-class citizens or bars them from citizenship entirely. Some therefore argue that any immigrants or long-term guest-workers admitted into a nation must be granted the franchise and other rights of citizenship.[11] As Michael Walzer puts it, a democracy must ensure that such entrants are "given a say, and ultimately an equal say," or else exclude them—"[a]nd those are their only choices."[12]

This is a false dichotomy. Even if Walzer is right to conclude that long-term exclusion from the franchise is unjust to immigrants, it is still a lesser injustice than excluding them from living in the country entirely. Exclusion would force many into a lifetime of poverty and oppression in their countries of origin—many of them ones where the would-be migrant has no influence over public policy either. The latter is especially true of the many who come from nations that are themselves undemocratic. For them, emigration may be the only feasible way to exercise any form of political choice at all.[13]

These points also count against claims that long-term exclusion from the franchise is unjust because it creates a permanent class of "denizens," which threatens a "social ethos characterized by an absence of caste distinctions."[14] Barring people from entering a society entirely—in large part based on their place of birth or national origin—is an even more severe "caste distinction" than denying them the franchise. This is especially true if the latter is not permanent, but lasts only until they can demonstrate adequate knowledge of the destination society's values and political institutions.

If the egalitarian "social ethos" of a liberal society is undermined by restrictions on the franchise based on the idea that the person in question may be a threat to liberal values, it is surely undermined even more by laws that bar people from entering the nation entirely based on the same sorts of considerations. This is especially true if the restrictions in question categorically bar people based on their ethnicity or country of origin (on the assumption that people of that background pose a threat), with little or no effort to make an individualized determination about the supposed danger they may pose. As discussed in Chapter 5, such classifications based on place of birth are caste-like in much the same way as domestic racial and ethnic classifications.[15]

To be sure, a society that bars people from entering may sometimes *feel* more egalitarian than one that allows those same people in, but bars them from voting. In the former case, the group shortchanged by the policy is often invisible to most members of the exclusionary society, because those excluded are on the other side of a border. But the fact that the victims are "out of sight, out of mind" does not change the essence of what is being done. It may even make it more pernicious, by enabling supporters of the policy to more easily ignore the consequences of what they have done.

Similarly, in a society that maintains rigid racial or ethnic segregation domestically, many members of the dominant group may rarely, if ever, encounter members of the subordinated one, that has been forcibly confined to less desirable areas. They might therefore think of themselves as maintaining an egalitarian ethos. But such a faux egalitarian sensibility would not change the true nature of the government's policies and the society they create.

Overall, even extended exclusion from the franchise is a lesser infringement on political freedom than exclusion from migration, and a less severe case of discrimination on the basis of place of birth. Being a second-class citizen—or noncitizen resident—of a first-class nation is far less unjust than being a "normal" citizen of a brutal dictatorship or a society mired in poverty and corruption. At the very least, migrants will have greater political freedom if the choice between these two admittedly flawed alternatives is left up to them rather than foreclosed by government policies that force them to remain where they are.

Admittedly, excluding immigrants from the franchise—or requiring them to meet standards not imposed on native-born citizens—is a form of discrimination based on parentage or place of birth. As such, it is presumptively unjust for reasons discussed in Chapter 5. The same is true for several other possible keyhole solutions analyzed later in this chapter, including discriminatory exclusion from welfare benefits, discriminatory income taxes, and entry tariffs.[16]

But all are less severe forms of place-of-birth discrimination than barring potential migrants from the country entirely. These forms of discrimination still allow migrants to live, work, and benefit from the political institutions of the destination nation. Total exclusion, by contrast, consigns them to what may well be lifelong poverty and oppression in their countries of origin. If a discriminatory policy is unavoidable, we should at least choose less harsh forms of discrimination over more severe ones.

A potential downside of keyhole mechanisms for addressing political externalities is that they may prevent migrants from having a *beneficial* effect on government policy rather than a harmful one. Migrants might have better political views than natives rather than worse ones. To the extent this is likely, governments would be wise to give them access to the franchise as soon as possible after arrival. But the analysis here is intended to address situations where migrants' political participation poses a potential threat to natives that the latter, by assumption, have a right to prevent. Where this is not the case, there is no problem to address in the first place.

Political externalities are also sometimes raised as an objection to internal foot voting within federal systems, though rarely to the extent of justifying barring such migration. Here too, the problem is manageable. Like international foot voters, domestic ones tend to have only a modest impact on the political balance of their new homes, in part because they participate in politics at a lower rate.[17]

Furthermore, migrants of either type would have to be both very numerous relative to the preexisting population and highly skewed in their political leanings to have a major impact.[18] For example, let us assume that recent migrants make up 10 percent of the population of a given area, and that they vote at the same rate as other residents. If the newcomers lean 60–40 to the Democratic Party, as opposed to the Republican Party, that would still give the Democrats only a net addition of 2 percent of the total vote. In a more realistic scenario, the newcomer vote is unlikely to be so lopsided, and newcomers are unlikely to vote at the same rate as previous residents.

There are rare cases when migration restrictions may indeed be the only way to prevent dire political consequences. This may be true in a scenario where the would-be migrants greatly outnumber the natives, have far more illiberal views than current voters, and it is politically infeasible to exclude recent arrivals from the franchise, but it *is* (for whatever reason), possible to bar entry.[19] The small nation of Estonia—faced with potential massive immigration from its very illiberal neighbor Russia—may be an example of such a case.[20] In such a tragic situation, political externalities caused by foot voting indeed "kill the goose that lays the golden egg" by destroying the freedom and opportunity that made the destination country attractive to migrants in the first place. Both migrants and natives could end up worse off, as a result. Fortunately, this combination of circumstances is likely to be rare.

Bruce Ackerman, a leading political theorist otherwise highly supportive of free migration, argues that immigration restrictions are nonetheless justified in a situation where accepting too many migrants is likely to cause an "illiberal upheaval" that severely undermines the destination countries' liberal democratic institutions.[21] The point is well taken. But in assessing such claims, it is important to consider whether an "illiberal upheaval" is truly a serious risk, and if so whether it can be prevented by means less draconian than barring migration.

Burdens on the Welfare State

Conservative—and some libertarian—opponents of increased immigration often argue that allowing in more immigrants is likely to lead to increases in the size of the welfare state.[22] In the extreme version of such scenarios, unconstrained immigration could lead to crushing burdens on taxpayers or even fiscal collapse.

The available evidence strongly suggests that increased immigration does not lead to increases in per capita welfare spending. In the United States, states with relatively high numbers of immigrants do not have higher levels of welfare state spending per capita than those that have lower percentages of immigrants in the population.[23] The same is true of European nations, where welfare spending may even be inversely correlated with ethnic diversity caused by relatively higher levels of immigration.[24] The perception that welfare benefits are going to recent immigrants reduces natives' support for redistributive welfare spending,[25] and the former generally have far more political clout than immigrants do.[26] A 2013 study of twenty-three advanced economies by the Organization of Economic Cooperation and Development (OECD) found that immigrants have a net positive fiscal impact in twenty of those countries—on average $4,400 per migrant per year, including $11,000 per migrant per year in the United States.[27] The National Academy of Sciences has found that immigrants with high school degrees or higher levels of education actually have a net positive average fiscal impact in the United States, and even high school dropouts do so as well, so long as they arrive before the age of twenty-five.[28]

Studies indicating that migrants tend to prefer nations with greater economic freedom (in the sense of lower levels of economic regulation and government spending)[29] suggest that most are seeking to improve their lot by finding jobs rather than opportunities to live off welfare benefits. This factor further reduces the likelihood that they will overburden the welfare state.

If immigration nonetheless does impose excessive burdens on the welfare state, receiving nations could abolish or reduce welfare payments to migrants, a policy that many countries have already adopted to varying degrees.[30] In the United States, even legal immigrants are already barred from a wide range of federal welfare benefits under the welfare reform act of 1996 and (in some cases) previous legislation.[31]

While generally favoring liberalization of immigration policy, the great libertarian economist Milton Friedman also famously said that "you cannot simultaneously have free immigration and a welfare state."[32] But Friedman was wrong, in part because he apparently did not consider the issue very carefully (an understandable omission given that it was outside the range of questions on which his academic work focused). In the very same 1999 interview where he made that statement, he also admitted that he "ha[dn't] really ever thought" of the possibility that immigrants could be permitted to legally live and work in the United States without being eligible for welfare state benefits.[33]

Selective exclusions from welfare benefits are appropriate from the standpoint of political theorists who argue that we have a special duty to provide welfare benefits to natives of our respective countries, and that immigrants' interests should subordinated to that goal when the two conflict.[34] If immigrants are barred from receiving all or most welfare benefits, their presence would not inhibit the provision of such benefits to natives. Indeed, the additional tax revenue provided by immigrants can actually help fund welfare benefits for the native-born poor.

Others, of course, argue that wealthy nations have a strong moral duty to redistribute wealth to the poor in underdeveloped nations, most of whom are vastly worse off than even the poorest native-born citizens of advanced liberal democratic states.[35] If so, it would be wrong to exclude poor immigrants from welfare benefits. Indeed, on such views, it would be wrong to deny redistribution to the foreign poor even if they never enter the territory of a wealthier nation.

But even from the standpoint of those who believe international redistribution is a moral imperative, excluding migrants from welfare benefits is still less harmful than barring them from entering a wealthier nation entirely. In the latter scenario, they are likely to be far worse off than in the former. Indeed, much of the moral imperative of alleviating poverty can be met simply by allowing immigrants to enter and take whatever jobs employers offer them, thereby vastly increasing their incomes compared to what they would likely be otherwise. As discussed in Chapter 3, this may be the best and most effective way for wealthy nations to reduce world poverty, since the efficacy of foreign aid transfers is highly questionable, at best.[36]

Arguments that we must limit immigration in order to ensure provision of welfare benefits to those immigrants we do admit have similar flaws.[37] They too founder on the reality that being completely barred from a more developed nation harms the immigrants in question far more than being admitted without access to welfare benefits, or with more limited access than that extended to natives. They also are at odds with the apparent preferences of most actual migrants, who tend to choose countries with relatively lower levels of regulation and government spending,[38] a strong sign that they value access to job markets over access to welfare, where the two might conflict.

In sum, excluding immigrants from welfare benefits may be unjust. But it is surely less so than forcing them to endure the much greater material deprivation of being condemned to far worse poverty in their countries of origin.

If keyhole solutions for possible fiscal burdens of immigration fail or turn out to be politically infeasible, there are several ways to defray these costs by tapping the wealth created by immigration. Perhaps the simplest such approach is to require immigrants to pay an entry tariff, intended to offset costs they might impose on the public fisc. The late Nobel Prize–winning economist Gary Becker proposed an immigration fee under which any immigrant who wishes could become a citizen of the United States, if he or she is willing to pay, say, $50,000.[39] Becker suggested that poor immigrants who cannot come up with the tariff immediately can be allowed access to credit markets in order to secure loans, and also that American citizens be allowed to subsidize payments for relatives (a notion that can be extended to potential employees and other connections, as well).[40]

A similar but more detailed proposal has been developed by legal scholar Eleanor Brown, who advocates using a system of bonds to pay entry fees.[41] As she points out, such bond arrangements were common in the late eighteenth and early nineteenth centuries, when "indentured servants" were required to work off over time the cost of their passage across the Atlantic.[42] In today's much wealthier society, with far more developed credit markets, repayment could be assured without the harsh arrangements of 200 years ago, under which indentured servants were forced to work without pay for one specific employer, until their loan was repaid.[43]

Yet another possibility would be to impose a surtax on immigrants' wages until they have contributed a set amount to the treasury.[44] Such a surtax can also be used to defray possible negative fiscal effects on the welfare state.

Like exclusion from some or all welfare benefits, entry tariffs and discriminatory taxes may well be unjust to migrants. From the standpoint of maximizing political freedom, it would likely be better to dispense with such measures. But they are far less unjust mechanisms for mitigating potential burdens on the welfare state than excluding the migrants entirely. Immigrants from a poor nation to a wealthy one who are required to repay a loan or pay a special surtax are still likely to end up with a far higher income—and far more opportunities generally—than if they had been forced to remain in their homeland.

Political philosopher Anna Stilz considers a hypothetical situation that is the exact opposite of the scenario that concerns those who fear that migration will lead to increased welfare spending: that migration of libertarian opponents of the welfare state to high-welfare countries such as Norway might enable the former to outvote natives, and thereby eliminate or at least greatly reduce welfare programs the latter value.[45] If this becomes a plausible scenario, and is legitimately considered a harmful outcome, it can be addressed by the same keyhole approaches as can be taken to other "political externalities," discussed earlier in this chapter.

Crime and Terrorism

The perception that immigration increases crime rates has been a major focus of political opposition to immigration in the United States and Europe. In many cases, this perception is the opposite of the truth— immigration actually lowers crime rates rather than increases it. Where immigration does increase crime, keyhole solutions and efforts to tap the wealth created by immigration can potentially help alleviate the problem.

In the United States, immigrants actually have a much lower crime rate than native-born citizens do.[46] Numerous studies support that conclusion.[47]

The finding holds true even if we focus solely on Mexican immigrants, who are often a particular major focus of public hostility. Mexican-born immigrant males aged eighteen to thirty-nine who lack a high school diploma actually had a lower incarceration rate in 2010 (2.8 percent) than all native-born males of the same age group (3.3 percent), *regardless* of education level. The incarceration rate for native-born men without a high school diploma was 10.7 percent in the same year (2010).[48] Guatemalan and Honduran immigrants—also often targets of especially severe political opposition— have even lower incarceration rates.[49] Overall, immigrants are only about one-fifth as likely to be incarcerated for crimes, and the difference is mostly due to a lower propensity to commit crime in the immigrant population rather than to deportation or other law enforcement measures that differen-tially target immigrants.[50]

Illegal migrants also have lower crime rates than native-born Americans. A recent overview of data from 1990 to 2014 for all fifty US states and Washington, DC, finds that undocumented migration is associated with lower crime rates, though the results are generally not statistically signifi-cant.[51] Studies also indicate that "sanctuary cities"—jurisdictions that refuse to help the federal government track down and deport undocumented immigrants, do not have higher crime rates, as a result, and may even have lower ones.[52] According to Census Bureau American Community Survey data, illegal migrants have lower incarceration rates than native-born Americans at every age range from eighteen to twenty-four up to fifty to fifty-four.[53]

For these reasons, claims that the United States could lower violent and property crime rates by reducing immigration or deporting more illegal migrants are fundamentally misplaced. Indeed, if reducing violent and prop-erty crime is really the goal, we could adopt the keyhole solution of shifting some of the vast resources currently devoted to keeping out and deporting peaceful migrants and reinvest them in combating violent crime and ter-rorism. The situation is similar in Canada. There, too, immigrants have sub-stantially lower crime rates than the native-born.[54]

But matters are more complicated in Europe. Data there are far less clear than in the United States because governments generally do not classify offenders based on nation of origin but instead based on citizenship, which means that immigrants who have become citizens are no longer classified as foreign-born in crime statistics.[55]

The available evidence is mixed, but it does suggest that immigration may increase crime in some countries. For example, the massive influx of Middle Eastern refugees into Germany in 2014–15 is often blamed for increased crime and has sparked a major political backlash. Some studies find no detectable increase in violent crime, though they do find evidence of modest increases in property crime.[56] A recent major evaluation finds small increases in violent crime, and somewhat larger, but still modest, increases in drug crime and other low-level offenses.[57] The authors sug-gest, however, that some of the recorded increase in crime in refugee-heavy areas may be due to authorities' devoting greater resources to reporting and investigation in those areas rather than to actual increases in under-lying rates.[58]

Even more recently, German violent crime rates have fallen to the lowest level since the early 1990s, but recent immigrants commit a disproportionate percentage of them because a high percentage of the migrants are young men under the age of thirty, who tend to have higher-than-average crime rates in any society.[59] While the most alarmist assessments of the refugee influx are likely wrong, it is probable that it has resulted in some increases in crime, nonetheless. A study of two large waves of immigration in the United Kingdom shows similar results, with increases in property crime in one of the waves but no increases in violent crime in either.[60]

Even if immigration generally does not increase crime, it is almost always possible to identify specific subsets of immigrants who are likely to have higher crime rates than natives. For example, young, unmarried males almost always have higher crime rates than other members of society. Governments can then target such groups for exclusion. Of course, the same thing is true of subsets of natives. The native population, too, can be divided into categories with higher and lower crime rates, and the internal migration of the former can be restricted.

To the extent that immigration does increase crime, governments can use some of the vast wealth created by immigration to invest in crime-reduction strategies. Research indicates, for example, that increasing the number of police on the streets can substantially reduce the incidence of violence and property crime.[61]

One potential keyhole strategy is to redirect resources currently devoted to immigration enforcement to conventional police dedicated to combating violent and property crime. In the United States, for example, the Immigration and Customs Enforcement agency devotes almost $4 billion annually to immigration enforcement, largely against undocumented immigrants found within the interior of the United States.[62] These funds alone could potentially pay the annual salaries of some 63,000 police officers,[63] enough for almost a 6 percent increase in the number of police officers in the United States (if nonsalary expenses are not considered).[64] And these figures do not count resources devoted to immigration enforcement by other federal and state government agencies.

What is true of crime is even more true for terrorism. The risks are low and can potentially be mitigated still further by keyhole solutions and tapping the wealth created by migration. The risk that an American will be killed by an immigrant terrorist in a given year is so infinitesimal that it is actually several times lower than the risk that he will be killed by a lightning strike during the same timeframe.[65] The risk in European countries is comparably low.[66] Even if these risks were to increase several-fold as a result of expanded immigration, they would still be extremely small.

Whether immigration increases the risk of terrorism at the margin is disputed by experts. Some studies find no effect on terrorism rates, even when migration increases from Muslim-majority nations and countries that themselves have terrorism problems.[67] Others conclude that while immigration generally does not increase terrorism, increased migration from nations with high terrorism rates can also modestly increase the risk in the destination country.[68] A recent analysis of European data from 1980 to 2004 concludes that increased immigration does not result in increased terrorism rates caused by the immigrants themselves, but *does* lead to an increase in terrorism by domestic right-wing terrorists hostile to migrants.[69]

If this last finding is sound, it suggests a pathway by which immigration does indeed increase terror. But it would be perverse to restrict migration for the purpose of limiting terrorist attacks generated by right-wing nativists. It would also set a dangerous precedent. By yielding to terrorist demands, it could incentivize more terrorism by other groups seeking to influence public policy.

Because terrorism risks are already so low, it may be very difficult to reduce them still further. However, tapping the vast new wealth created by immigration can potentially pay for extensive new security and counterterrorism operations, if necessary. Resources currently devoted to immigration enforcement can be repurposed as a keyhole solution here, as well.

Protecting the Culture

Immigrants can potentially introduce cultural values that are at odds with those of natives. This concern is often cited as a justification for restricting immigration. In Chapter 5, I criticized arguments to the effect that the dominant cultural group in a society has an inherent right to exclude migrants because of the principle of self-determination. That theory fails on multiple grounds.[70]

But even if nations have no general right to preserve existing cultures against potential change caused by migration, they might still have a legitimate interest in preventing the spread of cultural values that are likely to cause specific types of harm. For example, some cultures include invidious prejudice against women, gays and lesbians, and various religious and ethnic minorities. Others may promote violence and other types of crime.

Some immigration restrictionists also warn that unless migration is strictly regulated, culture clashes between immigrants and newcomers will lead to serious civil conflict.[71] In the extreme case, some contend it might even result in "civil war."[72]

Immigration restrictions can potentially inhibit the "importation" of various harmful cultural values. If the harm caused by them is great enough, the benefits of preventing it can potentially outweigh the benefits of allowing the group in question to immigrate—even including the benefit of enhancing political freedom.

Some of the danger potentially posed by migrants with harmful cultural values can be mitigated through restrictions on the franchise.[73] If the migrants are not able to vote until they have become significantly assimilated into their new country's culture, their potentially problematic values are unlikely to significantly influence government policy.

But culture can potentially influence society even if its bearers have little or no influence on public policy. If immigrants with "bad" values do not assimilate, they can have a negative impact on society over time, even if they cannot vote.

Fortunately, the problem is not nearly as severe as often claimed. Despite concerns about the supposed unwillingness of immigrants to assimilate,[74] social science research indicates that recent immigrants to the United States have assimilated at least as quickly and thoroughly as those of past eras.[75] It simply is not the case that they and others like them pose any significant threat of corrupting America's culture and values. Complaints about current immigrants are no more defensible than very similar indictments of past immigrants, including the Irish, Eastern European Jews, and Asians, all of whom were once widely regarded as unassimilable threats to American values.[76]

The situation in Western Europe is more complicated, with some arguing that Muslim immigrants, in particular, pose a danger to European culture, citing polling data showing high levels of anti-Semitism, homophobic hostility to gays and lesbians, and other prejudices among Muslims living in European nations.[77] Europe has clearly had greater difficulties dealing with Muslim immigration than the United States and Canada. However, it is far from clear that this is because Muslim immigrants' culture is inherently inimical to Western liberal values.

The experience of Muslim immigrants in the United States suggests otherwise. Assimilation of Muslim migrants in the United States has proceeded
apace, and most now accept liberal democratic principles and integrate with
the non-Muslim population.[78]

Recent survey evidence even finds that 51 percent of American Muslims
(over 80 percent of whom are immigrants or children of immigrants) support
same-sex marriage (compared to 34 percent opposed), a rate only modestly
lower than that of the general population (61 percent), and much higher than
that of adherents of conservative Christian denominations.[79] Whatever one
otherwise thinks of same-sex marriage, widespread support for it is a clear
contrast to the homophobic attitudes prevalent in many Muslim-majority
nations. It strongly suggests that Muslim immigrants are not inherently unwilling to adopt liberal values.

If Muslim immigrants in Europe are less assimilated than in the United
States, it may in large part be a result of the exclusion of many of them from the
labor market, due to highly restrictive labor regulations in many European
nations. Participation in the economy is a major facilitator of assimilation,
and its absence fosters alienation and conflict between immigrants and
natives.[80]

To the extent this is true, the cultural assimilation challenges posed by
Muslim immigrants in Europe could be significantly mitigated by a keyhole solution: reducing labor market regulations that make it difficult for
immigrants to find work. This would both diminish cultural conflict and
increase immigrants' contributions to European economies. European
governments and civil society – including the Muslim community—can
also take a variety of other steps to facilitate better integration of immigrants
from Muslim nations.[81]

Other, more traditional, keyhole solutions include using education and
outreach to smooth the path of assimilation for migrants. To the extent these
are costly to the state, they can be funded, in significant part, through using
some of the extra wealth generated by immigration itself.[82]

Even if immigrants' cultural values are not especially harmful (or at least
not more so than those of natives), increasing cultural and ethnic diversity
could potentially lower social trust—defined as generalized trust in other
members of society, a concern popularized by a well-known article by political scientist Robert Putnam finding that trust is inversely correlated with
ethnic diversity.[83] To the extent that social trust really does decline as a result
of diversity, the magnitude of the effect is small.[84] Moreover, it is far from clear

that reduction in social trust is necessarily a bad thing, as the connection between trust and positive social outcomes is often weak or nonexistent.[85] High trust might even have negative effects, including slowing economic growth and causing people to be more easily susceptible to con artists.[86]

Legal scholar Liav Orgad, who rejects most other cultural justifications for excluding immigrants, contends that liberal democracies can require "knowledge" and "acceptance" of basic liberal principles, such as equality before the law and a duty to obey laws passed by "just institutions," as "a prerequisite to admission" for voluntary migrants.[87] Presumably, this requirement can be imposed even in cases where there is no danger that the migrants in question will corrupt the society as a whole with their flawed values, and even if they do not have plans to act on them in violent or illegal ways.

This idea seems intuitively appealing. A liberal democratic society surely requires support for liberal principles by the population if it is to remain liberal. But notice that the point of this policy is to exclude people from society based on their "politically intolerant *beliefs*," as Orgad himself puts it—either because such beliefs are inherently unworthy of toleration, or because of the assumption that they are likely to lead to "intolerant behavior."[88] Orgad does moderate the requirement by suggesting that the "acceptance" prong might be met simply by declaring acceptance, without necessarily meaning it.[89]

If the government has the power to determine what qualifies as an "intolerant belief" and expel those who hold such views (or at least refuse to say that they do not), that itself has deeply illiberal implications. One of the main justifications for freedom of speech and religion is the assumption that individuals have the right to decide their own beliefs for themselves, and that governments cannot be trusted with broad power to determine which beliefs are acceptable.

And, as Orgad himself asks, if commitment to liberal beliefs is so fundamental, "why not require compliance with them from every native-born citizen," as well as from immigrants?[90] The answers he gives are not very persuasive. Orgad first mentions that such compliance is required of native-born citizens, but enforced by means less restrictive than expulsion, such as criminal and civil sanctions.[91] This answer conflates belief with action, as native-born citizens generally are *not* punished in liberal democracies merely for failing to have—or state "acceptance" of—the right beliefs, though they may of course be punished for some types of illiberal actions.

Orgad also defends the native-immigrant distinction because "there is a presumption that native-born citizens are not alien to basic principles of political liberalism by virtue of their birth and residence in a liberal state."[92] But, as he also notes, that presumption is open to challenge.[93] History shows that many native-born citizens of liberal democracies clearly do not accept liberal principles, as evident by the existence of racist, sexist, authoritarian, and other illiberal political movements in many such countries. Other things equal, illiberal natives pose a more serious threat to liberal institutions than recent immigrants do. The former generally have much greater political influence than the latter, and are more readily able to convert their harmful beliefs into public policy.[94] Yet even in such cases, liberal states—and Orgad himself—do not claim that these people should expelled.

Finally, Orgad claims that the distinction is justified because governments' have differing obligations to immigrants as opposed to natives.[95] But this theory assumes the very point that needs to be proved: that immigrants with illiberal beliefs are subject to the severe penalty of expulsion, even if natives with similar views are not sanctioned at all. Ultimately, the distinction here is a morally arbitrary one based on parentage or place of birth.[96]

A potentially more compelling justification for expelling illiberal immigrants, but not similar natives, is that denial of admission to a new nation is a less severe harm than expulsion from one where you have lived your whole life. But that is not uniformly true, as there is likely to be great variation between different individuals. Moreover, Orgad's theory could potentially justify revoking residency rights even from migrants who have been in the host nation for a long time, if they have not yet become citizens.[97]

Perhaps, as advocates of "hate speech" laws contend, liberal democratic governments have both a right and a duty to suppress the expression of certain types of illiberal views, such as the promotion of racial, ethnic, or religious bigotry.[98] I am skeptical that such restrictions are justified, but will not defend that view here. But if such policies are justified at all, they should be applied on an equal basis to both immigrants and natives, and the extreme penalty of banishment from the nation will rarely, if ever, be appropriate merely as a punishment for improper expression or belief.

The issue of whether illiberal immigrants can be expelled should be distinguished from the question of whether such people can be denied citizenship or voting rights. The latter is a far less severe restriction than the former, and might potentially be defensible in a wider range of circumstances.[99]

We cannot categorically rule out the possibility that there can be situations where an immigrant group with illiberal values is both highly resistant to assimilation and large enough to pose a serious danger grave enough to outweigh the harms caused by barring them. In such an extreme case, as with the extreme political externality situation described earlier in this chapter, constraints on migration may be the lesser of the available evils. But such policies should be adopted only if there is strong evidence of both the gravity of the threat and the host nation's inability to address it by less restrictive means.

Wage Competition and Displacement of Native Workers

Some argue that immigration must be restricted in order to limit displacement of native workers or reductions in their wages through competition.[100] How much immigration actually affects native workers is a point of some contention among economists. Most research suggests that immigration, on average, has little effect or actually slightly *increases* the wages of native workers. That is because many native workers are actually complements rather than substitutes for immigrants: they do tasks in which immigrant labor can make native workers more productive, and thereby actually increase their wages.[101] To take a simple example, native-born chefs can become more productive if combined with immigrant assistants who can help with food preparation. Native-born accountants or architects can be more productive if combined with immigrant tech specialists who make their computers function more efficiently. Native-born professionals with small children can do more work if some of the child care is done by immigrant nannies.[102] And so on.

In addition, natives benefit greatly from the often massive additional production created by immigrant workers.[103] They also benefit from increased income accruing to nonlabor assets owned by natives, such as pensions and real estate.[104]

There are, however, larger negative wage and displacement effects on some subcategories of workers, principally the least-educated native workers, such as high school dropouts.[105] While natives as a group gain economically from immigration, its impact on labor markets does create at least some substantial number of "losers" among native workers.

Thus, the supposed negative effects of immigrant workers on native ones are modest, at most, and likely outweighed by positive effects. In addition, much of the wage competition created by new immigrants is actually with other relatively recently arrived immigrants.[106] Even if a preference for natives over immigrants is warranted, it is hard to see why recently arrived immigrants deserve protection from wage competition from *other* immigrants.

More generally, it is far from clear that anyone deserves protection against job competition, regardless of who the competitor is. In most domestic contexts, we do not believe that any moral wrong has occurred if a person loses a job to a competitor who is more efficient or willing to do the work more cheaply. Perhaps workers deserve a guarantee of a minimal standard of living, or wages and working conditions that reach some minimum standard. But, subject to that constraint, it is not clear why they deserve protection from competition, as such.[107] If applied generally, this principle would make society vastly poorer by protecting inefficient workers and firms from more effective competitors and by stifling innovation.

Let us assume, for the sake of argument, that native workers (or some subset thereof) are morally entitled to protection against wage decreases caused by immigration. If so, there is a simple way to alleviate the problem by tapping wealth created by immigration, proposed by economist Bryan Caplan: impose special surtaxes or admissions fees on immigrant workers and use the proceeds to compensate natives who have been displaced by immigrant labor or had their wages reduced as a result.[108] In this way, both immigrant and native workers will be better off than before, and no one suffers a (supposedly) unjust reduction in income as a result.

Such discriminatory taxation of immigrants would, in my view, be unjust. But it is far less so than excluding them from the nation entirely, thus condemning most to a lifetime under far worse conditions (and, in most cases, far lower wages) than they could get in a more advanced nation.

Immigrants Destroying the Environment

Concerns that immigration might destroy the environment have not played as prominent a role in public debate as fears that it might undermine political institutions, overburden the welfare state, or "import" dangerous cultural values. But such fears have attracted greater attention in recent years. In 2019, claims that immigration destroys the environment were notoriously cited as justification by the perpetrators of two horrific mass shootings—one directed at Muslim immigrants in Christchurch, New Zealand, and another at Hispanics in El Paso, Texas.[109] The fact that such claims have been made by terrorists does not in and of itself prove that they are wrong. Similar arguments have been made by more intellectually respectable commentators and must be assessed on their own merits.[110]

The key concern of those who advance environmental justifications for restricting migration is that migrants typically seek to move from poor nations to wealthy ones, and residents of wealthy countries use more resources and generate more pollution.[111] This in turn potentially exacerbates environmental problems, including even ones that might lead to catastrophic consequences, such as global climate change.[112]

The main flaw in this line argument is that environmental quality actually improves as nations approach what are now considered First World levels of income. The so-called Environmental Kuznets Curve (EKC), supported by extensive empirical evidence, shows that pollution increases during early stages of economic growth but goes down again as nations become richer still and begin to approximate the income levels of the most advanced developed nations, such as the United States, Western Europe, and Japan.[113] EKC effects have also emerged even in middle-income countries, as they get wealthier.[114] Reasons for the EKC phenomenon include the fact that people are willing to devote more resources to environmental protection as they get wealthier, and that wealthier societies have more resources available to them to control pollution.[115]

Reducing barriers to immigration will enable to more people to migrate to advanced economies from poor ones, thus increasing the percentage who live in areas with better pollution controls. In addition, the immense new wealth produced by expanded migration can enrich both natives and immigrants, thereby making both more willing to devote resources to environmental protection.

To the extent that migration does increase pollution in some areas, there is an obvious keyhole solution: impose targeted taxes on pollution-generating activities. This is the standard prescription for reducing pollution offered by mainstream economists.[116]

Instead of reducing immigration generally, including that which has a neutral or even positive effect on environmental quality, the more efficient and more humane alternative is to tax activities that specifically generate pollution, whether engaged in by immigrants or natives. That both increases incentives to reduce pollution and avoids penalizing activities that are not actually causing environmental degradation.

Another often-useful keyhole solution is establishing private property rights in scarce resources, such as water and fisheries, that might otherwise be overexploited in a "tragedy of the commons" scenario in which there are incentives for overuse.[117] In situations where anyone can use the relevant resource at any time but no one can prevent others from doing the same thing, there is often a strong tendency to overuse it.

For example, I might overfish in a lake to which all have access, because if I restrain myself, other fishermen will just take the fish for themselves. Where property rights exist, owners have strong incentives to conserve relevant resources and also to produce more of them in order to meet demand.[118] In privately owned fisheries, the owner has incentives to restrict her take in order to allow the fish to reproduce and even increase their population; she can then profit from the increased stock and continue to do so as it replenishes itself over time.[119] The same point applies to various environmental amenities, such as clean water, which can also be conserved and expanded better with private property rights.[120]

Private property rights cannot deal with all conceivable environmental problems. Some are so large-scale that privatization of the relevant resource may not be feasible, given constraints of current technology. International air pollution—particularly global warming—is an example.[121] But they can be useful in many situations.

Where private property rights over scarce resources can be established, they give both immigrants and natives incentive and opportunity to conserve them and find ways to produce more. This approach can have great value even aside from any concerns raised by immigration. It can also serve to cope with increasing demand for resources that may be created by immigration.

Finally, to the extent that additional taxation or other regulatory measures might be necessitated by migration, such efforts can be financed using some of the wealth that immigration generates. Here, as elsewhere, instead of killing the golden goose, we can instead use it to pay to offset its own negative side effects.

Immigrants "Swamping" Natives

The danger of immigrants completely "swamping" natives is the most extreme form of scenario in which immigration causes harmful cultural and institutional change. Potentially, so many migrants might come so quickly that natives become a minority and chaos ensues, rapidly undermining cultural cohesiveness and economic and political institutions. Gallup poll data from 2017 suggest that about 750 million people worldwide say they would migrate to a different country if they could, including some 158 million who name the United States as their preferred destination.[122] Critics fear that if all of these people could migrate freely, they would rapidly destabilize their destination countries, potentially destroying the institutions that make them attractive in the first place.[123]

The fear of swamping is the opposite of the concern that international migration has little value for most poor and oppressed people, because the costs of moving are too great and would remain so even if legal restrictions were abolished.[124] If the moving costs critique is correct, concerns about swamping are likely baseless—and vice versa. On the other hand, it is entirely possible that moving costs are low enough to permit large numbers to benefit from the abolition of migration restrictions but not so low as to make swamping a realistic scenario.

One key flaw in "swamping" scenarios is that they do not take account of the fact that migration is usually a gradual process, in which migrants of a given ethnic group only gradually increase their numbers through "diaspora" dynamics: the presence of a small group of migrants from a given group makes it easier for more to arrive, which in turn attracts others. More risk-averse migrants, and those who most fear cultural adjustment, are likely to come only after a substantial number of others from the same group have already shown that adjustment to the area in question is feasible.[125] The case of Puerto Rico, whose population has had a completely unimpeded right to migrate to the far wealthier United States since 1904, is a telling example, as the actual rate of migration built up only slowly over a period of many years.[126] This gives time for social institutions and labor markets to adjust, and also for cultural and linguistic assimilation to occur. There is little if any reason to believe that swamping is a serious threat under plausible assumptions about migration rates, even if legal barriers were quickly dropped.[127]

A second reason for skepticism about "swamping" scenarios is that even rapid migration waves do not seem to have damaged the institutions of destination countries, if those institutions were even modestly robust to begin with. As a result of the crisis leading up to the first Gulf War in 1990–91, Jordan took in a massive wave of refugees amounting to some 10 percent of its total population, and Jordanian law allowed the refugees to take jobs and vote almost immediately. Nonetheless, the quality of the nation's political and economic institutions did not deteriorate as a result and may even have improved.[128] A similar story played out in Israel during the 1990s, when rapid immigration of Jews and many non-Jewish family members from the former Soviet Union increased the nation's population by some 20 percent, yet without thereby damaging political and economic institutions.[129]

In both the Jordanian and Israeli cases, the migrants in question came from deeply illiberal societies (the Soviet Union and Iraq and Kuwait, respectively) and were far poorer than the preexisting native population. And both nations had small populations, of under 6 million people in 1990.[130] Yet the predicted negative institutional impacts of "swamping" did not materialize. In the case of Jordan, they failed to do so despite the fact that Jordan's institutions were themselves questionable and of lower initial quality than those of developed liberal democracies.[131]

One can argue that the Jordanian and Israeli examples do not qualify as true "swamping" because the Russian immigrants were Jews, and Israel is a majority-Jewish nation; similarly, Palestinian refugees coming to Jordan were Arabs, as were most Jordanian natives. But this way of dismissing the evidence overlooks the major cultural differences between Russian Jews and native-born Israeli Jews, and the fact that both the Soviet Union and most of its successor states were and are illiberal societies of precisely the kind that skeptics claim are likely to generate illiberal migrants who could degrade institutional quality in host societies. Moreover, Russian immigration to Israel actually included a large number of non-Jews, as well.[132] Palestinian migrants to Jordan likewise have significant political and cultural differences from other parts of the population of that country.[133]

This experience suggests that "swamping" is even less likely in larger countries with better-developed institutions. The bigger the host nation, the harder it is for any given number of migrants to have a major impact on its institutions. The more robust those institutions are to begin with, the harder it is for them to be undermined by migration, even if rapid.

Despite these points, swamping cannot be definitively ruled out in the case of nations with fragile institutions and relatively small populations. Fortunately, several keyhole solutions are potentially available for such situations.

One obvious one, already discussed in relation to concerns about welfare and voting, is to temporarily limit migrants' access to specific institutions that are seen as potentially likely to fail under pressure, such as welfare state benefits or access to some types of political participation and the like. If the "swamping" concern is about culture or language, tests of linguistic competency or cultural knowledge could be imposed as conditions for residency, or perhaps passing scores could be required to stay in the country for more than a certain period of time.[134]

In extreme cases where a small nation with weak institutions faces a truly vast influx, it is possible that even the best possible keyhole strategies will fail.[135] But such extreme scenarios do not apply to migration to most developed nations.

Does Exit Undermine Voice? Albert Hirschman's Critique of Foot Voting

In contrast to most other criticisms of foot voting considered in this chapter, economist Albert Hirschman's classic critique is focused primarily on the internal variety rather than on international migration.[136] Hirschman contends that exit rights are damaging to self-determination by means of "voice" through the political process. That is because those individuals most likely to use voice effectively to promote needed reforms may instead exit the system.[137] In this sense, the exercise of political freedom by some through exit rights undermines that of others through the use of the traditional political process.

To address this problem, foot-voting rights could potentially be weakened or even abolished entirely. For example, legal scholar Erwin Chemerinsky has argued that the United States should abolish private schools and home-schooling entirely, so that wealthier and politically influential parents would have a stronger incentive to lobby for increased funding and quality improvements in public schools.[138]

It is important to recognize that Hirschman's argument applies only in a narrow range of circumstances. In order for it to hold true, a subset of participants in a political institution must (1) be able to force through reforms beneficial to other participants where the others could not impose the reforms in their absence; (2) prefer to exit rather than exercise voice despite the likelihood that their use of voice will be successful; and (3) possess exit options that are not available to the others.

The more foot-voting opportunities become available to all citizens, the more the third precondition is weakened. The kinds of measures described in chapters 2 and 4 of this book suggest ways to increase such options. That is a better approach than forcing people who might leave to stay, in the hope that their political activism might have a beneficial "trickle down" effect.

To the extent that widespread voter ignorance makes effective reform through the ballot box unlikely, condition 1 is also undermined. And, as we have seen, public ignorance is widespread indeed.[139] Should reform through voice be possible in relatively short order, the potential reformers might well choose to stay and fight rather than leave.

Finally, even if all three preconditions are met, foot voting by even some participants could give policymakers an incentive to enact needed reforms of their own accord in order to retain tax revenue or for other reasons. This seems to have occurred when it comes to the paradigm case that gave rise to Hirschman's theory: school vouchers that give parents funds to transfer their kids to private schools or better-performing public schools.[140] Peer-reviewed studies of the effects of vouchers generally find that they actually improve the quality of public schools "left behind" by those who exit.[141] By contrast, simply increasing funds for traditional public schools, without expanding exit rights, has little or no educational benefit.[142]

The ability to exit might actually facilitate investment in "voice" rather than undermine it. Exit enables foot voters to move to jurisdictions that fit their needs and preferences better than their original homes. The new home, presumably, is one they value more. And the more value people place on a resource, the more likely they are to invest in its maintenance and potential improvement.

Research suggests that political participation is greater in small suburbs, where residents have relatively extensive exit rights, than in larger ones, where moving costs are likely to be higher.[143] While this may be partially due to the higher likelihood of making a decisive difference to the outcome in a small electorate, it is also likely to be due to the ability of residents with many options to find a jurisdiction that meets their preferences.

To make an admittedly oversimplified analogy, the ability to freely choose a marriage partner does not necessarily lead to lower investment in the marriage than a system under which marriages are forcibly arranged by parents or by the state. Freedom of choice increases the likelihood that you can find a partner who is genuinely compatible with you. The resulting relationship is thereby one you would make more effort to maintain.[144] Far from devaluing the importance of being part of a good political community, strong exit rights can help ensure that many more people have access to one that is good for them.

This certainly does not prove that the sorts of trade-offs Hirschman posits never exist. But it does suggest that they are a comparatively special case, not a general weakness of foot voting. Even where they are present, it does not necessarily follow that exit rights should be constrained. As in the case of international migration and various types of internal foot voting, the justice of forcing some people to stay in place so they can work for the benefit of others is questionable at best.[145]

The Big Sort

A criticism of internal foot voting that has become significant in recent years in the United States arises from fears of the "Big Sort": the supposed tendency of people to cluster in communities of the politically like-minded. In a famous 2008 book of the same name, journalist Bill Bishop argued that this trend increases political polarization and our already strong tendency to ignore or dismiss opposing points of view.[146] While foot voting might help express political freedom for potential migrants, it could, on this view, undermine effective self-government at the national level. Expanding opportunities for foot voting could potentially make the situation even worse.

Ironically, the Big Sort argument is the reverse of the usual concern about political externalities. Instead of changing the public policies of migrants' destination jurisdictions, the fear here is that migrants will support the status quo even more than the native population and perhaps entrench status quo policies further.

This issue should not be lightly dismissed, especially in an age of rampant and growing partisan bias that has helped to poison American politics.[147] Nonetheless, the concern is overstated.

One flaw of the Big Sort theory is that the data do not seem to support the notion that we are more ideologically segregated than we were several decades ago. That does not rule out the possibility that increased foot voting would cause more of a big sort than currently occurs. But it should make us more skeptical of the theory.[148]

There is evidence that many states and congressional districts are more reliably Democratic or reliably Republican than in previous decades.[149] But this is not because people are more ideologically segregated than in the past, but because social issues—which correlate more with regional divisions than many other political issues do—have become more salient in national elections than before and therefore have a bigger impact on electoral outcomes.[150]

A deeper problem with the Big Sort theory is that people who vote with their feet do not in fact tend to make choices that align neatly on a left-right or Democratic-Republican spectrum. For example, the data suggest that many movers gravitate toward jurisdictions that are both socially tolerant and have relatively free market policies that lead to cheaper housing and more job opportunities.[151]

Many are also willing to move to jurisdictions that do not match their partisan biases, because they have specific policies that the migrants expect to benefit from. In recent years, "red" Republican-dominated states like Texas have attracted many migrants from liberal states on the East and West coasts because their less restrictive zoning rules lead to lower housing costs.[152]

More generally, there is considerable diversity in the amount of diversity (of many types) that people prefer to have in their communities. That, too, cuts against any monolithic tendency to move toward areas largely populated by those who have the same political views as the movers themselves.

To the extent that migration decisions are often driven by economic issues more than the social issues that have fueled geographic partisan polarization in recent years, it might even modestly mitigate such polarization, as social liberals move to areas with economically conservative policies that offer lower taxes and housing costs. The movement of social liberals to traditionally conservative Texas is a notable example, though such moderating effects are likely to be modest in scope and gradual in timing.[153]

A recent study finding that people who migrate away from politically extreme counties are disproportionately likely to move to destinations with similar political orientations should not be interpreted as strong support for the "Big Sort" theory.[154] If relative extremists move from one politically extreme area to another, they make the destination county even more extreme than it would be otherwise. But, at the same time, their departure slightly reduces the extreme tendencies of their previous location. Moreover, the same analysis finds that people moving from moderate counties do not disproportionately favor destinations with any particular political orientation.[155] To the extent some of these relative moderates move to more ideologically extreme areas, they would actually reduce the extremism of their destination at the margin.

Even if foot voting does increase ideological segregation to some substantial degree, that might not be such a bad thing. Sadly, data show that most Americans rarely discuss politics with people who hold significantly different views from their own—even if they live in politically diverse areas.[156] Greater residential segregation by ideology may not make that tendency much worse because people are very good at avoiding challenges to their views even in its absence.

Some degree of increased ideological segregation may, however, increase diversity in policies *between* jurisdictions. Diminished diversity *within* jurisdictions can sometimes promote beneficial diversity across institutions, by making each more distinctive from the rest. Such "second-order" diversity, as legal scholar Heather Gerken calls it,[157] can expand the range of choices available to foot voters and potentially stimulate greater interjurisdictional competition.

Implications for Internal Foot Voting

Much like the issues discussed in Chapter 5, many of the objections to foot voting covered in this chapter are—in modern times—usually raised only against international migration. At least in advanced liberal democracies, few argue that issues such as crime, burdens on the welfare state, and cultural change justify barring internal migration.

Historically, of course, such claims have often been used to justify internal migration restrictions, such as those associated with racial segregation in the United States and apartheid South Africa. Today, however, most modern Westerners consider these to be shameful episodes in our history, not examples to be emulated.

But the logic of most of these justifications for exclusion *does* often apply to internal migration, whether we want to admit it or not. Those who accept this type of reasoning as a justification for immigration restrictions but reject it as a justification for constraints on internal migration have a deep contradiction in their positions, one that in most situations cannot be resolved without applying the same standards to both types of migration.

As discussed earlier in this chapter, internal mobility can cause political externalities at least as readily as international migration can. Indeed, the risk might be greater, since internal migrants usually gain the right to vote at their new location much faster than international migrants. In the United States, for example, the Supreme Court has ruled that it is generally unconstitutional for states to impose duration of residency requirements on migrants from other states, striking down even those that last a few months to a year.[158] By contrast, federal law imposes a five-year waiting period before immigrants from abroad can get citizenship, and even then they must pass a civics test most Americans would fail.[159]

In many federal systems, there are significant divergences in political views between residents of different jurisdictions. Thus, migrants from liberal California could potentially have a substantial impact on the politics of conservative states.[160] Conservative southern migrants could similarly change the politics of more liberal northern states. Yet few argue this would justify restricting internal migration in the United States.

Residents of different regions and members of different ethnic groups often also differ greatly in their crime rates and the extent to which they use welfare benefits. Migrants from a poor region could potentially consume welfare benefits in a wealthier one, thereby increasing the burden on taxpayers in the latter. Migrants from a high-crime region could potentially increase the crime rate in lower-crime areas they choose to move to. The comparatively high crime rates of African Americans were in fact historically cited as justifications for racial segregation by the state and for restrictive zoning intended to keep blacks out of majority-white neighborhoods.[161]

Similar reasoning could be used to justify coercive restrictions on fertility.[162] After all, children—particularly those born into poor families—might increase burdens on the welfare state. Some may also be disproportionately likely to grow up to become criminals.

Protecting current residents against migrants with harmful cultural values is also a theory readily applicable to internal migration. There are often significant cultural differences between residents of different regions of the same country, some of them deeply rooted.[163] The supposedly harmful cultural values of African Americans (often claimed to be rooted in inherent racial inferiority) and the prospect of conflict between them and whites was a justification commonly offered to support racially based residential segregation laws in the early twentieth-century United States, an idea that spread rapidly until invalidated by a Supreme Court decision in 1917.[164]

Similarly, internal migration can potentially exacerbate environmental problems as well. It could lead to increases in air and water pollution in a given area or to overuse of scarce resources.

Finally, it is clear that internal migration can potentially cause wage competition between newcomers and natives of particular regions. If workers move from comparatively impoverished West Virginia to neighboring Virginia, which is much wealthier, they can cause increased competition for jobs, leading to declining wages in some sectors. Once again, however, few view this as a legitimate reason to prevent residents of relatively poor regions from moving to more affluent ones.

Conclusion

In most cases, potential downsides of migration are either overstated, can be addressed by keyhole solutions, or can be mitigated by tapping the wealth created by migration itself. At the very least, we should carefully consider these three possibilities before concluding that restricting migration is the best way to address some problems supposed to be caused by foot voting.

None of the points made in this chapter prove that freedom of movement must be completely unlimited. In a variety of situations, adherents of nearly all political ideologies would agree that movement can be restricted regardless of the citizenship or place of birth of the persons in question. For example, few doubt that governments can legitimately block the movement of people traveling for the purpose of committing crimes such as murder, rape, or assault, or in order to perpetrate terrorist attacks. Similarly, it may well be justified to impose quarantine restrictions on persons who are carriers of deadly diseases, if that is the only feasible way to prevent the spread of those diseases.

But in situations like these, the key point is that restrictions on freedom of movement can be justifiably imposed irrespective of whether the movement in question is internal or across international boundaries, and irrespective of the citizenship and parentage of the persons involved. By contrast, a theory that seeks to justify *selective* restrictions that apply only to international migrants cannot be defended on the basis of reasoning that applies with equal force to internal migration.[165]

7

The Foot-Voting Constitution

Foot voting is a valuable mechanism for expanding political freedom. How can constitutions be designed in ways that maximize its potential, while mitigating potential downsides? This chapter addresses that question. It is not a complete theory of constitutional design and certainly not one that can be applied in all times and all places. Nonetheless, there are some general principles that can help guide nations in designing constitutional frameworks that facilitate foot voting. Existing constitutional systems could adopt some of these ideas as adjustments at the margins. These include devolving substantial amounts of power to regional and local governments and giving them incentives to compete for residents. At the same time, regional and local governments should, as much as possible, be prevented from themselves restricting mobility.

Constitutional systems can also be structured in ways that facilitate international migration. Relevant rules might include limits on the central government's power to exclude migrants, and devolving some authority over immigration to subnational governments, as for example by permitting them to sponsor visas for immigrants and guest-workers.

Finally, constitutional frameworks that facilitate foot voting will generally feature some types of strong individual rights, and a robust system of judicial review. These can help facilitate foot voting—especially in the private sector—and also offer protection to immobile people and owners of immobile assets, which cannot as easily take advantage of many foot-voting opportunities.

The purpose of this chapter does not include determining the correct interpretation of any currently existing constitution. I also do not intend to assess the relative merits of competing theories of constitutional interpretation, such as originalism, living constitutionalism, and different variants thereof. Rather, the goal is to explain how constitutions can be structured in ways that facilitate foot voting. The extent to which current constitutions in the United States and elsewhere achieve that goal is a separate question that cannot be systematically considered here.

It is also important to remember that protecting and expanding foot-voting opportunities is not the only objective of constitutional design. I cannot here provide anything approaching a comprehensive assessment of how foot voting should be balanced against other relevant objectives. But it deserves greater consideration in discussions of constitutional design than is now generally the case.

Foot Voting and Constitutional Federalism

Constitutional Limits on Central Government Power

The most obvious way in which constitutional systems can facilitate foot voting is by promoting federalism: the decentralization of political power to subnational governments. As a general rule, the more authority is devolved to lower levels of government, the more issues will be subject to foot-voting options, at relatively lower moving costs. The key exceptions to the rule are local and regional policies that themselves inhibit mobility, an issue discussed in more detail later in this chapter.

The appropriate extent of decentralization of power depends on a variety of factors other than foot voting. This chapter cannot possibly do them full justice, though some related issues are addressed in Chapters 2, 5, and 6, which consider a number of standard objections to decentralization and mobility rights. But facilitating foot voting is an important consideration that should be given greater focus in debates over the allocation of power in federal systems. Other things equal, the value of facilitating foot voting counsels in favor of greater decentralization than might be preferred otherwise.[1]

Another important constitutional constraint that can facilitate foot voting is the limitation of fiscal transfers from central governments to regional and local ones. The greater the extent of such grants, the less subnational governments must rely on raising tax revenue from their own residents in order to meet their fiscal needs. That, in turn, diminishes their incentive to compete for migrants by adopting policies likely to attract them, and their incentive to promote economic development that attracts foot voters seeking jobs and opportunity. For these reasons, "hard budget constraints" that restrict central government transfers to regional and local authorities are extremely valuable tools for facilitating foot voting and economic development.[2]

Hard budget constraints do not necessarily require a complete ban on intergovernmental transfers. But they do require the imposition of relatively tight restrictions on their extent that are relatively difficult to breach. Otherwise, subnational governments will have strong incentives to look to central governments to meet their revenue needs rather than take the more politically difficult option of raising tax rates or increasing their tax base by fostering development.[3]

Hard budget constraints are also entirely compatible with using the central government to redistribute wealth to the poor. Such redistribution can be undertaken by transfers that give funds directly to the poor rather than using subnational governments as intermediaries. Doing so might even be more efficient, insofar as it might help reduce the risk of "capture" of the funds in question by local or regional interest groups.[4]

Devolving Authority to Local Governments

Most debates over the allocation of power in federal systems focus on conflicts between national and regional governments. But there is also a strong case for increasing the autonomy of local governments from regional ones. This too, can potentially do much to enhance opportunities for foot voting.

In recent years, in the United States, rural conservative "red" localities in liberal "blue" states and urban liberal blue localities in red states have both increasingly clashed with politically hostile state governments.[5] Both red enclaves in blue states and blue enclaves in red states could potentially benefit from increased local autonomy from their respective states.

The more autonomy local governments have from states, the more room there would be for potential policy variation for foot voters to choose from. In addition, there are simply many more local governments in the United States than states—89,000 compared to 50.[6] The more issues are left to the discretion of the former, the greater the range of potential options for foot voters. In Heather Gerken's influential phrasing, devolution of power to local government pushes "federalism all the way down."[7] By devolving authority to the seemingly lowest level possible, it enables a wider array of options to flourish than is possible when power is devolved only to the regional level.

In the United States today, the federal Constitution offers localities very little protection against their state governments. The former are essentially creatures of the latter, who can dispose of them largely as they wish.[8] But it may be possible to give localities greater protection under state constitutions, some of which already give them a measure of autonomy.[9]

It is neither possible nor desirable to devolve every issue to the local level. As with devolution from national to regional governments, the appropriate extent of regional-local decentralization will depend on a variety of issues other than foot voting. Some problems are so large-scale that they can only be handled at the state, national, or even international level.[10]

It will often be necessary to restrict local control over immobile assets, such as property in land, which cannot be moved in response to exploitative local policies. Such policies also often have the effect of eliminating valuable opportunities for foot voting, most notably in the case of restrictive zoning rules that lock out the poor and lower middle class, cutting them off from valuable job opportunities.[11] More generally, constitutional constraints on state and local governments can sometimes actually promote greater, rather than lesser, decentralization by empowering private individuals and organizations.[12] Still, there are large potential gains from devolving power to local governments over a wide range of issues where there is little risk of losing economies of scale or destroying foot voting opportunities.

Enforcing Federalism through Judicial Review

Since determining the size and degree of centralization of government involves many complex trade-offs, it is possible that legislatures will be in a better position to balance the relevant considerations than constitutional drafters or courts exercising the power of judicial review. The extent to which this is true may potentially vary between countries.

Despite this concern, there is reason to believe that ordinary legislative activity will undervalue the informational benefits of both decentralization and limited government. Perhaps "political safeguards of federalism" would make constitutional limits on central government power unnecessary. Some scholars argue that the political power of state governments is sufficient to prevent excessive centralization, because the regions can use their clout to prevent it, and voters will punish overcentralization at the polls.[13]

Unfortunately, some of the very same factors that make decentralization and limitations on national government power desirable also reduce the chance of achieving it through the ordinary legislative process.

Most voters have little understanding of federalism, and fewer still are likely to be aware of the interconnection between limits on federal government power and "foot voting."[14] For these reasons, they may be unlikely to punish elected officials who promote overcentralization.

This might not be a problem if central and regional governments had other incentives that would lead them to avoid excessive centralization. In fact, however, both regional and federal governments often have strong political incentives to facilitate the concentration of power at center. Central governments have incentives to expand their power in order to capture more revenue and use it to buy political support; subnational governments have incentives to lobby for central government grants and to use the central government as a cartel enforcer that suppresses competition between them.[15]

Strikingly, subnational governments in most federal systems get the vast majority of their funds from central government grants.[16] This occurs despite the fact that dependence on such grants severely reduces state incentives to compete for foot voters in order to attract tax revenue, and increases the central government's ability to use grants to suppress regional policy diversity.[17]

The political reality that overexpansion of central government power often advances the interests of regional governments undermines claims that "political safeguards" are enough to ensure an optimal level of decentralization. Virtually all such arguments rely on the political power of regional governments to serve as a check on the center. But if regional governments actually help promote centralization, their influence in the national legislature becomes a liability for federalism rather than an asset.

For these reasons, the political process is unlikely to generate the appropriate level of decentralization and limits on central government power. This suggests that constitutional restraints on centralization and the growth of government are needed.

How strict should those constraints be? As already noted, that will in part depend on considerations other than fostering foot voting. But this analysis does suggest that the need to combat the effects of political ignorance justifies stronger constitutional constraints on centralization and the growth of government than we might otherwise wish to impose.

Foot Voting and Individual Rights

The structural organization of regional and central government power is not the only aspect of constitutions that can facilitate foot voting. Constitutional protections for individual rights can help do so as well—particularly when it comes to facilitating private sector foot voting.

It is probably impossible to fully enumerate all of the types of individual constitutional rights that can help promote foot voting. But, as a general rule, they fall into two major categories: those that facilitate mobility directly, thereby making it easier for individuals to engage in foot voting between jurisdictions in a federal system, and those that protect individuals' abilities to enter into voluntary private arrangements of various types, thereby enhancing their ability to vote with their feet in the private sector. Some rights, of course, facilitate both. By decentralizing power to an even lower level than is possible through devolution to local government, constitutional rights that protect both social and economic liberties of individuals enable the creation of a wider range of foot-voting options, often accessible with lower moving costs than is possible through federalism alone.[18]

As in the case of constitutional arrangements relating to federalism, the proper scope of individual rights to be protected by a constitution cannot be resolved by reference to foot voting alone. A variety of other considerations may weigh for or against protecting a particular right, and for or against giving it a broad scope. But foot voting should at least be an important consideration in any such analysis.

Constitutional Rights that Directly Protect Mobility

The most obvious individual right that can help facilitate foot voting is, of course, the right of freedom of movement. As early as 1867, the US Supreme Court interpreted the Constitution as incorporating an implicit right of freedom of movement across state boundaries, even though it was nowhere explicitly stated.[19] After the enactment of the Fourteenth Amendment in 1868, the Court eventually interpreted its protections for liberty as forbidding state government efforts to restrict interstate movement: "Undoubtedly the right of locomotion, the right to remove from one place to another according to inclination, is an attribute of personal liberty, and the right, ordinarily, of free transit from or through the territory of any state is a right secured by the 14th Amendment."[20] As late as the 1940s, some states still attempted to block in-migration. In 1941, the Supreme Court struck down a California law making it a crime to bring into the state any "indigent" person who was not already a resident.[21] If either the central government or regional ones are able to block migration, foot voting becomes more difficult—and in the extreme case—completely impossible.

Foot voting is also obviously enhanced by constitutional restrictions on laws that forbid some members of the population from residing in particular areas, such as racial residential segregation laws. *Buchanan v. Warley*, the 1917 decision in which the US Supreme Court struck down such restrictions, was, among other things, a notable triumph for foot voting.[22] If people belonging to particular races, ethnicities, or other social groups are forbidden to settle in a given area, that obviously restricts their foot-voting options as well as being unjust for other reasons.

More controversial is the status of constitutional rules forbidding state and local governments from restricting the provision of welfare benefits to recently arrived migrants from other parts of the country.[23] On one hand, exclusion from welfare benefits can potentially deter migrants from entering a jurisdiction, thereby impeding mobility. On the other, such exclusion is a potentially useful "keyhole solution" for a possible negative side effect of migration: the pressure it can put on the welfare system.[24] While subnational governments generally do not have the legal authority to exclude internal migrants entirely, they can adopt various policies that might deter them indirectly, so as to avoid becoming "welfare magnets."[25]

The proper resolution of this issue turns in large part on the extent to which we believe jurisdictions are morally required to redistribute to people outside their territory.[26] But it is also worth noting that, to the extent limiting welfare benefits for migrants makes migration more politically feasible, it could be in the interest of migrants themselves. One of the biggest benefits of free migration—both internal and international—is the opportunities it creates for migrants to increase their productivity and find more lucrative employment, thereby greatly reducing the need for them to subsist off welfare benefits in the first place.[27]

Other Constitutional Rights that Facilitate Foot Voting

Some other standard individual rights included in the American Constitution and many others also have clear relevance to foot voting. For example, freedom of speech and press, of the sort protected by the First Amendment,[28] helps create a free flow of information, which in turn is of great value to potential foot voters in choosing between jurisdictions.

Freedom of religion also has great value in enhancing foot voting. For obvious reasons, people may not be able to migrate to jurisdictions where their religious beliefs are subject to persecution by the state. In addition, religious institutions often provide valuable private sector foot-voting opportunities, such as religious schools and social services.

The right to be free of arbitrary arrest and imprisonment without due process is another common constitutional guarantee that has a fairly obvious connection to foot voting. A person who is arrested or imprisoned is clearly not free to engage in foot voting for as long as state authorities choose to detain him or her.

For similar reasons, foot voting is facilitated by constitutional rights that prevent state interference with voluntary intimate relations, such as laws banning same-sex sexual relationships and marriages.[29] Persons involved in such relationships and marriages often cannot easily reside in jurisdictions that forbid them.

Constitutional protection for property rights and economic liberties can also often facilitate foot voting. In the case of property rights, restrictions on zoning and land use regulations that make it difficult or impossible to build new housing in areas otherwise highly attractive to migrants can help facilitate foot voting.[30] A series of US Supreme Court decisions beginning with *Euclid v. Ambler Realty* in 1926 have largely exempted zoning laws from the constraints of the Takings Clause of the Fifth Amendment, which might otherwise require "just compensation" for severe restrictions on owners' use of their own land.[31] Whatever the legal merits of these decisions, they have resulted in massive constraints on foot voting in the United States, especially by the poor and disadvantaged.[32]

The Supreme Court's near-total gutting of constraints on the purposes for which governments may take private property by eminent domain has also impeded foot voting. It has allowed numerous condemnations of residential property for purposes of removing "blight" and facilitating "economic development" that have led to the expulsion of many thousands of people—mostly poor and minorities—from their homes.[33] Similar problems have occurred in other nations where government has had free rein to use takings to displace homes and small businesses for the benefit of more powerful interest groups.[34]

Forcible displacement is not quite the same thing as blocking people from moving to an area in the first place. But in both cases, it is an example of the government's using force to prevent people from residing in the location where they would otherwise choose to be.

Stronger constitutional protection for property rights can also help forestall a potential negative side effect of mobility: the possibility that governments will target immobile assets for exploitation, as a result of limitations on their ability to target mobile ones, due to the fact that the latter can exit the jurisdiction.[35]

In addition to facilitating interjurisdictional mobility, constitutional protection for property rights can also often help promote foot voting in the private sector. If property owners have greater ability to use their land as they see fit, they can offer potential consumers a wider range of services and residential options. For example, they can establish more private planned communities, with a broader variety of institutional frameworks and services.[36]

What is true for property rights is also often true for some types of protection for economic liberties. As noted in Chapter 2, licensing regulations intended to protect incumbent producers against competitors are a significant obstacle to interstate mobility in the United States. In recent years, federal courts have begun to strike down at least a few of the most egregious examples of such regulations when evidence suggests there is no even remotely plausible consumer protection justification for these rules, whose only real purpose is therefore to protect incumbents from competition.[37]

A relaxation of licensing rules and other constraints on economic transactions can also expand individuals' abilities to foot vote in the private sector. It can facilitate contractual and other relationships with employers, producers of goods and services, and so on.[38]

Obviously, there are a variety of plausible justifications for restricting property rights and economic liberties,[39] and for denying them all or most constitutional protection. Since the 1950s, the US Supreme Court has imposed very strict limits on judicial protection for economic liberty,[40] and for some types of property rights—particularly those that limit the range of reasons for which government can take property.[41] These rulings have no shortage of modern defenders, on both doctrinal and consequentialist grounds.

The utility of constitutional protections for property rights and economic liberty for foot voting is a consideration in their favor but far from the only one that must be weighed. Still, it deserves greater attention than it has so far gotten.

As in the case of judicial protection for structural federalism, there are often good reasons to use strong judicial review to protect constitutional rights that facilitate foot voting. There are compelling reasons to suspect that such rights will often get short shrift in the political process because of a combination of political ignorance, prejudice, interest group lobbying power, and other well-known problems.

I will not attempt to review the voluminous literature on these subjects here.[42] But it is important to emphasize that, in the case of rights intended to protect foot voters who do not, at present, reside in the jurisdiction adopting the law in question, the political process may often ignore their interest precisely because they are not part of the electorate and also have far less ability to influence the political process by means other than voting.

The same point, of course, applies to those who are expelled from a jurisdiction by government action. That occurs if the government uses eminent domain to seize their homes or businesses, or forces them out through the use of more subtle regulatory measures. They are likely to be gone by the time of the next election, and therefore unable to use the political process to punish the public officials who forced them out.[43] In addition, many of those who stand to gain the most from foot voting are poor, members of historically discriminated against minorities, and otherwise disadvantaged.[44] That further reduces their political influence and strengthens the case for using judicial review to protect their rights.

For these reasons, the case for using judicial review to protect rights that are important to potential foot voters may often be even stronger than the standard rationale for using it to protect "discrete and insular minorities" and other groups that historically have had little influence in the political process.[45] If these groups' relative lack of influence entitles them to "representation-reinforcing" judicial review even when they have at least some access to the franchise and other conventional mechanisms of political influence,[46] the same is even more true of potential migrants, a group that is often excluded from such participation almost entirely.

A wide range of government policies can potentially impede mobility to one degree or another. Constitutional limits on government power cannot and should not forbid them all. Considerations other than freedom of movement must be weighed in determining the appropriate scope of government regulatory authority in various fields, and the optimal balance might well differ as between different countries.

In this book, I cannot offer a comprehensive account of the appropriate scope of constitutional rights. But the difficulty of drawing a precise line between the permissible and the impermissible should not divert attention away from the enormous gains to be had from curbing policies that massively inhibit foot voting for little or no gain, such as direct restrictions on mobility, and zoning laws that literally exclude millions of society's poorest members from housing and job opportunities.

Designing Constitutions to Facilitate International Migration

In addition to including features that facilitate domestic interjurisdictional and private sector foot voting, constitutions can also be structured in ways that enhance opportunities for international migration. Possible steps in that direction include limits on the power of national governments to exclude migrants and devolution of authority over immigration to subnational jurisdictions.

Limiting the Power to Exclude Immigrants

The most obvious way to bolster migration rights through constitutional design would be to impose constraints on the government's power to exclude immigrants. This may seem like a radical idea. But it is far from unprecedented. During most of the first century of American history, the dominant view (advocated by such Founding Fathers as James Madison and Thomas Jefferson, among others) was that the Constitution did not grant the federal government a general power over immigration,[47] and there was very little federal legislation restricting migrants entering from abroad.

While it may not be politically feasible for most modern governments to adopt a similar approach, constitutional constraints can still impose incremental limits on the extent to which national governments can restrict migration. At the very least, they can ensure that antidiscrimination rules that constrain other exercises of government power also apply to immigration policy. Thus, if the constitution forbids or severely limits government policies that discriminate on the basis of race, ethnicity, gender, or religion, those constraints should apply equally to immigration law and should be enforced by courts without any special deference of a kind that applies only to immigration restrictions. This idea is reinforced by the similarities between the place-of-birth discrimination inherent in many immigration restrictions and invidious racial and ethnic discrimination, as well as the fact that many immigration restrictions have historically been motivated in part by racial, ethnic, and religious prejudice.[48]

From this standpoint, the United States Supreme Court's decision in *Trump v. Hawaii* (2018),[49] the "travel ban" case, was a step in the wrong direction. It upheld President Donald Trump's policy of banning nearly all entry into the United States by citizens of several Muslim-majority nations, despite strong evidence that the ban was motivated by religious bigotry against Muslims. Religion-based discrimination of this type would almost certainly have been invalidated by the Court if it had occurred in any domestic context. It is unfortunate that the justices took a far more deferential approach because the travel ban was a type of immigration restriction.[50]

Constitutions can also be designed in ways that facilitate keyhole solutions to possible negative side effects of migration. For example, where there is a risk of harmful political externalities from immigrant voters, the government can be given the power to restrict eligibility for the franchise.[51] The same applies to the power to restrict immigrant welfare benefits, impose surtaxes on immigrant wages to compensate native workers, and other keyhole solutions discussed in Chapter 6. These sorts of discriminatory powers are potentially problematic in that they can lead to unjust discrimination against immigrants. But, as discussed in Chapter 6, in some situations they are the lesser of the available evils, if the only feasible alternative is barring the immigrants in question entirely.[52]

Devolving Power Over Immigration to Subnational Governments

Federal constitutions can be designed to give subnational governments the authority to authorize immigration of migrants and guest workers without prior approval by the central government. While such arrangements are unusual in modern times, they are not unprecedented. Under the Canadian Constitution, for example, immigration is a concurrent power jointly exercised by both the federal and provincial governments, and the latter exercise a degree of autonomy in selecting and authorizing migrants.[53]

Australia also has a program of state-based visas for workers.[54] In the United States, states had the primary role in setting immigration policy until the late nineteenth century.[55]

More recently, Republican Senator Ron Johnson and Representative Joe Buck have proposed a system under which state governments would have the power to authorize three-year renewable guest-worker visas.[56] Unlike the current H1-B employment visa system, the Johnson-Buck proposal would not require workers to stay with any particular employer and thus offers them far greater freedom of choice. While the Johnson-Buck proposal is limited to worker visas, one can imagine similar systems that offer longer-term visas and even residency rights unrelated to specific job skills.

Economists Adam Ozimek, Kenan Fikri, and John Lettieri have proposed a system of "place-based visas," in which some worker visas could be allocated by local governments in areas in need of additional labor.[57] This idea, versions of which were recently endorsed by Democratic presidential candidates Joe Biden and Pete Buttigieg, could potentially help revitalize struggling communities.[58]

Policies under which subnational governments are given discretion to admit migrants whom the central government would otherwise reject, should be distinguished from proposals to give the former authority to veto migrants who would otherwise be admitted.[59] For obvious reasons, the former expand foot-voting opportunities at the margin, while the latter have the exact opposite effect.

Decentralization of immigration policy to the regional or local level does not offer as much potential expansion of political freedom as the even more complete decentralization that would occur if these decisions were made by individual migrants themselves and their potential employers. Among other things, these proposals limit migrants' options to a particular region, or even to a specific community. If the latter is relatively small, that might in practice tie them to a single employer (or a choice of just a few employers) as well.

But regional or local visa programs could still be a major improvement over the status quo in the United States and many other countries. Migrants seeking access to a given country would have multiple jurisdictions to which they could apply for a visa, not just one. And regional and local governments more open to immigration would no longer be blocked from accepting migrants by a hostile national government or by other regions. Devolving such authority to a lower level of government could thereby help reduce political conflict over immigration while simultaneously allowing relatively pro-immigrant jurisdictions to take in more migrants than they would be permitted otherwise.[60]

Conclusion

No one constitutional framework is ideal for all nations at all times. Maximizing opportunities for foot voting is not the only factor that must be taken account in designing constitutions. But proper constitutional design can do much to expand foot-voting opportunities while helping to mitigate possible downsides of expanded migration rights.

8

Implications for International Law and Global Governance

The case for expanded foot voting set out in this book has important implications for international law and global governance. The two main ones are expanding the range of people who should qualify for refugee status, and guarding against the establishment of world government and strong forms of "global governance."

These two ideas may seem contradictory. But both flow naturally from a concern with the importance of foot voting, especially for people threatened by oppressive regimes. Expanding refugee status to cover a broader category of victims of oppression increases the range of people who can use foot voting to escape tyranny. Avoiding world government precludes a state of affairs where there would be no exit rights at all—an especially severe danger if the world government turns out be repressive, or even totalitarian. It is by no means certain that a world government would be a repressive authoritarian state. But, for reasons to be discussed below, the risk is great enough to be a serious consideration weighing against world government.

Proponents of world government contend that it is the only feasible way to prevent potential global catastrophes, such as global warming and large-scale nuclear war. If so, that might justify establishing it, despite the dangers to foot voting. Indeed, such a catastrophe might render foot voting itself infeasible, or ineffective. But the argument that world government is the best or the only way to solve the world's problems has serious flaws.

Expanding Protection for Refugees

As amended by a 1967 protocol, the 1951 Convention Relating to the Status of Refugees defines a refugee that governments have an obligation to refrain from expelling as "[a] person who owing to a well-founded fear of being persecuted for reasons of race, religion, nationality, membership of a particular social group or political opinion, is outside the country of his nationality and is unable or, owing to such fear, is unwilling to avail himself of the protection of that country."[1] US domestic law has a similar definition.[2] The principle of "non-refoulment" bars states from expelling people defined as refugees under the 1951 Convention "to the frontiers of territories where his life or freedom would be threatened on account of his race, religion, nationality, membership of a particular social group or political opinion."[3]

The Universal Declaration of Human Rights, signed by the vast majority of the nations of the world, mandates that "Everyone has the right to leave any country, including his own, and to return to his country."[4] There is very broad, though not universal,[5] agreement that people have a right to emigrate.

But that right is of little value to the many people who are prevented from moving to better locations by immigration restrictions. Expanding the range of people protected against such barriers can make the right to exit meaningful for large numbers of people who are currently effectively barred from using it.

Proposals for Reform

Scholars and refugee advocates have advanced a variety of proposals for expanding the categories of migrants entitled to refugee-like protection under international law. In a notable recent article, Jill Goldenziel argues that it should be expanded to cover "displaced persons," defined as those "fleeing violence, but not persecution."[6] As she explains, such people face serious dangers even if they are not threatened with persecution of the sort covered by the 1951 convention.[7] The latter does not, she argues, offer protection to the vast majority of the estimated 46 million people in the world, who are currently displaced by violence.[8]

Other scholars would go further in expanding the refugee protection system. For example, Michael Walzer and Niraj Nathwani argue for an expansion to all persons forced to migrate due to severe humanitarian needs, regardless of the reasons why that need came about,[9] though Walzer might limit this to situations where the number of refugees is not so great as to "have any significant impact upon the character of the political community."[10] Seyla Benhabib, a prominent political theorist, argues that states generally have a duty not to expel anyone "whose life, limb, and well-being" would be endangered as a result.[11]

All of these proposals and other similar ones[12] derive additional support from the argument of this book. People threatened by war and other types of violence are clearly lacking in political freedom in any of the forms considered here.[13]

Violence is an obvious threat to negative liberty. A person under threat of arbitrary violence also faces "domination" at the hands of those who have the power to kill or injure her. It is similarly easy to understand how violence threatens positive freedom, in the sense of expanding human capabilities. If the violence is undertaken by or supported by the government, it also renders the rule of that government nonconsensual and thereby undermines political freedom in the sense of consent. I set aside here the unlikely scenario where the people in question have meaningfully consented to the violence at issue.

Similar points apply to other threats to "life, limb, and well-being," at least in cases where those threats either emanate from the state or have its support. In that event, they too threaten all four conceptions of political freedom discussed in this book. Some forms of non-state threats can also undermine at least three of the conceptions: negative freedom, positive freedom, and nondomination (if the threat is grave enough to reach the level of domination). A nongovernmental threat, by contrast, generally does not implicate the ideal of political freedom as government by consent unless the government supports or connives in it.

The argument of this book suggests that refugee status should be extended to a much wider range of potential migrants than these proposals. People who live under repressive regimes suffer serious human rights violations even if they are not targeted for special persecution on the basis of the categories currently specified in refugee law. And the same is true even of some people who are not covered by any of the proposals for expanding refugee-like protections described above.

Moreover, those unable to leave nations ruled by undemocratic regimes often have little chance at political freedom of any kind, except through emigration to a freer society. Thus, at the very least, presumptive refugee status should be extended to migrants fleeing authoritarian regimes and governments that impose severe restrictions on a variety of liberties, whether or not the migrants in question have been specifically targeted on the basis of race, religion, nationality, and other similar criteria.

Destination countries need not be required to provide welfare rights to such migrants. Or at the very least, no such obligations are implied by the arguments advanced in this book.[14] But they should at least not be allowed to expel or deport them, absent some dire exigency that cannot be addressed in any other way.[15]

In the short to medium term, any expansion of eligibility for refugee status is likely to be incremental. Political feasibility almost certainly precludes it from swiftly going as far as described above. One or more of the incremental proposals advanced by other scholars might turn out to be a more politically viable path of progress. Alternatively, it could be that the best short-term political strategy lies elsewhere. In this book, I do not attempt to map out such a strategy. Others are far better positioned to do so than I am.

But the long-run objective should be a strong presumptive (though probably not absolute) right to immigrate, at least for all those fleeing repressive authoritarian regimes. That is the most complete way to protect political freedom against severe forms of oppression that prevail in all too many parts of the world.

Principles for Setting Priorities

In the meantime, it may be useful to consider the issue of which types of oppressed migrants should get priority if, for political reasons, it is not possible to grant refugee-like protection to all.

People threatened with a high likelihood of death, imprisonment, or forced labor (for reasons other than their status as combatants in war or perpetrators of crimes) should obviously rank high on any scale of priorities. These sorts of human rights violations massively undermine the subjects' political freedom as well as being unjust for other reasons. The US Justice Department's recent decision to deny asylum to slave laborers coerced into forced labor by insurgent or terrorist groups is a dramatic example of the kind of policy whose reversal should be a high priority.[16]

The exclusion of people threatened with punishment for crimes is potentially a tricky one. Authoritarian societies routinely criminalize a wide range of activities that should not be forbidden under liberal democratic principles, such as speaking out against the government or practicing a dissenting religion. On the other hand, even within a liberal democratic context, there is a wide range of disagreement as to what sorts of activities can legitimately be criminalized and punished. I do not propose to address that long-standing debate here and must therefore acknowledge that the proper application of asylum priorities may in, some cases, hinge on resolving the issue of whether the person's home state is seeking to punish him or her for a genuine crime or an activity that should not be one.

Here, it is sufficient to emphasize that a wide range of people whom authoritarian states define as criminals are not legitimately subject to punishment on any minimally defensible theory of the scope of criminal law and that such people therefore should not be denied refuge on the grounds of their supposed status as wanted "criminals." Such persons should be treated no differently than other refugees threatened with death, imprisonment, or other similar horrors.

Beyond people seeking refuge from death, imprisonment, forced labor, and other comparable harms, priority should be given to migrants fleeing authoritarian states with particularly oppressive regimes: those that deny a wide range of human liberties beyond "merely" restricting political opposition to the government. For example, refugees from North Korea's totalitarian state, which has committed large-scale mass murder by famine and imposes severe controls on nearly every aspect of its people's lives,[17] deserve priority over those fleeing comparatively run-of-the-mill authoritarian states or seriously flawed democracies, such as those in Central America. A state-created famine in North Korea accounted for some 1 to 3 million deaths in the 1990s, out of a total population of just 23 million.[18]

For fairly obvious reasons, such comprehensive totalitarian oppression and mass murder imposes still greater impositions on political freedom than less extensive repression does. That is clearly true with regard to negative freedom, positive freedom, and nondomination. Because of the near-total absence of limits on its control over the population, the North Korean state dominates its subjects more completely than more conventional dictatorships do.

It is, perhaps, arguable that such a state is not necessarily less consensual than any other dictatorship. In both types of societies, ordinary citizens have no way to alter government policy or escape its control, except— where feasible—by leaving. But the more extensive that authority is, the more nonconsensual impositions on liberty it can thereby impose on its citizens. In this sense, a totalitarian state is more nonconsensual than other dictatorships.

The arguments advanced in this book also call into question the traditional distinction between refugees and "economic" migrants, under which the former are entitled to protection while the latter can generally be deported or denied entry at will.[19] Migrants motivated by the hope of improving their "economic" circumstances are still very often victims of severe injustices inflicted by their nations' governments, including ones that impinge on political freedom.

In many cases, would-be migrants' severe economic deprivation is in large part the result of government policies that they have little hope of changing or escaping, except by emigration. The key role of policy in determining economic development is one of the main conclusions of modern development economics.[20]

Economic privation imposed by government policy constrains political freedom in multiple ways. From the standpoint of negative freedom, government-imposed restrictions on trade, entrepreneurship, and employment are major constraints. State-created poverty also obviously restricts positive freedom and the associated enhancement of capabilities. Economic privation similarly creates conditions in which the government can more readily violate principles of nondomination by establishing control over vital resources. To take one example, the economic crisis caused by the policies of the oppressive socialist government of Venezuela has enabled it to render much of the population dependent on government-issued food rations that are denied to those who oppose the ruling party.[21]

Severe restrictions on political freedom imposed as a result of government economic policies might be more serious forms of oppression than relatively modest types of persecution based on categories protected under the traditional definition of "refugee." The point is not that economic migrants necessarily deserve priority over traditional refugees, or vice versa. It is, rather, that the distinction between the two is a dubious standard for determining which potential migrants deserve priority in a case in which not all can be admitted.

Obviously, the application of these principles of priority to particular cases may often be controversial. Few countries offer as clear-cut a situation of massive oppression as North Korea.

Here, I cannot give a comprehensive account of how to assess more ambiguous situations. As a practical matter, moreover, it will be difficult to keep political calculations from influencing such decisions. But the general principles described here can at least provide some guidance as to the sorts of factors that deserve consideration in cases where political constraints require governments to prioritize some refugees over others.

The Foot-Voting Case Against World Government

The debate over world government and "global governance" typically pits cosmopolitan supporters of globalization against nationalist champions of state sovereignty. The latter fear world government because of the threat it poses to nationalism and the autonomy of nation-states. They also typically view free trade and international migration with suspicion.

However, one need not be a nationalist to oppose world government. Cosmopolitans who support free migration also have good reason to take a dim view of world government and other similar proposals. These positions are not contradictory; indeed they are mutually reinforcing. Precisely because they see great value in free migration and the opportunity to "vote with your feet," consistent cosmopolitans should oppose the creation of a global state whose authority would be almost impossible to escape. This is by no means an entirely new point.[22] But the importance of foot voting to political freedom gives it additional force.

A world government would necessarily close off opportunities for foot voting with respect to whichever policy issues it has control over. It would also undermine valuable interjurisdictional competition and exacerbate some key weaknesses of the democratic process. In the worst-case scenario, it could establish a global tyranny from which there may be no escape. As the famed political philosopher Hannah Arendt put it, a world government "could easily become the most frightful tyranny ever, since from its global police force, there would be no escape, until it finally fell apart."[23] Despite the claims of advocates, it also probably is not necessary to solve the world's great problems. Indeed, it might even exacerbate those dangers.

Why the Debate over World Government Matters

Concern about the perils of world government may seem ridiculous at this point in history. Critics of world government always run the risk of looking like paranoid fanatics who believe that the UN, the Council on Foreign Relations, or the Zionist-Masonic conspiracy is about to take over the world.

This perception may be even stronger in light of recent events such as the rise of powerful nationalist movements in several European countries, and Donald Trump's unexpected victory in the 2016 US presidential election, on a platform opposed to numerous international treaties, and "globalism" more generally. In the aftermath of these developments, the debate over world government may seem like an irrelevancy that can safely be left to utopians and conspiracy theorists.

It is certainly true that world government is unlikely to be established in the near future and that recent political events have made it less likely still. But current political trends may not continue. Survey data indicate that younger voters in both the United States and Europe are less nationalistic than their elders.[24] The same is true of highly educated voters relative to less-educated ones[25]—an important trend at a time when education levels continue to rise. And some influential opinion leaders and political elites are warming to the idea of world government and strong "global governance" because of fear caused by international problems such as global warming and recurring financial crises. They believe that such institutions are necessary to address the world's most serious challenges.[26]

While the establishment of world government is unlikely in the near future, trends favoring it could easily accelerate over time, while opposition might gradually wane. At the very least, it is an idea worthy of serious consideration. If we come to a better understanding of its dangers now, we are more likely to avert the peril before it becomes a serious threat. And sadly, that peril will be very real if the movement for world government makes significant progress.

In ascending order of gravity and descending order of likelihood, world government poses three major dangers: stifling of diversity and competition; elimination of the possibility of exit, and the rise of global despotism, perhaps even culminating in totalitarianism. These dangers are exacerbated by the ways in which a world government might exacerbate the impact of a key weakness of democracy at the national level: widespread political ignorance. All of these problems also pose a clear threat to foot voting.

Stifling Diversity and Competition

The whole world is far more diverse than any one nation-state. A world government will necessarily have to trample some of this diversity in order to impose one-size-fits all policies. If it does not do so, there would be no point in establishing a world government in the first place. Given the incredible diversity of the world's people and cultures, it will be difficult to adopt any policy that does not inflict severe harm on at least some groups. The problem of dissident minorities has been difficult to address within individual nation-states. It would be far more severe under a world government.

Stifling diversity might also undermine beneficial competition between nation-states. Currently, national governments compete with each other to attract business, investment, trade, and productive workers. This to some degree incentivizes states to adopt more effective economic policies and reduces their ability to impose excessive taxes and regulations. It also promotes policy innovation, as a successful innovator can get ahead in the economic race. Examples include Britain in the nineteenth century, the United States in the twentieth, and the "Asian Tigers" more recently. A world government would not be subject to this kind of competitive pressure. By definition, it would have little if any opportunity to learn from the achievements of other states.

The example effect of freer societies often helps stimulate liberalization in more oppressive ones. To take the most obvious case, the example effect of the West played an important role in the fall of communism in Eastern Europe.

Reductions in diversity and competition are likely to diminish opportunities for foot voting. The former diminishes the range of choice available to potential migrants. The latter reduces jurisdictions' incentives to try to attract them.

Exacerbating the Problem of Political Ignorance

The enormous size and complexity of world government would also exacerbate one of the already serious flaws of democracy at the nation-state level: widespread political ignorance. As described in Chapter 1, political ignorance is already a serious problem even in conventional nation-state democracies. Rational ignorance ensures that most voters will make relatively little effort to seek out information on government and public policy. The danger of political ignorance is exacerbated by the enormous size, scope, and complexity of modern government, which makes it difficult for voters to keep track of more than a small fraction of its activities.[27]

In a democratic world government, public ignorance is likely to be an even more serious menace than it is now. A world government would unavoidably deal with a much larger and more diverse society than any national government currently does. It will be even harder for rationally ignorant voters to understand government policy for the entire world than to grasp what is happening in their own country. How well are American voters likely to understand the problems of the Chinese, and vice versa?

The increase in the danger posed by ignorance increases the likelihood that a world government would adopt harmful policies and potentially degenerate into oppression or tyranny. Voters will be less able to monitor such a government effectively than in the case of national, regional, or local governments.

The problem of ignorance is one of a number of reasons why the efficiency and accountability of democratic government tends to decrease with scale.[28] A world government, is by definition, the largest-scale polity possible, thereby making democracy especially difficult to implement.[29]

A Government with No Exit

Throughout history, the option of emigration has been a tremendous boon to people forced to live under corrupt, backward, or oppressive regimes. The United States has taken in millions of such migrants from all over the world. Other relatively free societies have also served as important refuges for the oppressed, including Australia and Canada, among others.

If a world government becomes oppressive, falls victim to corruption, or adopts economic policies that stifle opportunity, *there will be nowhere else to go.* We will all be stuck with that regime for as long as it lasts, which could potentially be a very long time indeed. All or most of the advantages of foot voting as a mechanism for political freedom discussed in this book will be lost.

Political philosopher Rochelle DuFord resists this sort of seemingly common-sense conclusion on the basis that the lack of exit rights under a world government would be no more severe than that which already exists today for many people living under oppressive regimes who are barred from moving elsewhere because of immigration restrictions.[30] She points out that "many people" suffering under unjust regimes already "lack viable exit options" that would enable them to "relocate in order to be free of political and economic injustice."[31]

In an important sense, she is correct. Much of the rest of this book is devoted to criticizing current political arrangements for precisely the reason she mentions. But DuFord downplays the fact that under world government, *everyone in the world* would be in the position of lacking exit rights from any unjust policies that government might adopt. And, with respect to that government, everyone would lack the kind of political freedom that can be best realized through foot voting.[32]

Perhaps this is just a difference of degree rather than kind. But if so, it is a very large difference of degree. For as long as a world government exists and humanity is effectively confined to a single planet, there will be no exit from it for anyone, anywhere.

What if the World Government Were Democratic?

The dangers of world government might be somewhat mitigated if the world government were democratic.[33] If we cannot exercise exit rights against it, we can still resort to "voice." Defenders of strong global governance and eventual world government recognize that, as one puts it, a world state would "only be worth having . . . if its liberal democratic ideals. were sound."[34] But, as we shall see later in this chapter, there is no guarantee that a world government actually will be democratic or that it will stay democratic over time even if it is initially set up that way.

Moreover, even democratic regimes can and often do adopt pathological policies for a variety of reasons, including the widespread political ignorance discussed previously. It is dangerous to trust even a democratic government so much that we are willing to forgo any possibility of exit if things go wrong. We should not put all of humanity's eggs in a single political basket, no matter how enticingly democratic it might seem.

Federalism as a Possible Constraint on World Government

The threat that world government poses to diversity and competition might be mitigated if the government in question had a federal structure, with strong constitutional constraints on the expansion of centralized power.[35] Some degree of foot voting might be maintained in a world government if it had a federal system.

Many issues could potentially be left in the hands of individual nations, now transformed into regional governments. Like the sorts of national constitutions described in Chapter 7, the constitution of the world government could potentially impose restrictions on central government power, possibly ones enforced by judicial review.

Constitutional safeguards for federalism can have great value. But they nonetheless often buckle and break in the face of crises that seem to demand greater centralization. In day-to-day politics, federalism often falls prey to partisan agendas that subordinate constitutional structure to short-term political considerations. "Fair weather federalism" is ubiquitous in American politics and could well emerge in a federal world government as well.[36]

Perhaps constitutional structure can keep world government within strict federalist bounds. Yet history gives only modest grounds for optimism on that score. Federalism at the national level has had its share of successes, and in many cases it has kept government from becoming as centralized as it might have been under a unitary state. But constitutionally limited federalism is not easy to maintain over time.

And the history of federal states suggests that it is often difficult to prevent central governments' powers from expanding over time, even if there are constitutional guarantees against it.[37] For example, central government power often expands beyond previous constitutional limits during periods of crisis, and then does not revert back again.[38] The same thing could easily happen over time with a world government. There is good reason to believe that a federal world government would be subject to many of the same pressures to increase centralization that nation-state governments have experienced in the past.[39]

While such a government would not face pressures arising from external national security threats, it would still be subject to internal incentives for centralization, including a variety of possible crises.[40] Indeed, the task of enforcing compliance with its directives on an enormously large and diverse polity could itself stimulate pressure for greater centralization in order to ensure that the world government had enough power to enforce its laws and regulations.

Even if constitutional safeguards for global federalism worked perfectly, there would still be no exit rights with respect to whatever issues are controlled by the central government. As long as that government continued to exist and humanity continues to be restricted to a single planet, there would be at least some important functions of government from which no exit is possible—and thus no political freedom in the form of foot voting.

A world government could potentially expand foot-voting opportunities by breaking down barriers to migration currently enforced by nation-states. In this scenario, a world state could increase opportunities for foot voting on issues that remain under the control of national governments. But even this is far from certain, since many governments tolerate or even enforce barriers to internal migration.[41] A world government might well follow in that tradition rather than in the footsteps of more liberal states that promote internal freedom of movement.

Moreover, there are strategies to expand migration rights without taking the risks associated with world government. Much can be done to reduce barriers to immigration, both at the national level and by expanding international agreements that protect the rights of migrants and refugees.[42]

Ultimately, protecting and enhancing migration rights no more requires world government or some other sort of supranational governance, than the protection of a wide range of other human rights against national governments.[43] While international arrangements can potentially be helpful in some cases, they are neither the exclusive nor necessarily the best path to success. And it would be self-defeating to give a world government, or other supranational entity, broad enough power to threaten the very rights it is supposed to protect.

The Menace of Global Despotism

As problematic as a democratic world government might be, things will be even worse if it becomes a dictatorship, or even a totalitarian state. A world government might well start off as some sort of democracy and is at the very least highly unlikely to begin as a totalitarian nightmare. But history shows that authoritarian and totalitarian political movements can seize power in a previously relatively free society, especially during a crisis.

In the early twentieth century, totalitarian movements exploited crises to seize power in Germany, Russia, and elsewhere. More recently, democracy has been subverted by authoritarians in states such as Russia, Turkey, and Venezuela.

The likelihood of a descent into autocracy may be very low at any given time. But over decades or centuries, the cumulative risk that it will happen sooner or later rises. Consider a democratic world government that has only a 1 percent chance of succumbing to dictatorship in any given year. Over the course of a century, there is a cumulative 37 percent chance that the state in question will become despotic.[44]

Moreover, the odds of succumbing to dictatorship are much higher in a society where liberal democratic norms are relatively weak and much of the population is poor and ill-educated. In such a society, the odds of degeneration may well be much higher than 1 percent per year.

That gives us still more reason to worry about the potential degeneration of world government. Any world government established in the next few decades or so is likely to preside over a population whose members for the most part have never lived under democracy at all or have experienced it only relatively briefly. The average level of political development in the world is a lot closer to Germany under the Weimar Republic or Russia in 1917 than to the modern United States or Western Europe. And it is likely to remain that way for a long time to come. The median member of the world population lives under a "partly free" government that is far from a fully developed democracy, and about one-third of the world's people live under governments that are not democratic at all.[45]

Even if the average level of political development in the world were higher than it is, there might still be cause for concern. Some scholars argue that well-established democracies are still susceptible to "deconsolidation" of liberal democratic norms.[46] That is what seems to have happened in Poland and Hungary over the last few years, admittedly states where democracy is not as established as in the West. It is not yet clear whether deconsolidation is a serious prospect in the wealthiest and longest-established democratic polities. But the fact that such a scenario is even plausible should decrease our confidence in the prospects for indefinitely stable democracy in a world government.

The widespread political ignorance that is likely to undermine the quality of day-to-day governance in a world state is also likely to increase the danger of degeneration into despotism. Demagogic authoritarian movements can use public ignorance to their advantage, as has actually happened in many of the democratic nation-states that descended into authoritarianism.

In the worst-case scenario, a world government would not only degenerate into dictatorship, but become a full-fledged totalitarian state. And that totalitarianism could potentially be far worse and more long-lasting than any oppressive regime we have seen before.

Historically, the greatest threat to the longevity of totalitarian regimes has been the presence of rival, relatively free societies. Such rivals might forcibly overthrow the totalitarian regime (as happened with Nazi Germany). Even if they do not do so, their example might lead to restiveness among the totalitarian state's subjects and to the adoption of reforms that bring the system down, as happened in the Soviet bloc in the late 1980s.

Once established, a global totalitarian regime would not face either of these risks. There will be no rival government that could overthrow it or provide an example of a successful, relatively free society. For that reason, a worldwide totalitarian state could easily last longer and be more oppressive than any we have seen before. As economist Bryan Caplan explains in a fascinating article,[47] the combination of world government and future technological developments could greatly increase the likelihood of a global totalitarian state.

Is this scenario actually likely to happen? Even given the initial establishment of world government, I would guess that the probability of global totalitarianism within the next century or two is far less than 50%. Nonetheless, the consequences are so catastrophic that even a relatively small risk of global totalitarianism should give us pause.

For all of these reasons, it is overoptimistic to assume that a world government is likely to be democratic— or remain that way. As political theorist Ian Shapiro puts it, world government is "a pretty high-risk bet from a democratic point of view."[48]

Advocates of world government claim that it is needed to cope with a variety of potential catastrophes, many of which also have a relatively low probability of occurring (e.g., an environmental disaster so severe that it might destroy modern civilization) but should still be taken seriously, given the massive harm that would ensue if they ever did occur. The point cuts both ways. If it is valid at all, the "precautionary principle" advocated by many environmentalists should apply to political risks no less than to environmental ones. The principle counsels avoiding actions that might potentially cause great harm in situations where the outcome is uncertain.[49] The risk of global tyranny surely qualifies as such a risk. In the words of George Orwell in *1984*, global totalitarianism would be "a boot stamping on a human face— forever."[50] We should think long and hard before accepting even a small risk of that kind.

The risks of world government are also relevant to strong forms of "global governance" that fall short of officially establishing a world state.[51] The more powerful and centralized the institutions of global governance become, the more likely they are to turn into a world state in all but name.

In one sense, a world government that does not initially label itself as such might even be a greater menace than one that openly proclaims its true nature. The former is less likely to alert rationally ignorant voters to the potential danger,[52] thus making it harder to mobilize opposition.

Do We Need World Government to Solve
the World's Problems?

Even if world government poses grave risks, perhaps we have no choice but to take them. That may be true if world government is the only way to overcome even worse dangers than the ones it is likely to create. If, for example, world government is the only feasible way to prevent nuclear war or some other massive catastrophe, that would be a strong reason to support it, despite the potential negative effects on foot voting. Indeed, a world where such a catastrophe has occurred is also one where foot voting itself would likely become extremely difficult or impossible for most people.

The upsurge of concern over climate change, the 2008 financial crisis, and other international perils have given ammunition to advocates of world government who claim that it is the only way to solve global problems that cross state boundaries. Left to themselves, individual states might "free-ride" on the efforts of others, and the issue in question might remain unaddressed.[53]

This case for world government is superficially appealing but seriously flawed. Even if world government advocates are right to assume that some global problems are too big for any one nation to solve, it does not follow that world government is needed to address them. The problems in question can potentially be addressed equally effectively through cooperation between a few major powers.

For example, the United States, the European Union, India, Japan, and China produce the lion's share of the world's greenhouse gas emissions.[54] An agreement between these major powers could greatly reduce emissions, even if other states sought to free-ride. Similarly, these major powers have the vast majority of the world's banks and other financial institutions and could therefore cooperate with each other to address future financial crises (assuming, for the sake of argument, that such international regulation is necessary).

Both economic collective action theory and basic common sense suggest that cooperation between a small number of like-minded actors is not difficult to achieve and is not likely to be plagued by free-riding.[55] Free-riding would be inhibited by the fact that each of players knows that the whole arrangement is likely to fall apart if they refuse to do their share (i.e., each is big enough that its failure to contribute would have a decisive impact on the outcome). In other words, efforts at free-riding would be prevented by the knowledge that if they are attempted, there will be nothing left to free-ride on.[56]

Obviously, cooperation might be prevented not by free-riding but by honest disagreement over the nature of the problem, the kind of action needed to address it, and whether or not the costs of action exceed the benefits. But such disagreement can also arise even within the confines of a single worldwide government. Unless that government takes the form of an absolute dictatorship or a narrow oligarchy, it too will sometimes be prevented from acting by internal disagreement.

And we cannot assume that the advocates of stronger action are necessarily right. In cases where action is likely to cause more harm than good, the possibility that disagreement might block it is actually a good thing.

In sum, there is no a priori reason to believe that a world government can act to solve global problems more effectively than a consortium of the world's major powers. To the extent that honest disagreement might inhibit the actions of a concert of great powers more than those of a world government, that is as likely to be beneficial as harmful.

It is also essential to consider the possibility that a world government might exacerbate some of the very dangers it is meant to curb. For example, advocates claim that world government will avert the danger of nuclear war between nation-states[57] and perhaps also the use of other weapons of mass destruction (WMDs). This is indeed a genuine peril. But it is worth remembering that, since 1945, the use of nuclear weapons has been prevented in large part by deterrence: governments fear retaliation by other states armed with similar weapons—including nuclear-armed allies of nonnuclear states that might otherwise be vulnerable to atomic coercion.[58]

Mutual deterrence would be eliminated if nuclear weapons were under the exclusive control of a world government. If such a state descended into tyranny, there would be little to deter it from using its monopoly over nuclear arms to suppress potential dissent. For example, it could be tempted to incinerate a recalcitrant city or region as a warning to other would-be rebels. Lacking nuclear weapons or other weapons of mass destruction of their own, the rebels would be unable to respond in kind.

If, on the other hand, control of weapons of mass destruction were not monopolized by the world government, in order to provide a check on its potential abuses of power, then the WMD-control rationale for world government would be undermined. The whole point of it is to reduce the danger of their use by monopolizing their possession.

We cannot definitively rule out the possibility that world government or some strong form of global governance will turn out to be the only possible solution to some grave danger. Perhaps it will indeed be the only way to address either our current global problems or horrifying new ones that we cannot yet fully foresee.[59] But we should be more skeptical of such claims than world-government enthusiasts tend to be. And we should carefully weigh these risks against the very real dangers posed by world government itself.

Conclusion

International law can potentially be of great value in expanding foot-voting opportunities. In particular, much might be gained from incremental expansion of the range of people entitled to refugee status that protects them from being forcibly returned to their countries of origin.

At the same time, however, we should be wary of expanding international institutions to the point of establishing a world government or strong forms of global governance. Foot voting cannot protect us against a government from which there is no escape.

Conclusion

Prospects for a Foot Voting Future

Much can be done to enhance political freedom by expanding opportunities for foot voting. The arguments advanced in this book explain why doing so is an important moral imperative. There are few, if any, other ways to expand human freedom so greatly. And few, if any, other policy changes can do so much to help the poor and oppressed of the world.

This is particularly true if we can combine expansions in all three types of foot voting: interjurisdictional foot voting in federal systems, private sector foot voting, and foot voting through international migration. The former two types of foot voting can do much to reduce moving costs and expand the range and variety of opportunities available to people within their own countries. The latter can greatly benefit many of the most oppressed people in the world.

Interjurisdictional and private sector foot voting can also expand the range of opportunities available to international migrants, as they can choose between a number of different options in their destination countries. Similarly, private sector foot voting can expand the options available to people who move between regions within a given nation.

Thus, incremental expansions of one type of foot voting can augment the effectiveness of the other two. Operating in tandem, the three types of foot voting can enhance political freedom far more than is possible through any one alone.[1]

Opportunities for Incremental Progress

But can we actually achieve a world of greatly expanded foot voting? It is unlikely that we will realize the full potential benefits of foot voting in the near future. But there is a great deal of room for incremental progress with respect to all three major types of foot voting. Even modest expansions of foot-voting opportunities could be a boon to the cause of political freedom and transform the lives of millions of people.

The greatest room for progress is available in the field of international migration. Even relatively small incremental liberalization in migration policy could make an enormous difference. For example, the United States currently accepts just under about 1 million immigrants per year.[2] Even a 10 percent increase in this figure means 100,000 additional people per year will have access to vastly greater freedom and opportunity—most of them coming from poor and often repressive societies. Similarly dramatic results could be achieved if other advanced democracies were to increase their openness to immigration at the margin.

Despite the myth that the United States is the most "generous" country when it comes to openness to refugees fleeing oppression, it in fact accepts far fewer refugees relative to population than many other advanced democracies.[3] For example, Sweden takes fifteen times more by this measure.[4] The United States, therefore, has plenty of room for incremental improvement.

Progress could also be made by allowing subnational governments, such as American states and Canadian provinces, to sponsor more immigration, refugee, and guest worker visas, without prior approval by national governments.[5] The same goes for allowing private organizations to sponsor refugees without relying on government subsidies and permission, as is already the case in Canada.[6]

As discussed in Chapter 6, there are also many opportunities to use "keyhole solutions" to diminish possible negative side effects of expanded migration. This could potentially help weaken political opposition to such moves.

Incremental improvements can also be used to expand opportunities for internal migration. For example, state and local governments in the United States can reduce zoning regulations that lock out millions of people from jurisdictions where they could find better housing and job opportunities.[7] The city of Minneapolis recently achieved an important breakthrough in this respect, by abolishing single-family home requirements that severely restricted new housing construction over 75 percent of the city.[8] Other cities and states could potentially imitate this example, as the state of Oregon has recently done.[9] Each such reform in a major city or state could potentially open up foot-voting opportunities for thousands of people.

Domestic foot-voting opportunities can also be expanded by devolving more authority to regional and local governments so as to expand the range of issues subject to foot voting, and in many cases by giving more leeway to the private sector.[10] Here too, relatively modest changes could potentially make a big difference.

In developing countries that still retain legal barriers to internal migration, the removal of such constraints can do much to promote foot-voting opportunities for people who are far worse off than almost anyone in the United States.[11] In China, for example, many millions of people are blocked from seeking out valuable job opportunities by the *Hukou* system of residency permits, which is only very slowly being reformed.[12]

Political and Technological Prospects for Expanded Foot Voting

Recent years have seen both encouraging and troubling political trends for foot voting. In the United States, public opinion has shifted in a more pro-immigration direction, with younger and more highly educated voters supporting immigration more strongly than other parts of the population.[13] These latter two groups will be disproportionately influential in future years, since younger voters will gradually displace older ones through generational replacement and education levels continue to rise.

The young and highly educated also tend to be more pro-immigration than the general public in Canada and major European countries, such as France, Germany, and the United Kingdom,[14] though in most of these countries there is not a general trend toward a more favorable view of immigration. A recent study of public opinion in twenty-five European nations shows that these differences between age groups are "cohort effects" arising from the fact that each succeeding generation is more open to immigration than the one before, not "life cycle" effects in which people are relatively pro-immigration when young but become more hostile as they get older.[15] That suggests that generational succession will, over time, move public opinion in a more pro-immigration direction. The greater openness of the young and highly educated to immigration is at least in part a result of their being, on average, much less nationalistic and less prone to racial and ethnic prejudice than older and less educated voters.[16]

Ironically, some of the same trends in public opinion that might be long-term risk factors for world government are currently beneficial for the political prospects of foot voting through immigration. But the degree of movement in public opinion needed to expand immigration significantly is almost certainly much less than that needed to make world government politically feasible.

On the other hand, it is undeniable that strong anti-immigrant nationalist movements have emerged in both the United States and many European countries in recent years, as reflected in greater electoral success for parties advocating such stances.[17] Hostility toward immigration was a key factor in generating support for Donald Trump in the 2016 presidential election, even if that hostility was shared by only a minority of the electorate.[18]

Whether this rising nationalism will ultimately prevail over the pro-immigration sentiments of younger, more highly educated voters remains to be seen. The outcome may depend in considerable part on whether Western nations can restore stronger economic growth. Historically, hostility toward immigrants and racial and ethnic minorities is stronger in periods of economic recession or stagnation, perhaps because voters then have a stronger perception that the world is a zero-sum game pitting natives against immigrants and other foreigners.[19]

It is also not clear whether political factors will lead the United States and other nations to adopt reforms facilitating greater internal foot voting. But one positive trend is the growing understanding among a cross-ideological group of experts, and some policymakers, that zoning rules must be loosened to facilitate greater freedom of movement for the poor and lower-middle class.[20] In recent years, reforms to loosen up zoning restrictions have been enacted or at least seriously considered in several different parts of the United States.[21]

Should political obstacles to foot voting be reduced, technological developments help ensure that it will be easier for more people to take advantage of these opportunities than in the past. The internet and other modern technologies ensure that information about conditions and opportunities in almost every part of the world is more easily accessible than ever before in human history. That can enable potential migrants to quickly identify attractive destinations and to be matched with possible employers and other useful contacts. Future developments in information technology may improve things in this regard even further.

Declining transportation costs have also made migration cheaper and easier than before.[22] Future technological advances might reduce those costs even more.

The future of foot voting remains uncertain. The potential gains are vast. But the extent to which we can overcome political obstacles to them is uncertain. It will not be easy to secure what Frederick Douglass called "the right of migration; the right which belongs to no particular race, but belongs alike to all and to all alike."[23] The struggle may not be fully won for a long time, if ever. But it is a cause worth striving for, even so.

Notes

Introduction

1. Quoted in "A Better Way," *The Economist*, Oct. 7, 2010, available at http://www.economist.com/node/17173919.
2. Caglar Ozden et al., *Moving to Prosperity: Global Migration and Labor Markets* (Washington, DC: World Bank, 2018), 3. The phrase is adapted from Michael Clemens, "Economics and Emigration: Trillion Dollar Bills Left on the Sidewalk?" *Journal of Economic Perspectives* 25 (2011): 83–106.
3. Clemens, "Economics and Emigration." See also discussion of this issue in Chapter 3.
4. Lawrence H. Summers, "Rethinking Global Development Policy for the 21st Century," Speech at the Center for Global Development, Nov. 8, 2017, available at https://www.cgdev.org/publication/rethinking-global-development-policy-for-the-21st-century.
5. See discussion in Chapters 2 and 3.
6. For an overview, see Morton H. Halperin, Joseph Siegle, and Michael M. Weinstein, *The Democracy Advantage*, rev. ed. (New York: Routledge, 2010).
7. For a modern exposition of a utilitarian approach to morality, see, e.g., Peter Singer, *Practical Ethics*, 3d ed. (Cambridge: Cambridge University Press, 2011). On virtue ethics, see Liezl van Zyl, *Virtue Ethics: A Contemporary Introduction* (New York: Routledge, 2018).
8. See discussion of these types of arguments in Chapters 5 and 6.
9. Frederick Douglass, "Our Composite Nationality: An Address Delivered in Boston, Massachusetts, 7 December 1869," in *The Frederick Douglass Papers: Series One: Speeches, Debates and Interviews*, Vol. 4, ed. John Blassingame and John McKivigan (New Haven, CT: Yale University Press, 1991), 240–59; 252.
10. Ibid., 250–51.
11. See discussion of the parallels between immigration restrictions and racial and ethnic classifications in Chapter 5.
12. Frederick Douglass, *Selected Speeches and Writings*, ed. Philip S. Foner and Yuval Taylor (Chicago: Lawrence Hill Books, [1886] (1999), 702.
13. I recounted my experience of immigration in Ilya Somin, "A Road to Freedom," in *HIAS at 130: The Best of My Story* (New York: Hebrew Immigrant Aid Society, 2012). For the longer, more detailed version of this memoir, see Somin, "A Road to Freedom," unpub. manuscript, George Mason University, Nov. 2010, available at https://www.law.gmu.edu/assets/files/faculty/Somin_HIASMemoir.pdf.
14. J. D. Vance, *Hillbilly Elegy: A Memoir of a Family and Culture in Crisis* (New York: Harper, 2016).
15. Ibid., 172–77, 180–88, 198–206, 216–34 (describing the impact of these experiences).

16. Ibid., 242–46.
17. Ibid., 252.
18. Ibid., 253.
19. For a previous overview of the three types on which this one is modeled, see Ilya Somin, "Foot Voting, Federalism, and Political Freedom," in *Nomos: Federalism and Subsidiarity*, ed. James Fleming and Jacob Levy (New York: New York University Press, 2014).
20. For a wide-ranging overview of the relevant history, see Massimo Livi-Bacci, *A Short History of Migration* (London: Polity, 2012), chs. 5–6.
21. For an overview of private planned communities, see Robert Nelson, *Private Neighborhoods and the Transformation of Local Government* (Washington, DC: Urban Institute, 2005); cf. Edward Peter Stringham, *Private Governance: Creating Order in Economic and Social Life* (New York: Oxford University Press, 2015), 131–32.
22. Community Associations Institute, *Statistical Review for 2016* (2017), 2, available at https://www.caionline.org/AboutCommunityAssociations/Statistical%20 Information/2016StatsReviewFBWeb.pdf.
23. See George Glasze, Chris Webster, and Klaus Frantz, eds., *Private Cities: Global and Local Perspectives* (London: Routledge, 2006).
24. Ibid., and Nelson, *Private Neighborhoods*.
25. See discussion of this point in Chapter 4, and in the Conclusion.
26. See Albert O. Hirschman, *Exit, Voice, and Loyalty: Responses to Decline in Firms, Organizations, and States* (Cambridge, MA: Harvard University Press, 1970).
27. The relevance of some other "voice" mechanisms is discussed in Chapter 1.
28. Charles Tiebout, "A Pure Theory of Local Expenditures," *Journal of Political Economy* 64 (1956): 516–24.
29. For other differences between Tiebout's theory and mine, see discussion in Chapter 2.
30. This aspect of foot voting is discussed in more detail in Chapter 2.
31. See, e.g., Christopher Heath Wellman, "Freedom of Movement and the Right to Enter and Exit," in *Migration in Political Theory: The Ethics of Movement and Membership*, ed. Sarah Fine and Leah Ypi (New York: Oxford University Press, 2016), 83, 87.
32. Hirschman, *Exit, Voice, and Loyalty*, ch. 4.
33. Convention Relating to the Status of Refugees, Article 1 (1951, as amended in 1967).
34. See discussion in the Conclusion.
35. See, e.g., John B. Judis, *The Nationalist Revival: Trade, Immigration, and the Revolt against Globalization* (New York: Columbia Public Affairs Council, 2018).
36. See discussion in Chapter 2.
37. Tom Phillips, "Venezuela's 'Staggering' Exodus Reaches 4 Million, UN Refugee Agency Says" *The Guardian*, June 7, 2019, available at https://www.theguardian.com/ world/2019/jun/07/venezuela-exodus-4-million-un-refugee-agency.
38. See, e.g., Manuel Madrid, "Trump Is Tough on Venezuela—but Won't Let Fleeing Venezuelans into the US," *American Prospect*, Feb. 12, 2019, https://prospect. org/article/trump-tough-on-venezuela-wont-let-fleeing-venezuelans-us.
39. See, e.g., "Refugee Crises in the Arab World," Carnegie Endowment for International Peace, Oct. 2018, available at https://carnegieendowment.org/2018/10/18/ refugee-crises-in-arab-world-pub-77522.

40. Since 2017, the United States has cut annual cap for refugee admissions from 110,000 to a planned 18,000 in 2020. . See Jim Watson, "Trump Approves Plan to Cap Refugee Admissions at 18,000 in 2020," ABC News, Nov. 2, 2019, available at https://abcnews. go.com/Politics/wireStory/trump-approves-plan-cap-refugees-18000-2020-66718373; Michael D. Shear and Zolan Kanno-Youngs, "Trump Slashes Refugee Cap to 18,000, curtailing US Role as Haven," *New York Times*, Sept. 26, 2019, available at https://www. nytimes.com/2019/09/26/us/politics/trump-refugees.html. European nations have also cut refugee admissions. Some European governments have also sought to block migrants from entering, and incentivize refugees to go back to their countries of origin. See, e.g., Paul Taylor, "EU to Migrants: Go Home and Stay Home," July 3, 2018, available at https://www.politico.eu/article/europe-migration-refugees-drop-dead-angela-merk el-matteo-salvini-libya-italy-germany-refugees/.

Chapter 1

1. See discussion in the last section of this chapter.
2. Andrew Gelman, Nate Silver, and Aaron Edlin, "What Is the Probability That Your Vote Will Make a Difference?" *Economic Inquiry* 50 (2012): 321–26. For more detailed discussion of this and alternative methods of estimating the odds that a vote might be decisive, see Ilya Somin, *Democracy and Political Ignorance: Why Smaller Government Is Smarter*, rev. ed. (Stanford, CA: Stanford University Press, 2016), 75–79. The bottom line is that the odds of decisiveness are low by any reasonable metric.
3. Russell Hardin, *How Do You Know? The Economics of Ordinary Knowledge* (Princeton, NJ: Princeton University Press, 2009), 93.
4. Ibid., 93.
5. For a discussion of a few examples, see Eric Levenson, "Coin Flips, Poker Hands, and Other Crazy Ways in Which America Decides Tied Elections," CNN, Jan. 4, 2018, available at https://www.cnn.com/2018/01/04/us/tie-elections-history-lots-coins-dr aws-trnd/index.html.
6. In a classic article, economist James Buchanan made the related point that "the greater degree of certainty " of the impact of market choices as opposed to voting decisions "seems clearly to produce more rational behavior" in the sense of incentivizing decision-makers to exercise better-quality judgment. James M. Buchanan, "Individual Choice in Voting and the Market," *Journal of Political Economy* 62 (1954): 334–43, 341. He also noted that "[t]his difference [between market decisions and voting] tends to guarantee that a more precise and objective consideration of alternative costs takes place in the minds of individuals choosing in the market," ibid., 337. Foot voting shares this characteristic with market decisions.
7. AMA Code of Medical Ethics, Opinion 8.08 (2012), available at http://journalofethics. ama-assn.org/2012/07/coet1-1207.html.
8. For a more detailed discussion of the logical of rational ignorance, see Somin, *Democracy and Political Ignorance*, 75–91. The idea of rational political ignorance was first developed by Anthony Downs, *An Economic Theory of Democracy*, (New York:

Harper & Row, 1957), ch. 13.

9. This part of the chapter builds on my book *Democracy and Political Ignorance: Why Smaller Government Is Smarter*, which analyzes rational ignorance and its consequences in great detail (see esp. chs. 1–4). I addressed a variety of criticisms of the arguments advanced in that book in Ilya Somin, "The Ongoing Debate Over Political Ignorance: Reply to My Critics," *Critical Review* 27 (2015): 380–414.

10. See Somin, *Democracy and Political Ignorance*, ch. 3; Bryan Caplan, *The Myth of the Rational Voter* (Princeton, NJ: Princeton University Press, 2007), Ch. 5; and Bryan Caplan, "Rational Ignorance vs. Rational Irrationality," *Kyklos* 53 (2001): 3–21.

11. For a review of the evidence, see Somin, *Democracy and Political Ignorance*, 92–97.

12. For a more detailed discussion, see ibid., 78.

13. For more detailed discussion of the reasons why rational ignorance does not require careful calculation and is consistent with crude heuristics, see Ilya Somin, "Rational Ignorance," in *Routledge International Handbook of Ignorance Studies*, ed. Matthias Gross and Linsey J. McGoey (London: Routledge, 2015); and Brad R. Taylor, "The Psychological Foundations of Rational Ignorance: Biased Heuristics and Decision Costs," University of Queensland, unpublished paper, Aug. 31, 2019, available at https://papers.ssrn.com/sol3/papers.cfm?abstract_id=3443280.

14. For recent overviews of the evidence, see, e.g., Somin, *Democracy and Political Ignorance*, ch. 1; Jason Brennan, *Against Democracy* (Princeton, NJ: Princeton University Press, 2016); Christopher Achen and Larry Bartels, *Democracy for Realists: Why Elections Do Not Produce Responsive Government* (Princeton, NJ: Princeton University Press, 2016); Rick Shenkman, *Just How Stupid Are We? Facing the Truth about the American Voter* (New York: Basic Books, 2008).

15. For numerous examples, see Somin, *Democracy and Political Ignorance*, ch. 1.

16. Ibid., 1.

17. Ibid., 20. In more recent surveys, the number who can name the three branches varies from 26 to 39 percent. Annenberg Public Policy Center survey, Aug. 9–13, 2017, available at https://www.annenbergpublicpolicycenter.org/americans-are-poorly-informed-about-basic-constitutional-provisions/ (26 percent); Annenberg Public Policy Center survey, Aug. 16–27, 2019 (39 percent), available at https://www.annenbergpublicpolicycenter.org/americans-civics-knowledge-increases-2019-survey/.

18. Somin, *Democracy and Political Ignorance*, 18.

19. See, e.g., Ipsos-MORI, *Perils of Perception: A Fourteen-Country Study* (Ipsos-MORI, 2014) (detailing similar ignorance in many leading democracies): Ipsos-MORI, *Perils of Perception 2018* (Ipsos-MORI 2018) (same); Bobby Duffy, *The Perils of Perception: Why We're Wrong about Nearly Everything* (London: Atlantic Books, 2018), chs. 4–9.

20. For a recent argument along these lines, see Julia Maskivker, *The Duty to Vote*, (New York: Oxford University Press, 2019), 122–23. Maskivker cites studies indicating that inequality in political knowledge is less correlated with education in countries with greater economic equality. Ibid. But, even if this is the case, those countries still feature low absolute levels of political knowledge. See, e.g., Ipsos-MORI, *Perils of*

Perception and Ipsos-Mori, *Perils of Perception 2018.*

21. For more detailed discussion, see Duffy, *The Perils of Perception*, ch. 3.

22. Ibid., ch. 5, and Kevin Valier, "Exit, Voice, and Public Reason," *American Political Science Review* 112 (2018): 1120-24, 1122–23.

23. Somin, *Democracy and Political Ignorance*, ch. 5.

24. For arguments of this type, see, e.g., Susan Moller Okin, "'Mistresses of their Own Destiny': Group Rights, Gender, and Realistic Rights of Exit," *Ethics* 108 (2002): 661–85; Brian Barry, *Culture and Equality: An Egalitarian Critique of Multiculturalism* (Oxford: Polity, 2001), 147–53.

25. For examples and discussion of relevant literature, see Somin, *Democracy and Political Ignorance*, 93–96, 99–104.

26. Adam Przeworksi, *Democracy and the Limits of Self-Government* (Cambridge: Cambridge University Press, 2010), 101.

27. See discussion of these issues in Chapters 2, 3. and 4.

28. For defense of deliberative democracy, see, e.g., Robert Goodin, *Reflective Democracy* (New York: Oxford University Press, 2005); Ethan R. Lieb, *Deliberative Democracy in America: A Proposal for a Deliberative Branch of Government* (University Park: Pennsylvania State University Press, 2004); James Bohman, *Public Deliberation: Pluralism, Complexity, and Democracy* (Boston: MIT Press, 1996); John S. Dryzek, *Deliberative Democracy and Beyond: Liberals, Critics, Contestations* (New York: Oxford University Press, 2002); Amy Gutmann and Dennis Thompson, *Why Deliberative Democracy?* (Princeton, NJ: Princeton University Press, 2004); Amy Gutmann and Dennis Thompson, *Democracy and Disagreement* (Cambridge, MA: Belknap Press, 1996); and James S. Fishkin, "Deliberative Democracy and Constitutions," *Social Philosophy and Policy* 28 (2011): 242–60.

29. For detailed discussions of this point, see Ilya Somin, "Deliberative Democracy and Political Ignorance," *Critical Review* 22 (2010): 253–79, and Somin, *Democracy and Political Ignorance*, 58–62.

30. See John Locke, *Second Treatise on Government*, ed. Peter Laslett (New York: Cambridge University Press, 1963); Thomas Hobbes, *Leviathan*, ed. Richard Tuck (New York: Cambridge University Press, 1991). For a modern version of consent theory, see A. John Simmons, *On the Edge of Anarchy: Locke Consent and the Limits of Society* (Princeton, NJ: Princeton University Press, 1993); A. John Simmons, *Moral Principles and Political Obligation* (Princeton, NJ: Princeton University Press, 1979).

31. See, e.g., Steinberger, *Idea of the State*, 219–20.

32. In *Crito*, Socrates argues that he is required to obey Athens' laws because he chose not to leave the city. See Plato, *Crito*, in *The Collected Dialogues of Plato*, ed. Edith Hamilton and Huntington Cairns (Princeton, NJ: Princeton University Press, 1969), 27.

33. This example is adapted from Ilya Somin, "Creation, Consent, and Government Power over Property Rights," *Cato Unbound*, Jan. 2010, available at https://www.cato-unbound.org/2010/12/13/ilya-somin/creation-consent-government-po wer-over-property-rights.

34. See, e.g., John Plamenatz, *Consent, Freedom, and Political Obligation*, 2nd. ed. (Oxford: Oxford University Press, 1968), postscript; Peter Steinberger, *The Idea of the*

State (Cambridge: Cambridge University Press, 2004), 218.

35. See, e.g., Michael Huemer, *The Problem of Political Authority* (New York: Palgrave Macmillan, 2013), ch. 4; Simmons, *Moral Principles and Political Obligation*, 136–39.

36. Mario Puzo, *The Godfather* (New York: Fawcett Crest, 1969).

37. This issue is taken up in greater detail in Chapter 2.

38. See more extensive discussion of these issues in Chapters 2 and 4.

39. See Chapter 4.

40. For a leading modern work in this vein, See Robert Nozick, *Anarchy, the State and Utopia* (New York: Basic Books, 1974).

41. On the ways in which migration restrictions violate negative freedom, see Michael Huemer, "Is There a Right to Immigrate?" *Social Theory and Practice* 36 (2010): 429–61.

42. These points are discussed in greater detail in Chapter 3.

43. See, e.g., Amartya K. Sen, *Development as Freedom* (New York: Knopf, 1999); Phillippe Van Parijs, *Real Freedom for All* (Oxford: Oxford University Press, 1995); Charles Taylor, "What's Wrong with Negative Liberty," in *The Idea of Freedom*, ed. Alan Ryan (Oxford: Oxford University Press, 1979); cf. Isaiah Berlin, "Two Concepts of Liberty," in *Four Essays on Liberty* (Oxford: Oxford University Press, 1959).

44. Nondomination is discussed later in this chapter.

45. See the discussion of this issue earlier in this chapter, and also in Somin, *Democracy and Political Ignorance*, ch. 5.

46. See discussion of this point in Somin, *Democracy and Political Ignorance*, ch. 2.

47. For examples, see discussion in Chapters 2 and 3.

48. Michael Clemens, "Economics and Emigration: Trillion Dollar Bills Left on the Sidewalk?" *Journal of Economic Perspectives* 25 (2011): 83–106. See also discussion of this issue in Chapter 3.

49. For estimates of the massive effects of migration on the income of emigrants from poor nations, see Michael Clemens and Lant Pritchett, "Income per Natural: Measuring Development for People Rather than Places," *Population and Development Review* 34 (2008): 395–434.

50. This discussion of Rawls' theory and its relationship to foot voting is in part inspired by Kevin Vallier, "Rawls, Political Liberty, and Freedom of Exit," *Reconciled*, Dec. 16, 2019, available at https://www.kevinvallier.com/reconciled/the-rawlsian-priority-of-the-political-liberty-to-exit/.

51. John Rawls, *Political Liberalism* (New York: Columbia University Press, rev. ed. 1996), 327–30; see also John Rawls, *A Theory of Justice*, (Cambridge: Harvard University Press, 1971), 224–28.

52. Rawls, *Political Liberalism*, 327.

53. Ibid., 327–30; see also Rawls, *Theory of Justice*, 224–28.

54. See Rawls, *Theory of Justice*, 224–28, 233–34.

55. See also the discussion of foot voting and equality in this chapter, and in Chapter 2.

56. Rawls, *Theory of Justice*, 234.

57. See discussion of this issue in Chapter 2, and in Ilya Somin, "Foot Voting, Federalism, and Political Freedom," in *Nomos: Federalism and Subsidiarity*, ed. James Fleming and

Jacob Levy (New York: New York University Press, 2014).

58. See, e.g., Sen, *Development as Freedom*.

59. See, e.g., Phillip Pettit, *On the People's Terms: A Republican Theory of Democracy and Government* (Cambridge: Cambridge University Press, 2012); Philip Pettit, *Republicanism: A Theory of Freedom and Government* (Oxford: Clarendon Press, 1997); Frank Lovett, *A General Theory of Domination and Justice* (New York: Oxford University Press, 2010); James L. Fishkin, *Tyranny and Legitimacy: A Critique of Political Theories* (Baltimore: Johns Hopkins University Press, 1979).

60. Pettit, *On the People's Terms*, 2, 4.

61. See discussion of this point later in the chapter.

62. For a somewhat similar critique of democracy from the standpoint of nondomination theory, see Jason Brennan, *Against Democracy* (Princeton, NJ: Princeton University Press, 2016), 94–99.

63. See, e.g., Pettit, *On the People's Terms*, 64–74 (arguing that mere "noninterference" is not enough to avoid domination if the ruler in fact has the authority to impose restrictions on her subjects, but merely chooses not to use it); Lovett, *General Theory of Nondomination and Justice*, 97–98.

64. This is why, contra James Allan, my argument does not imply that taking the vote away from women or racial minorities would not be problematic. Extending it to them helps protect them against unjust discrimination by the government, even if it does little to promote political freedom, and does not satisfy the requirements of nondomination theory. For the claim that my theory does have such implications, see James Allan, "Reply to 'How Foot Voting Enhances Political Freedom,'" *San Diego Law Review* 56 (2020): 1121–28, 1127.

65. See, e.g., Chandler Davidson and Bernard Grofman, eds., *Quiet Revolution in the South: The Impact of the Voting Rights Act, 1965–90* (Princeton, NJ: Princeton University Press, 1994).

66. Somin, *Democracy and Political Ignorance*, chs. 4–5, and 262.

67. See, e.g., Pettit, "Freedom as Antipower," *Ethics* 106 (1996): 576–604, 578–81.

68. See, e.g., Kenneth Stampp, *The Peculiar Institution: Slavery in the Antebellum South* (New York: Vintage, 1956), ch. 4.

69. Pettit, *On the People's Terms*, 263–74.

70. See, e.g., Morton H. Halperin, Joseph Siegle, and Michael M. Weinstein, *The Democracy Advantage*, rev. ed. (New York: Routledge, 2010).

71. For a recent defense of this view, see Samuel Bagg, "The Power of the Multitude: Answering Epistemic Critiques of Democracy," *American Political Science Review* 112 (2018): 891–904.

72. For a recent discussion of the ways in which exit rights facilitate nondomination that makes similar arguments, see Robert S. Taylor, *Exit Left: Markets and Mobility in Republican Thought* (New York: Oxford University Press, 2017). See also Mark D. Warren, "Voting with Your Feet: Exit-Based Empowerment in Democratic Theory," *American Political Science Review* 105 (2011): 683–701, 686–92 (arguing that exit rights can help prevent domination in situations where it enables foot voters to escape monopoly provision of public services).

73. See, e.g., Donald Wittman, *The Myth of Democratic Failure* (Chicago: University of

Chicago Press, 1995); Hélène Landemore, *Democratic Reason: Politics, Collective Intelligence, and the Rule of the Many* (Princeton, NJ: Princeton University Press, 2013); James Stimson, "A Macro Theory of Information Flow," in *Information and Democratic Processes*, ed. John Ferejohn and James Kuklinski (Urbana: University of Illinois Press, 1990); Bernard Grofman and Julie Withers, "Information-Pooling Models of Electoral Politics," in *Information, Participation and Choice*, ed. Bernard Grofman (Ann Arbor: University of Michigan Press, 1993); James Surowiecki, *The Wisdom of Crowds: Why the Many Are Smarter than the Few* (New York: Doubleday, 2004), ch. 12; and Robert S. Erikson, Michael B. Mackuen, and James A. Stimson, *The Macro Polity* (New York: Cambridge University Press, 2002).

74. Somin, *Democracy and Political Ignorance*, ch. 4. I considered a number of possible critiques of my position in Somin, "Ongoing Debate Over Political Ignorance."

75. Morris Fiorina, *Retrospective Voting in American Presidential Elections* (New Haven, CT: Yale University Press, 1981), 5. For an early classic defense of retrospective voting, see V. O. Key, *The Responsible Electorate* (Cambridge, MA: Harvard University Press, 1966), 60–61.

76. Quoted in Lou Cannon, *Governor Reagan: His Rise to Power* (New York: Public Affairs, 2005), 547n.26.

77. See, e.g., Samuel L. Popkin, *The Reasoning Voter* (Chicago: University of Chicago, Press, 1991).

78. See, e.g., Downs, *Economic Theory of Democracy*, chs. 7–8; John H. Aldrich, *Why Parties?* (Chicago: University of Chicago Press, 1995), 47–49.

79. See, e.g., Arthur Lupia and Matthew McCubbins, *The Democratic Dilemma: Can Citizens Learn What They Need to Know?* (New York: Cambridge University Press, 1998); I criticized their analysis in my review of their book. See Somin, "Resolving the Democratic Dilemma," *Yale Journal on Regulation* 16 (1999): 401–16.

80. See, e.g., Achen and Bartels, *Democracy for Realists*, chs. 4–7; Andrew Leigh, *The Luck of Politics: True Tales of Disaster and Outrageous Fortune*, (Collingwood, Australia: Black, Inc. 2015), ch. 4. Andrew Leigh, "Does the World Economy Swing National Elections?" *Oxford Bulletin of Economics and Statistics* 71 (2009): 163–81.

81. Somin, *Democracy and Political Ignorance*, 117–19. Christopher H. Achen and Larry Bartels, "Blind Retrospection: Electoral Responses to Drought, Flu, and Shark Attacks," Jan. 2004, available at http://www.international.ucla.edu/media/files/PERG. Achen.pdf; Andrew Healy, Neil Malhotra, and Cecilia Hyunjung Mo, "Irrelevant Events Affect Voters' Evaluations of Government Performance," *Proceedings of the National Academy of Sciences* 107 (2010): 12804–9; Andrew Healy and Neil Malhotra, "Random Events, Economic Losses, and Retrospective Voting: Implications for Democratic Competence," *Quarterly Journal of Political Science* 5 (2010): 193–208.

82. Somin, *Democracy and Political Ignorance*, 119; Bryan Caplan, Eric Crampton, Wayne Grove, and Ilya Somin, "Systematically Biased Beliefs about Political Influence," *PS: Political Science and Politics* 46 (2013): 760–67.

83. See, e.g., Larry M. Bartels, "Beyond the Running Tally: Partisan Bias in Political Perceptions," *Political Behavior* 24 (2002): 117–50; Thomas Rudolph, "Triangulating Political Responsibility: The Motivated Formation of Responsibility Judgments,"

Political Psychology 27 (2006): 99–122; Michael Marsh and James Tilley, "The Attribution of Credit and Blame to Governments and Its Impact on Vote Choice," *British Journal of Political Science* 40 (2009) 115–34; Chistopher H. Achen and Larry M. Bartels, "It Feels Like We're Thinking: The Rationalizing Voter and Electoral Democracy," working paper, 2006, available at http://www.princeton.edu/~bartels/ papers; and Donald Green, Bradley Palmquist, and Eric Shickler, *Partisan Hearts and Minds: Political Parties and the Social Identities of Voters* (New Haven, CT: Yale University Press, 2002), vii–viii, 85–139. For recent overviews of this evidence, see Somin, *Democracy and Political Ignorance*, 120–22, and Achen and Bartels, *Democracy for Realists*.

84. Bartels, "Beyond the Running Tally."

85. For detailed discussion, see Somin, *Democracy and Political Ignorance*, ch. 4.

86. For more detailed discussion of this point, see ibid., 160–63.

87. I discuss these points in greater detail in Somin, *Democracy and Political Ignorance*, 10–12.

88. For a more extensive discussion of these points, see ibid., 11–12.

89. Ibid., 120–21.

90. For far more extensive analysis, see ibid., ch. 4.

91. For miracle of aggregation theories of this kind, see, e.g., Philip Converse, "Popular Representation and the Distribution of Information," in *Information and Democratic Processes*, ed. John Ferejohn and James Kuklinski (Urbana: University of Illinois Press, 1990), 383; and Wittman, *Myth of Democratic Failure*.

92. For a prominent recent defense of this sort of theory, see Landemore, *Democratic Reason*.

93. Ibid., ch. 4.

94. For a more detailed discussion of these points, see Somin, *Democracy and Political Ignorance*, 128–30.

95. Ibid., 130–31.

96. Landemore, *Democratic Reason*, 102.

97. See discussion of rational irrationality earlier in this chapter.

98. For more extensive analyses of these points, see Somin, *Democracy and Political Ignorance*, 131–33, and Ilya Somin, "How Political Ignorance Undermines the Wisdom of the Many," *Critical Review* 26 (2014): 151–69.

99. Somin, *Democracy and Political Ignorance*, 133.

100. Jennifer Oser, Jan Leightley, and Kenneth Winneg, "Participation, Online and Otherwise: What's the Difference for Policy Preferences?," *Social Science Quarterly* 95 (2014): 259–77.

101. See, e.g., Oser et al., "Participation, Online and Otherwise," in *Voice and Equality*, ed. Sidney Verba, Kay Schlozman, and Henry Brady (Cambridge, MA: Harvard University Press, 1995); Larry Bartels, *Unequal Democracy* (Princeton, NJ: Princeton University Press, 2010).

102. See the first part of this chapter.

103. For a discussion of this possibility, see Somin, "Deliberative Democracy and Political Ignorance."

104. See, e.g., Verba et al., *Voice and Equality*.

105. For surveys of the evidence, see, e.g., Diana Mutz, *Hearing the Other Side* (Cambridge: Cambridge University Press, 2006), 29–41; Somin, *Democracy and Political Ignorance*, 92–96; Brennan, *Against Democracy*, chs. 2–3.

106. See, e.g., Bruce Ackerman and James Fishkin, *Deliberation Day*, (New Haven, CT: Yale University Press, 2004); Claudio Lopez-Guerra, *Democracy and Disenfranchisement: The Morality of Electoral Exclusions* (Cambridge: Cambridge University Press, 2014); Claudio Lopez-Guerra, "The Enfranchisement Lottery," *Philosophy, Politics, and Economics* (Oct. 2010); Helene Landemore, "Deliberation, Cognitive Diversity, and Inclusiveness: An Argument for the Random Selection of Representatives," *Synthese* 190 (2013): 1209–31; Ethan Leib, *Deliberative Democracy in America: A Proposal for a Popular Branch of Government* (University Park: Pennsylvania State University Press, 2004).

107. See, e.g., Ackerman and Fishkin, *Deliberation Day*. For my analysis and critique of this proposal, see Somin, *Democracy and Political Ignorance*, 204–8.

108. See, e.g., Lopez-Guerra, "Enfranchisement Lottery"; Landemore, "Deliberation."

109. See discussion of this possibility in Somin, *Democracy and Political Ignorance*, 209–10.

110. See ibid., 204–11; and Ilya Somin, "Jury Ignorance and Political Ignorance," *William and Mary Law Review* 55 (2014): 1167–93, 1179–87.

111. See discussion earlier in this chapter.

112. On this point, see Somin, *Democracy and Political Ignorance*, 208–209.

113. Somin, "Jury Ignorance and Political Ignorance," 1179–87.

114. See Somin, *Democracy and Political Ignorance*, 210–11.

115. For a more detailed discussion, see ibid., 206–9.

116. Ibid., ch. 7. For recent claims that such means can be effective, see, e.g., Ben Berger, *Attention Deficit Democracy: The Paradox of Civic Engagement*, (Princeton: Princeton University Press, 2011), 153–57.

117. For more detailed discussion of these and related points, see Somin, *Democracy and Political Ignorance*, ch.7.

118. For more extensive discussion, see Somin, *Democracy and Political Ignorance*, ch. 5.

119. See, e.g., Robert C. Ellickson, "Legal Sources of Residential Lock-Ins: Why French Households Move Half as Often as U.S. Households," *University of Illinois Law Review* (2012): 373–404, esp. 395–97; Paul W. Rhode and Koleman S. Strumpf, "Assessing the Importance of Tiebout Sorting: Local Heterogeneity from 1885 to 1990," *American Economic Review* 93 (2003): 1648–77, 1649.

120. On the importance of zoning in determining housing availability and cost, see, e.g., Chang Tai-Hsieh and Enrico Moretti, "Housing Constraints and Spatial Misallocation," NBER Working Paper No. 21154 (2015), available at http://www.nber.org/papers/w21154. For an overview of the evidence, see Edward Glaeser, "Reforming Land Use Regulations," Brookings Institution, Apr. 24, 2017, available at https://www.brookings.edu/research/reforming-land-use-regulations/amp/. For more detailed discussion of the relevance of policy to foot voting decisions, see Somin, *Democracy and Political Ignorance*, 167.

121. See discussion in Chapter 3.

122. See discussion in Chapter 4.

123. For a recent overview of the ubiquity of crude economic retrospective voting, see Achen and Bartels, *Democracy for Realists*, chs. 6–7.

124. Cf. Buchanan, "Individual Choice in Voting and the Market," 336–37 (making the point that ballot box voting decisions are more likely to be motivated by public-interest considerations than market decisions.

125. For an important challenge to the conventional wisdom that political views are mostly the product of public-interest considerations rather than self-interest, See Jason Weeden and Robert Kurzban, *The Hidden Agenda of the Political Mind: How Self-Interest Shapes our Opinions and Why We Won't Admit it*, (Princeton, NJ: Princeton University Press, 2014). For criticisms, see Bryan Caplan, "Conspiracy Theory: *The Hidden Agenda of the Political Mind*," Econlog, Jan. 5, 2015, available at http://econlog.econlib.org/archives/2015/01/conspiracy_theo.html. Caplan's post led to a prolonged exchange with Weeden. For links to various posts by both sides, see Caplan, "Rejoinder to Weeden," EconLog, Jan. 14, 2015, available at http://econlog.econlib.org/archives/2015/01/a_few_replies_t.html; see also Somin, *Democracy and Political Ignorance*, 69.

126. Somin, *Democracy and Political Ignorance*, 69–70.

127. I discuss this point in more detail in ibid., 65–67, 70–71,

128. Heather K. Gerken, "Second-Order Diversity," *Harvard Law Review* 118 (2005): 1099–196. See also discussion of the problem of the "Big Sort" in Chapter 6.

129. See discussion earlier in this chapter. Cf. Achen and Bartels, *Democracy for Realists*, chs. 4–7

130. See sources referenced in Somin, *Democracy and Political Ignorance*, 267n.127.

131. On the difficulties of determining whether and to what extent a "mandate" exists, see Lawrence J. Grossback, David A. Peterson, and James A. Stimson, *Mandate Politics* (Cambridge: Cambridge University Press, 2006).

132. See, e.g., David. D. Friedman, *The Machinery of Freedom*, 2nd ed. (Chicago: Open Court, 1989); Huemer, *Problem of Political Authority*, chs. 9–13.

133. For this argument as a critique of my approach to foot voting, see Roderick M. Hills Jr. and Shitong Qiao, "Voice and Exit as Accountability Mechanisms: Can Foot-Voting Be Made Safe for the Chinese Communist Party?," *Columbia Human Rights Law Review* 48 (2017): 158–210, 174–76.

134. Ibid. But see the discussion of how to mitigate potential "political externalities" in Chapter 6.

135. Ibid. 175–76.

136. See, e.g., J. Kevin Corder, "Are Federal Programs Immortal? Estimating the Hazard of Program Termination," *American Politics Research* 32 (2004): 3–25.

137. See discussion in Chapter 2.

138. See discussion of this point earlier in this chapter.

139. See discussion of this example in Chapter 2.

140. I make a similar point about the ability of foot voting to enhance economic development in Ilya Somin, "Foot Voting, Decentralization, and Development," *Minnesota Law Review* 102 (2018), 1649–70.

141. For an overview, see Halperin et al., *Democracy Advantage*.

Chapter 2

1. U.S. Census Bureau, *2012 Census of Governments*, available at https://www.census. gov/newsroom/releases/archives/governments/cb12-161.html.

2. For example, Canada, with a population one-tenth the size of that of the United States, has some 3,600 different local governments, and 143 regional authorities, in addition to 10 provinces and 3 territories. See "Local Government in Canada," Commonwealth Governance, Commonwealth of Nations, available at http://www. commonwealthgovernance.org/countries/americas/canada/local-government/.

3. Charles Tiebout, "A Pure Theory of Local Expenditures," *Journal of Political Economy* 64 (1956): 516-24.

4. This issue is considered further, later in this chapter and in Chapter 7.

5. See discussion in Chapter 1.

6. See discussion below, and also see Ilya Somin, "Foot Voting, Federalism, and Political Freedom," in *Nomos: Federalism and Subsidiarity*, ed. James Fleming and Jacob Levy (New York: New York University Press, 2014).

7. See, e.g., Barry Weingast, "The Economic Role of Political Institutions: Market-Preserving Federalism and Economic Development," *Journal of Law, Economics & Organization* 11 (1995), 1-31; and Ilya Somin, *Democracy and Political Ignorance: Why Smaller Government is Smarter*, (Stanford: Stanford University Press, 2d. ed. 2016), 145-46.

8. For an overview, see Ray Allen Billington and Martin Ridge, *Westward Expansion: A History of the American Frontier*, 6th ed. (Santa Fe: University of New Mexico Press, 2001).

9. Daniel M. Johnson and Rex R. Campbell, *Black Migration in America: A Social Demographic History* (Durham, NC: Duke University Press, 1981), 74-75.

10. Ibid., 77.

11. Ibid., 114-23.

12. Quoted in Michael J. Klarman, *From Jim Crow to Civil Rights: The Supreme Court and the Struggle for Racial Equality* (New York: Oxford University Press, 2004), 164.

13. See Stephen Clark, "Progressive Federalism? A Gay Liberationist Perspective," *Albany Law Review* 66 (2003): 719-57.

14. See discussion in Chapter 1.

15. See Terry Anderson and Peter J. Hill, *The Not So Wild, Wild West: Property Rights on the Frontier* (Stanford, CA: Stanford University Press, 2004).

16. See, e.g., Akhil Reed Amar, *The Law of the Land: A Grand Tour of Our Constitutional Republic* (New York: Basic Books, 2015), 227. T. A. Larson, "Woman Suffrage in Wyoming," *Pacific Northwest Quarterly* 56 (1965): 57-66.

17. Jayme S. Lemke, "Interjurisdictional Competition and the Married Women's Property Acts." *Public Choice* 166 (2016): 291-313

18. See Bradley M. Gardner, *China's Great Migration: How the Poor Built a Prosperous Nation* (Oakland, CA: Independent Institute, 2017), 5; cf. Xiaochu Hu, "China's Young Rural-to-Urban Migrants: In Search of Fortune, Happiness, and Independence," Migration Policy Institute, Jan. 4, 2012, available at http://www.migrationpolicy.org/article/china s-young-rural-urban-migrants-search-fortune-happiness-and-independence (estimating a total of 145 million internal rural to urban migrants as of 2009).

19. See Thomas Gries et al., "Explaining Inter-provincial Migration in China," *Papers in Regional Science* 95 (2016), 4709–33.

20. Gardner, *China's Great Migration*, 72.

21. See Raj Chetty, Nathaniel Hendren, and Lawrence Katz, "Chetty, Raj, Nathaniel Hendren, and Lawrence Katz. 2016. "The Effects of Exposure to Better Neighborhoods on Children: New Evidence from the Moving to Opportunity Project." *American Economic Review* 106 (2016): 855–902.

22. Tiebout, "A Pure Theory of Local Expenditures."

23. Pew Research Center, *Who Moves? Who Stays Put? Where's Home?* (Washington, DC: Pew Research Center, Dec. 2008), 8, 13.

24. Somin, *Democracy and Political Ignorance*, 166.

25. See Erin O'Hara and Larry Ribstein, *The Law Market* (New York: Oxford University Press, 2009); Abraham Bell and Gideon Parchomovsky, "Of Property and Federalism," *Yale Law Journal* 115 (2005): 72–115, 101–13. Bruno Frey, "A Utopia? Government without Territorial Monopoly," *Independent Review* 6 (2001): 99–112; Bruno Frey, *Happiness: A Revolution in Economics* (Cambridge, MA: MIT Press, 2008), 189–97; Bruno S. Frey and Reiner Eichenberger, *The New Democratic Federalism for Europe: Functional, Overlapping, and Competing Jurisdictions*, new ed. (London: Edward Elgar, 2004); Gillian K. Hadfield, *Rules for a Flat World: Why Humans Invented Law and How to Reinvent it for a Complex Global Economy* (New York: Oxford University Press, 2016), ch. 7.

26. See O'Hara and Ribstein, *The Law Market*, chs. 3, 7.

27. See, e.g., Frey, "A Utopia," and other works cited in note 25, above.

28. Hadfield, *Rules for a Flat World*, 264–77.

29. Frey, "A Utopia?"

30. See Aurelia Chaudhury, Adam J. Levitin, and David Schleicher, "Junk Cities," *California Law Review* 107 (2019): 259–334; Christopher Berry, *Imperfect Union: Representation and Taxation in Multilevel Governments* (Cambridge: Cambridge University Press, 2009), 9–19, 84–86, 98–101.

31. On the ways in which increasing the number of issues addressed by a given government entity exacerbates the effects of voter ignorance, see Somin, *Democracy and Political Ignorance*, 160–63.

32. For an overview of agglomeration theory, see David Schleicher, "The City as a Law and Economic Subject," *University of Illinois Law Review* 2010 (2010): 1507–64, 1509–11, 1515–29, 1533–40; see also Edward L. Glaeser, *Cities, Agglomeration, and Spatial Equilibrium* (New York: Oxford University Press, 2008).

33. Schleicher, "Law and Economic Subject."

34. See Joan Siefert Rose, "How the Rest of America Is Competing with Silicon Valley," *Forbes*, Aug. 28, 2016, available at https://www.forbes.com/sites/joansiefertrose/2016/08/28/how-the-rest-of-america-is-competing-with-silicon-valley/#2f3b57b27c3f.

35. Ibid.

36. For evidence of decreasing mobility in the United States, especially among the poor, see David Schleicher, "Stuck! The Law and the Economics of Residential Stability," *Yale Law Journal* 127 (2018): 78–154, 81–86 (summarizing relevant studies). For some of the leading analyses, see Greg Kaplan and Sam Schulhofer-Wohl, "Understanding

the Long-Run Decline in Interstate Migration," *International Economic Review* 58 (2017): 57–94; Raven Molloy, Christopher L. Smith, and Abigail Wozniak, "Internal Migration in the United States," *Journal of Economic Perspectives* 25 (2011): 173–96; Raven Molloy, Christopher L. Smith and Abigail Wozniak, "Declining Migration Within the U.S.: The Role of the Labor Market," NBER Working Paper No.20065 (2014); Scott Winship, "When Moving Matters: Residential and Income Mobility Trends in the United States, 1880–2010," Manhattan Institute (Nov. 2015), 27–38, available at https://www.manhattan-institute.org/html/when-moving-matters-resi dential-and-economic-mobility-trends-america-1880-2010-8048.html.

37. For recent overviews of the evidence on zoning, see, e.g., David Schleicher, "Stuck! The Law and the Economics of Residential Stability," *Yale Law Journal* 127 (2018): 78–154, 114–16; Brink Lindsey and Steven M. Teles, *The Captured Economy: How the Powerful Enrich Themselves, Slow Down Growth, and Increase Inequality* (New York: Oxford University Press, 2017), ch. 6; Edward Glaeser, "Reforming Land Use Regulations," Brookings Institution, Apr. 24, 2017, available at https://www. brookings.edu/research/reforming-land-use-regulations/amp/.

38. See Schleicher, "Stuck!" 117-22; Ilya Somin, "Moving Vans More Powerful Than Ballot Boxes," *USA Today*, Oct. 18, 2016, available at www.usatoday.com/ story/opinion/2016/10/18/mobility-zoning-licensing-voting-minorities-c olumn/91990486/; Department of Treasury, Council of Economic Advisers, and Department of Labor, *Occupational Licensing: A Framework for Policymakers*, July 2015, 39–41 available at https://obamawhitehouse.archives.gov/sites/default/files/ docs/licensing_report_final_nonembargo.pdf; Morris N. Kleiner, "Reforming Occupational Licensing Laws," Hamilton Project, Brookings Institution, Mar. 2015, available at https://www.brookings.edu/wp-content/uploads/2016/06/THP_ KleinerDiscPaper_final.pdf.

39. Chang Tai-Hsieh and Enrico Moretti, "Housing Constraints and Spatial Misallocation," NBER Working Paper No. 21154 (2015), available at http://www. nber.org/papers/w21154. For recent overviews of the evidence, see Joseph Gyourko, Jonathan Hartley, and Jacob Krimmel, "The Local Residential Land Use Regulatory Environment Across U.S. Housing Markets: Evidence from a New Wharton Index," NBER Working Paper No. 26573 (Dec. 2019), available at https://www. nber.org/papers/w26573; and Edward Glaeser, "Reforming Land Use Regulations," Brookings Institution, Apr. 24, 2017, available at https://www.brookings.edu/research/ reforming-land-use-regulations/amp/.

40. See discussion of this point in the analysis of the "Big Sort" in Chapter 6. Cf. Heather K. Gerken, "Second-Order Diversity," *Harvard Law Review* 118 (2005): 1099–196.

41. See discussion earlier in this chapter.

42. For a number of reasons, capitalization is likely to be less of a problem for policies that are not regulations of the land itself. Cf. Somin, *Democracy and Political Ignorance*, 145–46.

43. See Ilya Somin, "Federalism and Constitutional Property Rights," *University of Chicago Legal Forum* 2011 (2011): 53–88.

44. On "subjective value" of property, see Ilya Somin, *The Grasping Hand: Kelo v. City of New London and the Limits of Eminent Domain*, rev. ed. (Chicago: University of Chicago Press, 2016), 206–8.

45. See Hannah Grabenstein, "Should 16-Year-Olds Be Allowed to Vote," PBS, Apr. 20, 2018; George Arnett, "Votes for 16- and 17-Year-Olds—Where Else Outside Scotland?" *The Guardian*, June 18, 2015, available at https://www.theguardian.com/politics/datablog/2015/jun/18/votes-for-16--and-17-year-olds-where-else-outside-scotland.

46. See, e.g., Joanne Lu, "Two Arguments for Child Enfranchisement," Political Studies 60 (2012): 860–76; Daniel Weinstock, "What Harms Should we Worry About in the Enfranchisement of Children,?" *Georgetown Journal of Law and Policy* (forthcoming); Matthew Weaver, "Lower Voting Age to Six, to Tackle Bias against the Young, Says Academic," *The Guardian*, Dec. 6, 2018, available at https://www.theguardian.com/politics/2018/dec/06/give-six-year-olds-the-vote-says-cambridge-university-academic. I have tentatively proposed this myself, in the case of minors with above-average levels of political knowledge. Ilya Somin, "Should We Let 16 Year Olds Vote," Volokh Conspiracy, *Washington Post*, Sept. 19, 2014, available at https://www.washingtonpost.com/news/volokh-conspiracy/wp/2014/09/19/should-we-let-16-year-olds-vote/?utm_term=.ea9529c2c42a.

47. For arguments that equality is an important attribute of political participation, see, e.g., Thomas Christiano, *The Constitution of Equality* (Cambridge: Cambridge University Press, 2010).

48. For discussions of this kind of inequality, see Somin, *Democracy and Political Ignorance*, 62–65.

49. See discussion in Chapter 1.

50. See Chapter 1.

51. See, e.g., Martin Gilens, *Affluence and Influence* (Princeton, NJ: Princeton University Press, 2012) (discussing how inequality of influence was at comparable levels from the 1960s to the 2000s, and even finding that it was lowest during the administration of George W. Bush in the 2000s). For a discussion of the evidence, see Ilya Somin, "Why Growing Government Is a Bigger Political Menace than Growing Inequality," *Boston University Law Review Online* 98 (2018): 21–26, 22–23.

52. G. A. Cohen, "The Structure of Proletarian Unfreedom," *Philosophy and Public Affairs* 12 (1983): 3–33.

53. Ibid.

54. See discussion Chapter 1.

55. For a recent overview of disagreements on redistribution by philosophers and political theorists, see, e.g., Serena Olsabetti, ed., *Oxford Handbook of Distributive Justice* (New York: Oxford University Press, 2018).

56. See, e.g., Paul E. Peterson, *The Price of Federalism* (Washington, DC: Brookings Institution, 1995).

57. For a summary and defense of the race to the bottom theory, see Kirsten H. Engel, "State Environmental Standard-Setting: Is There a 'Race' and Is It 'to the Bottom'"? *Hastings Law Journal* 48 (1997): 274–369. For other defenses, see, e.g., Kirsten Engel and Scott R. Saleska, "Facts Are Stubborn Things: An Empirical Reality Check in the

Theoretical Debate over State Environmental Rate-Setting," *Cornell Journal of Law and Public Policy* 8 (1998): 55–87; and Joshua D. Sarnoff, "The Continuing Imperative (But Only from a National Perspective) for Federal Environmental Protection," *Duke Environmental Law and Policy Forum* 7 (1997): 225–73.

58. For the classic theoretical critiques, see Richard Revesz, "Rehabilitating Interstate Competition: Rethinking the 'Race to the Bottom' Rationale for Federal Environmental Regulation," *NYU Law Review* 67 (1992): 1210–44; and Revesz, "The Race to the Bottom and Federal Environmental Regulation: A Response to Critics," *Minnesota Law Review* 82 (1997): 535–74. See also Wallace E. Oates, "Fiscal Competition or Harmonization? Some Reflections," *National Tax Journal* 54 (2001): 507–12.

59. For a more extensive discussion of the evidence, See Somin, *Democracy and Political Ignorance*, 168–69; cf. Marc Schneiberg and Tim Bartley, "Organizations, Regulation, and Economic Behavior: Regulatory Dynamics and Forms from the Nineteenth to Twenty-First Century," *Annual Review of Law and Social Science* 4 (2008): 31–61.

60. For some examples of such "capture" caused in part by misinformation, see, e.g., David Schultz, *American Politics in the Age of Ignorance: Why Lawmakers Choose Belief over Research* (New York: Palgrave Macmillan 2012).

61. For recent critiques of such claims, see, e.g., Hanna Kleider, "Fiscal Federalism and Social Policy," paper presented at the Symposium on Case Studies in Self-Governance, Centre For the Study of Governance and Society (CSGS), King's College London, Oct. 24–27, 2019 (on file with author); and Hanna Kleider, "Redistributive Policies in Decentralised Systems: The Effect of Decentralisation on Subnational Social Spending," *European Journal of Political Research*, 57 (2018): 355–77. For earlier studies arguing that race to the bottom effects undermine redistribution, see, e.g., Paul E. Peterson and Mark Rom, *Welfare Magnets* (Washington DC: Brookings Institution, 1989); Paul E. Peterson, *The Price of Federalism* (Washington, DC: Brookings Institution, 1995); Michael Bailey and Mark Rom, "A Wider Race? Interstate Competition Across Health and Welfare Programs," *Journal of Politics* 66 (2004): 326–47.

62. See discussion later in this chapter.

63. For a helpful summary of this conventional wisdom, see Douglas Laycock, "Protecting Liberty in a Federal System: The US Experience," in *Patterns of Regionalism and Federalism: Lessons for the UK*, ed. Jorg Fedtke and B.S. Markesisinis (London: Hart, 2006), 121–45.

64. William H. Riker, *Federalism: Origin, Operation, Significance,* (Boston: Little, Brown, 1964), 152–53, 55; Riker later developed a less negative view of American federalism. See William H. Riker, *The Development of American Federalism* (Boston: Kluwer Academic, 1987), xii–xiii. Cf. Craig Volden, "Origin, Operation, Significance: The Federalism of William H. Riker," *Publius* 34 (2004):89–107.

65. See Arthur Zilversmit, *The First Emancipation: The Abolition of Slavery in the North* (Chicago: University of Chicago Press, 1967); Joanne Pope Melish, *Disowning Slavery: Gradual Emancipation and "Race" in New England 1780–1860* (Ithaca, NY: Cornell University Press, 1998). Vermont had abolished slavery even before it became a state in 1791. Melish, *Disowning Slavery,* 64.

66. Some northern states and abolitionists even resisted the Fugitive Slave Acts on "states' rights" grounds. See Robert Kaczorowski, "The Tragic Irony of American Federalism: National Sovereignty versus State Sovereignty in Slavery and Freedom, *University of Kansas Law Review* 45 (1997): 1015–61, 1034–40.

67. For a brief review of the record, see Lynn Baker and Ernest Young, "Federalism and the Double Standard of Judicial Review," *Duke Law Journal* 51 (2001): 75–162, 143–47.

68. For an overview of segregationist federal policies during this period, see Desmond King, *Separate and Unequal: African-Americans and the US Federal Government*, rev. ed. (New York: Oxford University Press, 2007).

69. See Roger Daniels, *Concentration Camps, USA: The Japanese Americans and World War II* (New York: Holt, Rinehart and Winston, 1972); Sarah Barringer Gordon, *The Mormon Question: Polygamy and Constitutional Conflict in Nineteenth-Century America* (Chapel Hill: University of North Carolina Press, 2002).

70. For a summary of the evidence, see Somin, "Foot Voting, Political Ignorance, and Constitutional Design," *Social Philosophy and Policy* 28 (2011): 202–27, 215–21.

71. For an overview covering a variety of cases like this, see Luis Moreno and César Colino, eds., *Diversity and Unity in Federal Countries* (Montreal: McGill-Queen's University Press, 2010); see also Dawn Brancati, *Peace by Design: Managing Intrastate Conflict through Decentralization* (New York: Oxford University Press, 2009).

72. Edward L. Glaeser and Andrei Shleifer, "The Curley Effect: The Economics of Shaping the Electorate," *Journal of Law, Economics, and Organization* 21 (2005): 1–19.

73. Ibid., 9–12.

74. Ibid., 13–14.

75. See, e.g., Brancati, *Peace by Design* (discussing many such examples).

76. For other potential advantages of such a system, see Donald L. Horowitz, "The Many Uses of Federalism," *Drake Law Review* 55 (2007): 953–74.

77. For a discussion of Kurdish government, see Stephen Mansfield, *The Miracle of the Kurds* (Brentwood, TN: Worthy Publishing 2014).

78. For the classic study reading this conclusion, see Robert Dahl and Edward Tufte, *Size and Democracy* (Stanford, CA: Stanford University Press, 1973).

79. See discussion in Somin, *Democracy and Political Ignorance*, 227–28.

80. Ibid., 227.

81. Denmark and Luxembourg are members of the European Union (EU). Norway and Switzerland have arrangements under which EU citizens are free to move to these countries, even though neither country is a member of the EU. Adam Payne and Adam Bienkov, "What Is the Norway Model?," *Business Insider*, Dec. 5, 2018, available at https://www.businessinsider.com/what-is-the-norway-model-brexit-2018-4.

Chapter 3

1. Ilya Somin, "Tiebout Goes Global: International Migration as a Tool for Voting with Your Feet, *Missouri Law Review* 73 (2008): 1247–64, 1259 (symposium on federalism and international law). Similar gains are realized by other migrants from

poor nations to wealthy ones. See Michael Clemens and Lant Pritchett, "Income per Natural: Measuring Development for People Rather than Places," *Population and Development Review* 34 (2008): 395–434; Lant Pritchett, *Let Their People Come: Breaking the Gridlock on Global Labor Mobility* (Washington, DC: Center for Global Development, 2007); Caglar Ozden et al., *Moving to Prosperity: Global Migration and Labor Markets* (Washington, DC: World Bank, 2018); Sarai Kerr and William Kerr, "Economic Impacts of Immigration: A Survey," National Bureau of Economic Research (NBER) Working Paper No. 16736 (2011).

2. This argument should be differentiated from the claim that would-be migrants experience domination at the hands of the excluding state rather than their home governments. See Sarah Fine, "Non-Domination and the Ethics of Migration," *Critical Review of International and Social Philosophy,*" 17 (2014): 10–30, 19–23; and Alex Sager, "Immigration Enforcement and Domination: An Indirect Argument for Much More Open Borders," *Political Research Quarterly* 70 (2017): 42–54.

3. See discussion of this concept in Chapter 1.

4. See Maryam Nagesh Nejad and Andrew T. Young, "Want Freedom, Will Travel: Emigrant Self-Selection According to Institutional Quality," *European Journal of Political Economy* 45 (2016): 71–84; Nathan J. Ashby, "Freedom and International Migration," *Southern Economic Journal* 77 (2010): 49–62; Rosamaria Bitetti, "Voting vs. Moving: Exit and Voice Mechanisms in EU Federalism," *Arizona State Law Journal* 49 (2017): 867–82.

5. See studies cited in note 4.

6. See, e.g., Jonathan Hiskey, Jorge Daniel Montalvo, and Diana Orces, "Democracy, Governance, and Emigration Intentions in Latin America and the Caribbean," *Studies in Comparative International Development* 49 (2014): 89–111.

7. Maryam Nagesh Nejad and Andrew T. Young, "Female Brain Drains and Women's Rights Gaps: A Gravity Model Analysis of Bilateral Migration Flows," IZA Discussion Paper No. 8067 (2014), available at https://papers.ssrn.com/sol3/papers.cfm?abstract_id=2191658.

8. Freedom House, "Table of Country Scores," *Freedom in the World 2018* (New York: Freedom House, 2018), available at https://freedomhouse.org/report/freedom-world-2018-table-country-scores.

9. Freedom House, "Methodology," available at https://freedomhouse.org/report/methodology-freedom-world-2018.

10. Freedom House, "Table of Country Scores."

11. Since Fidel Castro established a communist regime in 1959, over 1 million Cubans have fled to the United States alone. On the history of Cuban emigration, see, e.g., Susan Eckstein, *The Immigrant Divide: How Cuban Immigrants Have Changed the US and Their Homeland* (New York: Routledge, 2009); Felix Masud-Piloto, *From Welcomed Exiles to Illegal Immigrants: Cuban Migration to the United States, 1959–95* (New York: Rowman and Littlefield, 1995).

12. See, e.g., Somin, "Tiebout Goes Global," 1260–61 , and discussion in Chapter 8.

13. Ilya Somin, "Justice Department Rejects Salvadoran Woman's Application for Asylum Because She Provided 'Material Support' to Terrorists—By Working as a Slave Laborer for Them," *Reason*, June 8, 2018, available at https://reason.com/volokh/2018/06/08/justice-department-rejects-salvadoran-wo.

14. Yael Tamir, *Why Nationalism* (New Haven, CT: Yale University Press, 2019), 36–37.

15. Tamir, *Why Nationalism*, 38.

16. United Nations, *International Migration Report 2017* (New York: United Nations, 2017), 4–5, available at http://www.un.org/en/development/desa/population/migration/publications/migrationreport/docs/MigrationReport2017_Highlights.pdf.

17. Neli Esipova, Anita Pugliese, and Julie Ray, "More Than 750 Million Worldwide Would Migrate if They Could," Gallup, Dec. 2018, available at https://news.gallup.com/poll/245255/750-million-worldwide-migrate.aspx.

18. Ozden et al., *Moving to Prosperity*, 1–2.

19. See Michael Clemens, "Economics and Emigration: Trillion Dollar Bills Left on the Sidewalk?" *Journal of Economic Perspectives* 25 (2011): 83–106.

20. For overviews, see Michael A. Clemens, Claudio Montenegro, and Lant Pritchett, "The Place Premium: Bounding the Price Equivalent of Migration Barriers," *Review of Economics and Statistics* 101 (2019): 201–13; Michael A. Clemens, Claudio Montenegro, and Lant Pritchett, "The Place Premium: Wage Differences for Identical Workers across the US Border," Center for Global Development Working Paper No. 148, (2009); Michael A. Clemens and Lant Pritchett, "Income Per Natural: Measuring Development for People Rather than Places," *Population and Development Review* 34 (2008) 395–434; see also Ilya Somin, "Foot Voting, Decentralization, and Development," *Minnesota Law Review* 102 (2018): 1649–70, 1651–55 (summarizing implications of the place premium for economic development).

21. For the suggestion that free trade might be sufficient, see James Allan, "Reply to 'How Foot Voting Enhances Political Freedom,'" *San Diego Law Review* 56 (2020): 1121–28, 1121.

22. This is a fairly plausible estimate for productivity increases resulting from migration from a poor developing nation to the US. See, e.g., Clemens, et al., "Place Premium," and Clemens and Pritchett, "Income per Natural."

23. See, e.g., George J. Borjas, "Immigration and Globalization: A Review Essay," *Journal of Economic Literature* 53 (2015): 961–74, 964–66; George Borjas, *Immigration Economics* (Cambridge, MA: Harvard University Press, 2014), 157–58.

24. See, e.g., Borjas, "Immigration and Globalization," 966–73; Paul Collier, *Exodus: How Migration Is Changing Our World* (New York: Oxford University Press, 2013); Yann Algan et al., "Inherited Trust and Growth," *American Economic Review*, 100 (2010): 2060–92; Brian Barry, "The Quest for Consistency: A Skeptical View," in *Free Movement: Ethical Issues in the Transnational Migration of People and Money*, ed. Brian Barry and Robert E. Goodin (University Park: University of Pennsylvania Press, 1992), 279–87.

25. See discussion of this case in Chapter 6.

26. See discussion in Chapter 6.

27. See discussion in Chapter 6.

28. See US Census Bureau, "Chart of US Population, 1790–2000," available at https://www.census-charts.com/Population/pop-us-1790-2000.html.

29. See, e.g., Antonio Spilimbergo, "Democracy and Foreign Education," *American Economic Review* 99 (2009): 528–43.

30. For an overview of these types of effects, see Michael A. Clemens, "What Do We Know about Skilled Migration and Development?" Migration Policy Institute Policy Brief No. 3 (Sept. 2013); see also discussion of remittances in Chapter 5.

31. Borjas, *Immigration Economics*, 251n.20.

32. Borjas, *Immigration Economics*, 84–88; see also Bas Van der Vossen and Jason Brennan, *In Defense of Openness: Why Global Freedom Is the Humane Solution to Global Poverty* (New York: Oxford University Press, 2018), 22–23 (summarizing studies on this).

33. Roger V. Daniels, *Coming to America: A History of Immigration and Ethnicity in American Life*, 2nd ed. (New York: Perennial, 2002), 124.

34. Ibid., 245–46, and ch. 10.

35. Ibid., ch. 11.

36. For an overview of the 1965 act and its consequences, see Tom Gjelten, *A Nation of Nations: A Great American Immigration Story* (New York: Simon and Schuster, 2015), esp. ch. 10.

37. David Bier, "Over 100 Million Immigrants Have Come to America since the Founding," Cato Institute, Dec. 4, 2018, available at https://www.cato.org/blog/over-100-million-immigrants-have-come-america-founding.

38. Pew Research Center, "Modern Immigration Wave Brings 59 Million to US, Driving Population Growth and Change through 2065, " Sept. 28, 2015, available at http://assets.pewresearch.org/wp-content/uploads/sites/7/2015/09/2015-09-28_modern-immigration-wave_REPORT.pdf.

39. For a recent summary of relevant studies, see Graziano Batistella, "Return Migration: A Conceptual and Policy Framework," Center for Migration Studies, Mar. 8, 2018, available at http://cmsny.org/publications/2018smsc-smc-return-migration/.

40. See Saara Koikkalainen, "Free Movement in Europe: Past and Present," Migration Policy Institute, Apr. 21, 2011, available at https://www.migrationpolicy.org/article/free-movement-europe-past-and-present.

41. Uuriintuya Batsaikhan, Zsolt Darvas, and Inês Gonçalves Raposo, *People on the Move: Migration and Mobility in the European Union* (Brussels: Bruegel, 2018), ch. 3. available at http://bruegel.org/wp-content/uploads/2018/01/People_on_the_move_ONLINE.pdf.

42. Ibid., 84.

43. Ibid., ch. 4.

44. Murray Leibbrandt and James Levinsohn, "Fifteen Years On: Household Incomes in South Africa," NBER Working Paper No. 16661 (Jan. 2011).

45. On the important role of employment for integration, see, e.g., Batsaikhan et al, *People on the Move*, 105–12; Mary Waters and Marisa Gerstein Pineau, *The Integration of Immigrants into American Society* (Washington, DC: National Academy of Sciences, 2015), ch. 6.

46. See Batsaikhan et al., *People on the Move*, 87–88 (surveying literature on this subject).

47. Thomas Pogge, "Migration and Poverty," in *Citizenship and Exclusion*, ed. Veit Bader (Basingstoke: Macmillan, 1997), 14–15. For a similar argument, see David Miller,

"Immigration: The Case for Limits," in *Contemporary Debates in Applied Ethics*, ed. Andrew Cohen and Christopher Heath Wellman (Oxford: Blackwell, 2005), 198–99.

48. For arguments to this effect, see, e.g., Peter Singer, *The Life You Can Save* (New York: Random House, 2010).

49. Joseph Carens, *The Ethics of Immigration* (New York: Oxford University Press, 2013), 234.

50. For extensive recent discussions of the relevant evidence, see Daron Acemoglu and James A. Robinson, *Why Nations Fail: The Origins of Power, Prosperity, and Poverty* (New York: Crown, 2013), 450–55; Angus Deaton, *The Great Escape: Health, Wealth, and the Origins of Inequality* (Princeton, NJ: Princeton University Press, 2013), 268–76; Christopher Coyne, *Doing Bad by Doing Good: Why Humanitarian Action Fails* (Stanford, CA: Stanford University Press, 2013); Hristos Doucouliagos, and Martin Paldam, "The Aid Effectiveness Literature: The Sad Results of 40 Years of Research," *Journal of Economic Surveys* 23 (2009): 433–61.

51. Acemoglu and Robinson, *Why Nations Fail*, 453.

52. Ibid., 453.

53. Ibid., 453.

54. See, e.g., Sebastian Mallaby, "The Politically Incorrect Guide to Ending Poverty," *The Atlantic*, Aug./Sept. 2010, available at https://www.theatlantic.com/magazine/archive/2010/07/the-politically-incorrect-guide-to-ending-poverty/308134/; Paul Romer, "Technologies, Rules, and Progress: The Case for Charter Cities," Center for Global Development, Working Paper, Mar. 2010.

55. See, e.g., Reihan Salam, *Melting Pot or Civil War? A Son of Immigrants Makes the Case against Open Borders* (New York: Sentinel, 2018), 144–48; Alexander Betts and Paul Collier, "Help Refugees Help Themselves," *Foreign Affairs*, Nov./Dec. 2015.

56. See Eric Kaufmann, *Whiteshift: Populism, Immigration, and the Future of White Majorities* (New York: Abrams Press, 2019); cf. Conor Friedersdorf, "A Once-Unthinkable Proposal for Refugee Camps," *The Atlantic*, June 12, 2019.

57. See sources cited in discussion of this issue in Chapter 5.

58. Chandran Kukathas, "Why Immigration Controls Resemble Apartheid in Their Adverse Consequences for Freedom," London School of Economics and Political Science, Sept. 16, 2015, available at http://blogs.lse.ac.uk/politicsandpolicy/why-immigration-controls-resemble-apartheid-in-their-adverse-consequences-for-freedom/.

59. Francisco Balderrama and Raymond Rodriguez, *Decade of Betrayal: Mexican Repatriation in the 1930s* (Santa Fe: University of New Mexico Press, 2006).

60. Jacqueline Stevens, "US Government Unlawfully Detaining and Deporting US Citizens as Aliens," *Virginia Journal of Social Policy and the Law*, 18 (2011): 606–720, 608.

61. Ibid., 629–33.

62. Matt Apuzzo and Michael S. Schmidt, "US to Continue Racial, Ethnic Profiling in Immigration Policy," *New York Times*, Dec. 5, 2014.

63. For examples, see, e.g., Stevens, "Unlawfully Detaining and Deporting," and Shikha Dalmia, "How Immigration Crackdowns Screw Up Americans' Lives," *Reason*, Dec. 2017, available at https://reason.com/archives/2017/11/12/how-immigration-crackdowns-scr.

64. For arguments along similar lines, see Frank Lovett, *A General Theory of Domination and Justice* (New York: Oxford University Press, 2010), 98; Sager, "Immigration Enforcement and Domination," 44–45.

65. For suggestions of possible reforms, see Stevens, "Unlawfully Detaining and Deporting," 713–17.

Chapter 4

1. Heather K. Gerken, "Foreword: Federalism All the Way Down," *Harvard Law Review* 124 (2010): 6–83.

2. I discuss this possible extension of Gerken's theory in Ilya Somin, "Taking Dissenting by Deciding All the Way Down," *Tulsa Law Review* 48 (2013): 523–34, 529–30 (symposium in honor of Heather Gerken).

3. Community Associations Institute, *Statistical Review for 2016* (2017), 2, available at https://www.caionline.org/AboutCommunityAssociations/Statistical%20Information/2016StatsReviewFBWeb.pdf. This is up from 62 million in 2010. See Edward Peter Stringham, *Private Governance: Creating Order in Economic and Social Life* (New York: Oxford University Press, 2015), 131.

4. Community Associations Institute, *Statistical Review for 2016*, 3.

5. Ibid., 3.

6. See, e.g., Barbara Coyle McCabe, "Homeowners Associations as Private Governments: What We Know, What We Don't Know, and Why It Matters," *Public Administration Review* 71 (2011): 535–42.

7. See Renaud Le Goix, "Gated Communities as Predators of Public Resources: The Outcomes of Fading Boundaries Between Private Management and Public Authorities in Southern California, in *Private Cities: Global and Local Perspectives*, ed. George Glasze, Chris Webster, and Klaus Frantz (London: Routledge, 2006)..

8. Community Associations Institute, *Statistical Review for 2016*, 3.

9. For an overview of the differences, see Jesse Dukeminier et al., *Property*, 8th ed. (New York: Aspen, 2014), 937–40.

10. See Fred Foldvary, *Public Goods and Private Communities* (Aldershot: Edward Elgar, 1994).

11. John Fraser Hart, Michelle Rhodes, and John T. Morgan, *The Unknown World of the Mobile Home* (Baltimore: Johns Hopkins University Press, 2002), 8–11, 128–32.

12. For overviews of how private planned communities work and the services they provide, see, e.g., Robert H. Nelson, *Private Neighborhoods and the Transformation of Local Government* (Washington, DC: Urban Institute, 2005); McCabe, "Homeowners Associations as Private Governments"; Robert H. Nelson, "Community Associations at Middle Age: Considering the Options," in *Oxford Handbook of State and Local Government Finance*, ed. Robert D. Ebel and John Petersen (New York: Oxford University Press, 2012).

13. Though, as discussed below, Robert Nelson has a proposal to relax this requirement.

14. Evan McKenzie, "The Dynamics of Privatopia: Private Residential Governance in the USA," in *Private Cities: Global and Local Perspectives*, ed. George Glasze, Chris Webster, and Klaus Frantz (London: Routledge, 2006).

15. McKenzie points out that it "seriously undermines the entire voluntarism rationale for the institution." McKenzie, "The Dynamics of Privatopia," 28.

16. Community Associations Institute, *Statistical Review for 2016*, 3; US Census Bureau, *2012 Census of Governments*, available at https://www.census.gov/newsroom/releases/archives/governments/cb12-161.html.

17. On the superior quality of many private planned community services, see, e.g., Robert H. Nelson, "The Puzzle of Local Double Taxation: Why Do Private Community Associations Exist," *Independent Review* 13 (2009): 345–65; Fred Foldvary, "The Economic Case for Private Residential Government," in *Private Cities: Global and Local Perspectives*, ed. George Glasze, Chris Webster, and Klaus Frantz (London: Routledge, 2006), and Foldvary, *Public Goods and Private Communities*.

18. Amanda Y. Agan and Alexander T. Tabarrok, "What Are Private Governments Worth?," *Regulation* 28 (2005): 14–17.

19. Foldvary, "The Economic Case for Private Residential Government," 43 (summarizing criticism without fully agreeing with it); see also Le Goix, "Gated Communities as Predators of Public Resources"; Robert B. Reich, "Secession of the Successful," *New York Times Magazine*, Jan. 20, 1991; Evan McKenzie, *Privatopia: Homeowner Associations and the Rise of Residential Private Government* (New Haven, CT: Yale University Press, 1994), ch. 3; Sheryll Cashin, "Privatized Communities and the 'Secession of the Successful': Democracy and Fairness beyond the Gate," *Fordham Urban Law Journal* 28 (2001); 1675–92; Teresa P. R. Caldeira, "Fortified Enclaves: The New Urban Segregation," in *Theorizing the City*, ed. Setha Low (New Brunswick, NJ: Rutgers University Press, 2005).

20. Reich, "Secession of the Successful." See also Cashin, "Privatized Communities and the 'Secession of the Successful.'"

21. See Randall Fitzgerald, *When Government Goes Private: Successful Alternatives to Public Services* (New York: Universe, 1988), 48; Foldvary, *Public Goods and Private Communities*, 191.

22. See Foldvary, "Economic Case," 43–44; Grazia Brunetta and Stefano Moroni, *Contractual Communities in the Self-Organising City* (Berlin: Springer, 2012), 33–34 (summarizing available evidence); McKenzie, "The Dynamics of Privatopia," 27–28 (noting concentration of homeowners associations in areas with relatively high-cost urban land).

23. Nelson, "The Puzzle of Local Double Taxation."

24. Foldvary, "Economic Case," 43.

25. See discussion in Chapter 2.

26. See discussion in Chapter 2.

27. See Nelson, "Community Associations at Middle Age," 974–75; Robert H. Nelson, "New Community Associations for Established Neighborhoods," *Review of Policy Research* 23 (2006); and Robert H. Nelson, "Privatizing the Neighborhood: A Proposal to Replace Zoning with Private Collective Property Rights to Existing Neighborhoods," *George Mason Law Review* 7 (1999): 827–81.

28. Nelson, "Community Associations at Middle Age," 974–75.

29. Ibid., 974–75.

30. See discussion in Chapter 2.

31. See G. A. Cohen, "The Structure of Proletarian Unfreedom," *Philosophy and Public Affairs* 12 (1983): 3–33. Cf. the discussion of Cohen's argument as it relates to foot voting in Chapter 2.

32. See also discussion of this issue in Chapter 2.

33. On the role of the earned income tax credit (EITC) as a large-scale program for subsidizing the wages of the poor, see Hilary Hoynes, "Building on the Success of the Earned Income Tax Credit," Brookings Institution (September 2014), available at https://www.brookings.edu/research/building-on-the-success-of-the-earned-income-tax-credit.

34. See Chapter 1.

35. See discussion in Chapter 1.

36. For descriptions, see, e.g., Nelson, *Private Neighborhoods*, chs. 3, 5.

37. Ibid., 77–80.

38. See discussion in Chapter 1.

39. Edward Stringham, Jennifer K. Miller, and J. R. Clark, "Internalizing Externalities through Private Zoning: The Case of Walt Disney Company's Celebration, Florida," *Journal of Regional Analysis and Policy* 40 (2010): 96–103.

40. See discussion in Stringham et al., "Internalizing Externalities," 100–102.

41. See Shruti Rajagopalan and Alexander Tabarrok, "Lessons from Gurgaon: India's Private City," in *Cities and Private Planning: Property Rights, Entrepreneurship, and Transaction Costs*, ed. David Emmanuel Anderson (Aldershot: Edward Elgar, 2014).

42. Rajagopalan and Tabarrok, "Lessons from Gurgaon," 216–24.

43. Chris Webster, "Gated Cities of Tomorrow," *Town Planning Review*, 72 (2001) 149–70.

44. For a detailed proposal of this type, see Fred Foldvary, "Small-Group, Multi-Level Democracy: Implications of Austrian Public Choice for Governance Structure," *Review of Austrian Economics* 15 (2002): 161–74.

45. Ibid. See also discussion of the problem of rational voter ignorance in Chapter 1.

46. For a recent analysis of a wide range of such private alternatives to public services, see Edward Peter Stringham, *Private Governance: Creating Order in Economic and Social Life* (New York: Oxford University Press, 2015).

47. See, e.g., Carmel Chiswick, "Competition vs. Monopoly in the Religious Marketplace: Judaism in the United States and Israel," IZA Discussion Paper No. 7188 (2013), available at https://papers.ssrn.com/sol3/papers.cfm?abstract_id=2210848.

48. Niall McCarthy, " Private Security Outnumbers the Police in Most Countries Worldwide," *Forbes*, Aug. 31, 2017, available at https://www.forbes.com/sites/niallmccarthy/2017/08/31/private-security-outnumbers-the-police-in-most-countries-worldwide-infographic/#671f2b0c210f.

49. See discussion in chapters 2 and 3.

Chapter 5

1. See, e.g., Andrew Altman and Christopher Heath Wellman, *A Moral Theory of International Justice* (Cambridge: Cambridge University Press, 2011), ch. 7; A. John Simmons, *Boundaries of Authority* (New York: Oxford University Press, 2016), 239–42; Stephen Kershnar, "There is no Moral Right to Immigrate to the United States," *Public Affairs Quarterly* 14 (2000): 141–58.

2. See, e.g., Michael Walzer, *Spheres of Justice* (New York: Basic Books, 1983), ch. 2; Michael Walzer, "Exclusion, Injustice, and the Democratic State," *Dissent* 40 (1993): 55–64; David Miller, "Immigration: The Case for Limits," in *Contemporary Debates in Applied Ethics*, ed. Andrew Cohen and Christopher Heath Wellman (Oxford: Blackwell, 2005); David Miller, *Strangers in Our Midst: The Political Philosophy of Immigration* (Cambridge, MA: Harvard University Press, 2016), 60–68,

3. Walzer, *Spheres of Justice*, 39.

4. Ibid., 39.

5. International Covenant on Civil and Political Rights, Article 1(1) (1966).

6. Ibid., 39.

7. For related criticisms of Walzer's argument, see Joseph Carens, *The Ethics of Immigration* (New York: Oxford University Press, 2013), 260–62, and Bas van der Bossen, "Immigration and Self-Determination," *Politics, Philosophy, and Economics* 14 (2015): 270–90,

8. Michael Clemens and Lant Pritchett, "The New Economic Case for Migration Restrictions: An Assessment," *Journal of Development Economics* 138 (2018): 153–64, 163.

9. Miller, *Strangers in Our Midst*, 63.

10. Walzer, *Spheres of Justice*, 39.

11. For a related criticism of Walzer for assuming greater unity within societies than can be justified by the facts, see David Luban, "Romance of the Nation State," *Philosophy and Public Affairs* 9 (1980): 392–97.

12. On this point, see Liav Orgad, *The Cultural Defense of Nations: A Liberal Theory of Majority Rights*, (New York: Oxford University Press, 2015), 178–81.

13. Anna Stilz, *Territorial Sovereignty: A Philosophical Exploration* (New York: Oxford University Press, 2019), 192.

14. Ibid.

15. Walzer, *Spheres of Justice*, 39.

16. Cf. Miller, *Strangers in Our Midst*, 60, who argues that the right inheres in a "groups with shared national identities that, over time, have transformed the land at stake, typically endowing it with both material and symbolic value; and Miller, "Immigration: The Case for Limits."

17. Jacob T. Levy, *The Multiculturalism of Fear* (New York: Oxford University Press, 1998), 219.

18. Ibid., 219.

19. See, e.g., Thomas B. Allen, *Tories: Fighting for the King in America's First Civil War* (New York: Harper, 2010); Maya Jasanoff, *Liberty's Exiles: American Loyalists in a Revolutionary World* (New York: Vintage, 2012).

20. In my view, the American Revolution was still preferable, on moral grounds, to continued British rule, despite the many shortcomings of the rebels and their new government. See Ilya Somin, "The Case Against the American Revolution," *Reason*, July 4, 2019, available at https://reason.com/2019/07/04/the-case-against-the-case-again st-the-american-revolution/.

21. For a discussion of the virtually insuperable difficulties in trying to determine which ethnic or cultural group deserves exclusive rights to a given territory, see Chandran Kukathas, *Immigration and Freedom* (forthcoming). For the argument that being a member of an ethnic group that settled an area first is a morally irrelevant characteristic that cannot justify immigration restrictions, see Bruce A. Ackerman, *Social Justice in the Liberal State* (New Haven, CT: Yale University Press, 1980), 89–93.

22. Yoram Hazony, *The Virtue of Nationalism* (New York: Basic Books, 2018), 89.

23. Ibid., 121.

24. For more detailed critiques of Hazony's theory of nationalism, see Mark Koyama, "A Nationalism Untethered to History," *Liberal Currents*, Sept. 25, 2018, available at https://www.liberalcurrents.com/a-nationalism-untethered-to-history/; and Alex Nowrasteh, "Ridiculous Claims in Yoram Hazony's *The Virtue of Nationalism*," Cato Institute, Nov. 1, 2018, available at https://www.cato.org/blog/ridiculous-claims-yora m-hazonys-virtue-nationalism. As Nowrasteh points out, Hazony's definition of legitimate nationalism turns out to be so narrow as to exclude virtually all the major European nations.

25. Hazony, *The Virtue of Nationalism*, 165.

26. See, e.g., Robert K. Fullwinder, "Achieving Equal Opportunity," in *Moral Foundations of Civil Rights*, ed. Robert K. Fullwinder and Claudia Mills (Totowa, NJ: Rowman and Littlefield, 1986).

27. In his iconic 1963 "I Have a Dream" speech, King famously said: "I have a dream that my four little children will one day live in a nation where they will not be judged by the color of their skin but by the content of their character." Martin Luther King Jr., *I Have a Dream: Writings and Speeches that Changed the World*, ed. James Melvin Washington (San Francisco: Harper, 1986), 103.

28. See, e.g., Randall Kennedy, *For Discrimination: Race, Affirmative Action, and the Law* (New York: Pantheon, 2013); David Boonin, *Should Race Matter: Unusual Answers to the Usual Questions* (Cambridge: Cambridge University Press, 2011), chs. 2–4.

29. See, e.g., Randall Kennedy, *Race, Crime, and the Law* (New York: Pantheon, 1997), 161 (arguing that racial profiling might be permissible in a case where it is the only way to prevent an imminent bombing, where "the social need is absolutely compelling: weighty immediate, and incapable of being addressed sensibly by any other means").

30. For discussion of a variety of possible scenarios where restrictions might be needed to forestall some type of harm, see Chapter 6.

31. Carens, *The Ethics of Immigration*, 226. See also Joseph Carens, "Aliens and Citizens: The Case for Open Borders," *Review of Politics* 49 (1987): 251–73; cf. Ayelet Shachar, *The Birthright Lottery: Citizenship and Global Inequality*, (Cambridge, MA: Harvard University Press, 2009).

32. See David Bier, "No One Knows How Long Legal Immigrants Will Have to Wait," Cato Institute, July 28, 2016, available at https://www.cato.org/blog/no-one-knows-how-long-legal-immigrants-will-have-wait.

33. Christian Jopke and Zeev Rosenheek, "Contesting Ethnic Immigration: Germany and Israel Compared," *European Journal of Sociology* 43 (2002): 303–35.

34. See, e.g., Matthew Cella and Alan Neuhauser, "Race and Homicide in America: By the Numbers," *US News and World Report*, Sept. 29, 2016, available at https://www.usnews.com/news/articles/2016-09-29/race-and-homicide-in-america-by-the-numbers.

35. See New America Foundation, *Terrorism in America after 9/11*, (2015), available at https://www.newamerica.org/in-depth/terrorism-in-america/.

36. Quoted in Ilya Somin, "Nations Can and Do Exist without Immigration Restrictions," Volokh Conspiracy blog, *Washington Post*, Aug. 18, 2015, available at https://www.washingtonpost.com/news/volokh-conspiracy/wp/2015/08/18/nations-can-and-do-exist-without-immigration-restrictions/?utm_term=.bcf2266338e5.

37. Chae Chan Ping v. United States, 130 U.S. 581, 603, 609 (1889).

38. Carens, *Ethics of Immigration*, 273.

39. See Chapter 8.

40. See Hajo Holborn, *A History of Modern Germany: The Reformation* (Princeton, NJ: Princeton University Press, 1959), 204–46.

41. On the influence of oppressive regimes on the content of international human rights law and some of its normative implications, see, e.g., John O. McGinnis and Ilya Somin, "Democracy and International Human Rights Law," *Notre Dame Law Review* 84 (2009): 1739–98.

42. Sarah Song, "Why Does the State Have the Right to Control Immigration?" *Nomos LVII: Immigration, Emigration, and Migration,* ed. Jack Knight (New York: New York University Press, 2013): 3–50, 38. See also Sarah Song, *Immigration and Democracy* (New York: Oxford University Press, 2019), chs. 3–4.

43. Song, *Immigration and Democracy*, 62.

44. Song, *Immigration and Democracy*, 63. Song also suggests that deciding "whom to admit into the territory" is an element of collective self-determination "regardless of the particular effects of immigration," i.e., even apart from the impact on political participation (ibid., 63, 73). But this argument, if indeed she makes it, is circular, as it assumes the very premise that needs to be proven: that self-determination entails a right to exclude.

45. Cf. Adam B. Cox, "Three Mistakes in Open Borders Arguments," in *Nomos LVII: Immigration, Emigration, and Migration,* ed. Jack Knight (New York: New York University Press, 2013), 63–64, (making a similar criticism of Song's argument).

46. For the distinction between "voice" and "exit," see Albert O. Hirschman, *Exit, Voice and Loyalty: Responses to Decline in Firms, Organizations, and States* (Cambridge, MA: Harvard University Press, 1970).

47. See discussion of this point in Chapter 1.

48. See also discussion in Chapter 1.

49. Arash Abizadeh, "Democratic Theory and Border Coercion: No Right to Unilaterally Control Your Own Borders," *Political Theory* 36 (2008): 37–65, 49; see also Arash Abizadeh, "On the Demos and Its Kin: Nationalism, Democracy, and the Boundary Problem," *American Political Science Review* 106 (2012): 867–82.

50. Song, *Immigration and Democracy*, 58.

51. Ibid., 60.

52. Ibid., 73.

53. Perhaps the deportation would have to include their parents as well.

54. Both analogies are advanced in Christopher Heath Wellman, "Freedom of Movement and the Right to Enter and Exit," in *Migration in Political Theory: The Ethics of Movement and Membership*, ed. Sarah Fine and Leah Ypi (New York: Oxford University Press, 2016), 83, 87; see also Christopher Heath Wellman, "Immigration and Freedom of Association," *Ethics* 119 (2008): 109–141.

55. Welllman, "Immigration and Freedom of Association," 123,

56. This distinction is also emphasized by Christopher Bertram, *Do States Have the Right to Exclude Immigrants?* (Cambridge: Polity, 2018), 79.

57. For related critiques of this sort of claim, see Bas Van der Vossen and Jason Brennan, *In Defense of Openness: Why Global Freedom Is the Humane Solution to Global Poverty* (New York: Oxford University Press, 2018), 48–50; and Loren E. Lomasky and Fernando R. Teson, *Justice at a Distance: Extending Freedom Globally* (Cambridge: Cambridge University Press, 2015), 110–11.

58. For this sort of argument on the left, see, e.g., Stephen Holmes and Cass R. Sunstein, *The Cost of Rights: Why Liberty Depends on Taxes* (New York: Norton, 1999), 210, 217.

59. See Ilya Somin, "Creation, Consent, and Government Power over Property Rights," *Cato Unbound*, Dec. 2010, available at https://www.cato-unbound.org/2010/12/13/ilya-somin/creation-consent-government-power-over-property-rights.

60. Michael Huemer, "Is There a Right to Immigrate?" *Social Theory and Practice* 36 (2010): 29–61. For related criticisms of the club argument, see Song, *Immigration and Democracy*, 43–46.

61. For similar criticisms of the club analogy, see also. Anna Stilz, "The Duty to Allow Harmless Migration," unpublished paper (2016), available at https://www.law.berkeley.edu/wp-content/uploads/2016/01/The-Duty-to-Allow-Harmless-Migration.pdf, 7–8.

62. Ibid., and Stilz, *Territorial Sovereignty*, 195–96.

63. Stilz, "Duty to Allow Harmless Migration," 7; see also Bertram, *Do States Have the Right to Exclude Immigrants?*, 79–80.

64. See discussion earlier in this chapter.

65. See, e.g., Richard A. Epstein, *Forbidden Grounds: The Case Against Employment Discrimination Laws* (Cambridge, MA: Harvard University Press, 1992).

66. See, e.g., Epstein, *Forbidden Grounds*, 421–33 (explaining that his case against anti-discrimination laws is largely limited to private settings, while government policies should be subject to much tighter antidiscrimination rules); David E. Bernstein and

Ilya Somin, "Judicial Power and Civil Rights Reconsidered," *Yale Law Journal* 114 (2004): 591–657, 602–9 (outlining important differences between public and private discrimination).

67. See, e.g., Jasanoff, *Liberty's Exiles*.

68. Cf. Huemer, "Is There a Right to Immigrate?"

69. This formulation is adapted from Jason Brennan, "Our Relationship to Democracy Is Nonconsensual," Princeton University Press Blog, Jan. 26, 2016, available at http://blog.press.princeton.edu/2016/01/26/jason-brennan-our-relationship-to-democracy-is-nonconsensual/.

70. For a classic example, see Robert Nozick, *Anarchy, the State and Utopia* (New York: Basic Books, 1974), Part I.

71. A. John Simmons, *Boundaries of Authority* (New York: Oxford University Press, 2016), 239.

72. Ibid., 241.

73. Ibid., 246.

74. Ibid., 246.

75. See Wellman, "Immigration and Freedom of Association," 109–41.

76. John Jay, "Federalist 64," in James Madison, Alexander Hamilton, and John Jay, *The Federalist Papers*, ed. Clinton Rossiter (New York: Mentor, 1961).

77. See Michael Blake, "Immigration, Jurisdiction, and Exclusion," *Philosophy and Public Affairs* 41 (2013): 103–30.

78. Ibid., 104.

79. Ibid., 113–14.

80. Ibid., 105–19.

81. Ibid., 104, 122–23.

82. Blake recognizes that the right to exclude based on avoiding unwanted obligations might be trumped in cases where entry is necessary to protect the migrant's own "basic rights" (104, 122–23). But this exception presumably does not apply to every case where exclusion would consign a migrant to a far worse situation than he or she would face otherwise.

83. See discussion of these issues in Chapter 3.

84. See discussion of this sort of approach to dealing with extra expenses created by migration in Chapter 6.

85. See discussion earlier in this chapter.

86. Blake, "Immigration, Jurisdiction, and Exclusion," 118–19.

87. See Mei Fong, *One Child: The Story of China's Most Radical Experiment* (Boston: Houghton Mifflin Harcourt, 2016).

88. Quoted in Nic Robertson, "Donald Trump's World View Was Laid Bare at the UN—And It Should Worry Anyone Who Understands History," CNN, Sept. 26, 2018, available at https://www.cnn.com/2018/09/25/world/robertson-trump-un-worldview/index.html. In fairness, Trump did not claim that home governments would be justified in forcing potential migrants to stay.

89. See, e.g., David Miller, *Strangers in Our Midst: The Political Philosophy of Immigration* (Cambridge, MA: Harvard University Press, 2016), 108–11; Thomas

Pogge, "Migration and Poverty," in *Citizenship and Exclusion*, ed. V. Bader (Basingstoke: Macmillan, 1997), 14–15; Kieran Oberman, "Can Brain Drain Justify Immigration Restrictions?, *Ethics* 123 (2013): 427–55; Paul Collier, *Exodus: How Migration Is Changing the World* (New York: Oxford University Press, 2013), chs. 9–10. Gillian Brock, "Part I," in Gillian Brock and Michael Blake, *Debating Brain Drain: May Countries Restrict Emigration* (New York: Oxford University Press, 2015); Anna Stilz argues that states may not be able to force skilled professionals to stay but can impose special exit taxes on them, so long as these are set at "reasonable" levels. Anna Stilz, "Is there an Unqualified Right to Leave?," in *Migration and Political Theory*, ed. Sarah Fine (New York: Oxford University Press, 2016), 66–75.

90. For an argument that brain drain justifies the latter, but not the former, see Miller, *Strangers in Our Midst*, 111.

91. The debate took place at the University of Calgary in April 2017.

92. On Trump's grandfather's emigration from Bavaria, see Gwenda Blair, "The Man Who Made Trump Who He Is," *Politico*, Aug. 24, 2015, available at https://www.politico.com/magazine/story/2015/08/the-man-who-made-trump-who-he-is-121647.

93. See, e.g., Somin, *Democracy and Political Ignorance*, and discussion of political ignorance in Chapter 1.

94. For an overview, see Rudolph J. Rummel, *Lethal Politics: Soviet Genocide and Mass Murder since 1917* (New Brunswick, NJ: Transaction, 1990).

95. Philippe Legrain, *Immigrants: Your Country Needs Them*, (Princeton, NJ: Princeton University Press, 2007), 189.

96. This example is adapted from a similar argument by Van der Vossen and Brennan, *In Defense of Openness*, 45.

97. Philippe Legrain makes a similar point, noting that many skilled workers rightly feel no obligation to stay and work on behalf of governments that are corrupt, unjust, and often "unfree." Legrain, *Immigrants*, 189.

98. For this example, see Van der Vossen and Brennan, *In Defense of Openness*, 46–47.

99. For an account of the role of the shah's policies in bringing on the 1979 revolution that overthrew him and led to the establishment of a more repressive regime, see, e.g., Abbas Milani, *Shah* (New York: St. Martin's Press, 2011).

100. Drew Desilver, "Remittances from Abroad Are Major Economic Assets for Some Developing Countries," Pew Research Center, Jan. 29, 2018, available at http://www.pewresearch.org/fact-tank/2018/01/29/remittances-from-abroad-are-major-economic-assets-for-some-developing-countries/.

101. Richard H. Adams and John Page, "Do International Migration and Remittances Reduce Poverty in Developing Nations?," *World Development* 33 (2005): 1645–69. For citations to numerous other studies on the benefits of remittances, see van der Vossen and Brennan, *Case for Openness*, 183nn.6–7.

102. For an overview of the literature, see Covadonga Meseguer and Katrina Burgess, "International Migration and Home Country Politics," *Studies in Comparative International Development* 49 (2014): 1–12.

103. On this point, see Ilya Somin, *Democracy and Political Ignorance: Why Smaller Government Is Smarter*, 2nd ed. (Stanford, CA: Stanford University Press, 2016), 221–22.

104. For an overview of relevant research on these points, see Michael A. Clemens, "What Do We Know about Skilled Migration and Development?," Migration Policy Institute Policy Brief No. 3 (Sept. 2013). On increasing innovation through greater interchange of ideas, see, e.g., Legrain, *Immigrants*, 190–97.

105. See, e.g. ibid. and Clarisa Pérez-Armendáriz, "Cross-Border Discussions and Political Behavior in Migrant-Sending Countries," *Studies in Comparative International Development* 49 (2014): 67–88.

106. For related argument emphasizing similarities between external and internal freedom of movement, see Carens, *The Ethics of Immigration*, 237–52.

107. A few defenders of international migration restrictions do concede the logical connection between their arguments and rationales for restricting internal freedom of movement. See, e.g., Brian Barry, "The Quest for Consistency: A Skeptical View," in *Free Movement: Ethical Issues in the Transnational Migration of People and Money*, ed. Brian Barry and Robert E. Goodin (University Park: University of Pennsylvania Press, 1992); see also discussion of Michael Blake's and Christopher Wellman's arguments argument later in this chapter.

108. Wellman, "Freedom of Movement and the Right to Enter," 89.

109. For a recent summary of studies on this subject, see Scott Beyer, "Why Has Detroit Continued to Decline?," *Forbes*, July 31, 2018, available at https://www.forbes.com/sites/scottbeyer/2018/07/31/why-has-detroit-continued-to-decline/#74a06083fbe1.

110. Christine MacDonald, "Detroit Population Rank Is Lowest since 1850," *Detroit News*, May 20, 2016, available at https://www.detroitnews.com/story/news/local/detroit-city/2016/05/19/detroit-population-rank-lowest-since/84574198/.

111. See J. D. Vance, "Why I'm Moving Home," *New York Times*, Mar. 16, 2017. For a more detailed response to Vance, see Ilya Somin, "Why Successful People Should Not Feel Guilty about Voting with Their Feet, but Should Instead Make It Easier for Others to Do the Same," Volokh Conspiracy, *Washington Post*, Mar. 30, 2017, available at https://www.washingtonpost.com/news/volokh-conspiracy/wp/2017/03/30/why-successful-people-should-not-feel-guilty-about-voting-with-their-feet-but-should-instead-make-it-easier-for-others-to-do-the-same/. My response to Vance attracted a critique by political scientist Mark Chou. See Chou, "'Foot Voting' and the Dilemma of Two Americas," *Governing*, Apr. 24, 2017, available at https://www.governing.com/gov-institute/voices/col-j-d-vance-hillbilly-legacy-foot-voting-dilemma-two-americas.html. I responded to Chou in Ilya Somin, "Is Voting with Your Feet Selfish? Does It Matter if It Is?" Volokh Conspiracy, *Washington Post*, Apr. 25, 2017, available at https://www.washingtonpost.com/news/volokh-conspiracy/wp/2017/04/25/is-voting-with-your-feet-selfish-does-it-matter-if-it-is/.

112. Vance, "Why I'm Moving Home."

113. Vance himself notes that it is "one of the fastest-growing cities in the country," J. D. Vance, *Hillbilly Elegy* (New York: HarperCollins, 2016), 179.

114. See discussion earlier in this chapter.
115. Blake, "Immigration, Jurisdiction, and Exclusion," 122–23. Though he does note that many federal systems will forbid such restrictions, for economic and political reasons, Blake recognizes that such a ban is not required under his theory.
116. Miller, *Strangers in Our Midst*, 54–56.
117. For a classic work on the latter, see Robert D. Putnam, *Making Democracy Work* (Princeton, NJ: Princeton University Press, 1993).
118. Joseph Carens makes a similar point. See Carens, *Ethics of Immigration*, 243.
119. On the white Australia policy, see, e.g., Gavin Jones, "White Australia, National Identity, and Population Change," in *Legacies of White Australia: Race, Culture, and Nation*, ed. Laksiri Jayasuriya et al. (Crawley: University of Western Australia Press, 2003). On US immigration policy discriminating against Asians, see, e.g., Gabriel J. Chin, "Segregation's Last Stronghold: Racial Discrimination and the Constitutional Law of Immigration," *UCLA Law Review* 46 (1998): 1–74; Gabriel J. Chin, "Chae Chan Ping and Fong Yue Ting: The Origins of the Plenary Power," in *Immigration Law Stories*, ed. David Martin and Peter Schuck (New York: Foundation Press, 2005). For a detailed recent account of the role of ethnic prejudice in the enactment of the landmark 1924 Immigration Act, which radically curtailed European migration to the United States, see Daniel Okrent, *The Guarded Gate: Bigotry, Eugenics, and the Law that Kept Two Generations of Jews, Italians, and Other European Immigrants Out of America* (New York: Scribner, 2019).
120. Miller, *Strangers in Our Midst*, 56.
121. Ibid., 56.
122. For a very similar point, see Carens, *Ethics of Immigration*, 243.

Chapter 6

1. See, e.g., Philip Cafaro, *How Many Is Too Many? The Progressive Argument for Reducing Immigration into the United States* (Chicago: University of Chicago Press, 2014); George Borjas, *Immigration Economics* (Cambridge. MA: Harvard University Press, 2014), chs. 4–7.
2. See, e.g., Samuel P. Huntington, *Who Are We? The Challenges to America's Cultural Identity* (New York: Simon and Schuster, 2005).
3. For examples of such proposals, see Bryan Caplan, "Why Should We Restrict Immigration?," *Cato Journal* 32 (2012): 5–21. The phrase "keyhole solution" was apparently first introduced by Tim Harford, *The Undercover Economist* (New York: Oxford University Press, 2005), 130–31.
4. See, e.g., the discussion of Estonia faced with potential Russian migration, later in this chapter.
5. Alex Nowrasteh and Zac Gochenour, "The Political Externalities of Immigration: Evidence from the United States," Cato Institute Working Paper, Jan. 2014, available at http://object.cato.org/sites/cato.org/files/pubs/pdf/working-paper-14-3.pdf. On the

term "political externalities," see Vipul Naik, "Political Externalities," Open Borders: The Case," (N.D.), available at https://openborders.info/political-externalities/.

6. See, e.g., Tova Andrea Wang, "Expanding Citizenship: Immigrants and the Vote," *Democracy: A Journal of Ideas* 28 (2013), available at https://democracyjournal. org/magazine/28/expanding-citizenship-immigrants-and-the-vote/; Caplan, "Why Should We Restrict Immigration," 13–14 (surveying various studies on this).

7. For an extensive overview, see Sam Wilson and Alex Nowrasteh, "The Political Assimilation of Immigrants and Their Descendants," Economic Development Bulletin No. 23, Cato Institute, Feb. 24, 2015, available at http://www.cato.org/publications/economic-development-bulletin/political-assimilation-immigrants-their-descendants.

8. Ilya Somin, *Democracy and Political Ignorance: Why Smaller Government is Smarter*, (Stanford, CA: Stanford University Press, 2nd ed. 2016), 212.

9. Woodrow Wilson National Fellowship Foundation Survey, October 2018, available at https://woodrow.org/news/national-survey-finds-just-1-in-3-americans-would-pass-citizenship-test/.

10. See Liav Orgad, *The Cultural Defense of Nations: A Liberal Theory of Majority Rights*, (New York: Oxford University Press, 2015), 101–20 (surveying Western European and US tests, and concluding that the latter impose fewer and easier requirements).

11. See, e.g., Michael Walzer, *Spheres of Justice: A Defense of Pluralism and Equality* (New York: Basic Books, 1983), 52–61. Anna Stilz, *Territorial Sovereignty: A Philosophical Exploration* (New York: Oxford University Press, 2019), 197.

12. Walzer, *Spheres of Justice.*, 61.

13. See discussion in Chapter 3.

14. Stilz, *Territorial Sovereignty*, 197.

15. See discussion in Chapter 5.

16. See discussion of these proposals later in this chapter.

17. For a more detailed discussion of these points, see Somin, *Democracy and Political Ignorance*, 172–76.

18. Ibid., 172–76.

19. For discussion of this sort of scenario as a justification for immigration restrictions, see, e.g., Stilz, *Territorial Sovereignty*, 193–94; Anna Stilz, "The Duty to Allow Harmless Migration," unpublished paper (2016), available at https://www.law.berkeley.edu/wp-content/uploads/2016/01/The-Duty-to-Allow-Harmless-Migration.pdf, at 7–8.

20. Russia's population is some 100 times larger than Estonia's, and the average Russian has very illiberal views on a wide range of issues. Due in part to Russia's power, Estonia might not be able to deny the franchise to Russian migrants for long, yet might find it feasible to continue to bar most of them. On Estonia's dilemmas with respect to its Russian minority, see Agnia Grigas, *The Politics of Energy and Memory Between Russia and the Baltic States* (New Haven, CT: Yale University Press, 2016), ch. 2; and Grigas, "Compatriot Games: Russian-Speaking Minorities in the Baltic States," *World Politics Review*, Oct. 21, 2014, available at http://www.worldpoliticsreview.com/articles/14240/compatriot-games-russian-speaking-minorities-in-the-baltic-states.

21. Bruce A. Ackerman, *Social Justice in the Liberal State* (New Haven, CT: Yale University Press, 1980), 94–95.

22. See, e.g., Mark Krikorian, *The New Case Against Immigration: Both Legal and Illegal* (New York: Penguin, 2008), ch. 5.

23. See, e.g., Alex Nowrasteh and Zac Gochenour, "The Political Externalities of Immigration: Evidence from the United States," Cato Institute Working Paper, Jan. 2014, available at http://object.cato.org/sites/cato.org/files/pubs/pdf/working-paper-14-3.pdf (evidence from American states).

24. Alberto Alesina and Edward L. Glaeser, *Fighting Poverty in the US and Europe: A World of Difference* (New York: Oxford University Press, 2004) (evidence indicating that European nations with greater immigration actually have lower welfare spending than those with more). Alberto Alesina, Edward Glaeser, and Bruce Sacerdote, "Why Doesn't the United States Have a European-Style Welfare State?," *Brookings Papers on Economic Activity* 2 (2001); 187–277.

25. See, e.g., Alberto Alesina, Armando Miano, and Stefanie Stantcheva, "Immigration and Redistribution," National Bureau of Economic Research, NBER 24733, Sept. 2019; Ann-Helen Bay and Axel West Pedersen, "The Limits of Social Solidarity: Basic Income, Immigration and the Legitimacy of the Universal Welfare State," *Acta Sociologica* 49 (2006): 419–36; Matz Dahlberg, Karin Edmark, and Helene Lundqvist, "Ethnic Diversity and Preferences for Redistribution," Research Institute of Industrial Economics, IFN Working Paper No. 860 (2011); Holger Stichnoth, "Does Immigration Weaken Natives' Support for the Welfare State? Evidence from Germany," Centre for European Economic Research, Discussion Paper No. 10-008 (2012).

26. See discussion of this point earlier.

27. Organization for Economic Cooperation and Development, "The Fiscal Impact of Immigration in OECD Countries," *International Migration Outlook 2013*, available at https://dx.doi.org/10.1787/migr_outlook-2013-6-en. For a discussion of other recent studies reaching similar conclusions, see Neeraj Kaushal, *Blaming Immigrants: Nationalism and the Economics of Global Movement*, (New York; Columbia University Press, 2019), 128–29; see also Philippe Legrain, *Immigrants: Your Country Needs Them*, (Princeton, NJ: Princeton University Press, 2007), ch. 7.

28. Francine Blau and Christopher Mackie, eds., *The Economic and Fiscal Consequences of Immigration*, (Washington, DC: National Academy of Sciences, 2016), 341.

29. See Maryam Nagesh Nejad and Andrew T. Young, "Want Freedom, Will Travel: Emigrant Self-Selection According to Institutional Quality," *European Journal of Political Economy* 45 (2016): 71–84; Nathan J. Ashby, "Freedom and International Migration," *Southern Economic Journal* 77 (2010): 49–62.

30. See, e.g., Martin Ruhs, *The Cost of Rights: Regulating International Labor Migration* (Princeton, NJ: Princeton University Press, 2014); Glen Weyl, "The Openness-Equity Tradeoff in Global Redistribution," *Economic Journal* 128 (2019): 1–36.

31. See Tanya Broder, Avideh Moussavian, and Jonathan Blazer, "Overview of Immigrant Eligibility for Welfare Programs," National Immigration Law Center, Dec. 2015, available at https://www.nilc.org/wp-content/uploads/2015/12/overview-immeligfedprograms-2015-12-09.pdf.

32. Quoted in Bryan D. Caplan, "Why Should We Restrict Immigration?," *Cato Journal* 32 (2012): 5–24, 9.

33. Quoted in Bryan Caplan, "Milton Friedman Opposed a Pareto Improvement," Econlog, June 7, 2008, available at http://www.econlib.org/archives/2008/06/milton_friedman_10.html. Friedman did apparently recognize that illegal migration avoided this problem, because such migrants are ineligible for most welfare benefits. He considered such migration beneficial "[b]ecause as long as it's illegal the people who come in do not qualify for welfare, they don't qualify for social security, they don't qualify for the other myriad of benefits that we pour out from our left pocket to our right pocket. So long as they don't qualify they migrate to jobs." Quoted in James Peron, "What Milton Friedman Actually Said About Illegal Immigration," The Radical Center, *Medium*, Apr. 21, 2018, available at https://medium.com/the-radical-center/what-milton-friedman-actually-said-about-illegal-immigration-6b19efaf7a5. Friedman may not have considered the possibility that the US could adopt similar policies for legal migrants.

34. See, e.g., Stephen Macedo, "The Moral Dilemma of US Immigration Policy: Open Borders vs. Social Justice," in *Debating Immigration Policy*, ed. Carol Swain (Princeton. NJ: Princeton University Press, 2007).

35. For the classic argument of this sort, see Peter Singer, "Famine, Affluence, and Morality," *Philosophy and Public Affairs* 1 (1972): 229–43. See also Peter Singer, *The Life You Can Save* (New York: Random House, 2010).

36. Peter Singer, perhaps the leading philosophical advocate of international redistribution, argues that wealthy nations have a moral duty to take as many poor refugees as they can, stopping only at the point where taking more could lead to a breakdown of societal order. Peter Singer and Renata Singer, "The Ethics of Refugee Policy," in *Free Movement: Ethical Issues in the Transnational Migration of People and Money*, ed. Mark Gibney (University Park: Pennsylvania State University Press, 1992).

37. See, e.g., Reihan Salam, *Melting Pot or Civil War? A Son of Immigrants Makes the Case against Open Borders* (New York: Sentinel, 2018), ch. 2.

38. See Nagesh Nejad and Young, "Want Freedom, Will Travel"; Ashby, "Freedom and International Migration."

39. See Gary S. Becker and Edward Lazear, "A Market Solution to Immigration Reform," *Wall Street Journal*, Mar. 1, 2013, available at https://www.wsj.com/articles/SB10001424127887323375204578271531542362850?mod=rsswn.

40. Ibid.

41. See Eleanor Marie Lawrence Brown, "Visa as Property, Visa as Collateral," *Vanderbilt Law Review* 64 (2011): 1047–105.

42. Ibid., 1053–54.

43. Ibid., 1053–54.

44. See discussion of this possibility earlier in this chapter.

45. Stilz, *Territorial Sovereignty*, 194; Stilz, " Duty to Allow Harmless Migration," 8.

46. For a review of the relevant studies and evidence, see Mary Waters and Marisa Gerstein Pineau, *The Integration of Immigrants into American Society* (Washington, DC: National Academy of Sciences, 2015), 326–32. See also Graham C. Ousey and

Charis E. Kubrin, "Immigration and Crime: Assessing a Contentious Issue," *Annual Review of Criminology* 1 (2018): 63–84.

47. For reviews of the relevant literature, see Ousey and Kubrin, "Immigration and Crime" Walter Ewing et al., "The Criminalization of Immigrants in the United States," *American Immigration Council* (2015), 4–8, available at http://www. immigrationpolicy.org/sites/default/files/research/the_criminalization_of_immigration_in_the_united_states.pdf; and Kaushal, *Blaming Immigrants,* 160-63.

48. Ewing et al., "Criminalization of Immigrants," 7–8: Kaushal, *Blaming Immigrants,* 162-63.

49. Ibid., 7–8.

50. Kristin F. Butcher and Anne Morrison Piehl, *Why Are Immigrants' Incarceration Rates so Low? Evidence on Selective Immigration, Deterrence, and Deportation* (Cambridge, MA: National Bureau of Economic Research, July 2007).

51. Michael T. Light and Ty Miller, "Does Undocumented Immigration Increase Violent Crime?," *Criminology* 56 (2018): 370–401; see also Michelangelo Landegrave and Alex Nowrasteh, "Criminal Immigrants in 2017: Their Numbers, Demographics, and Countries of Origin," Cato Institute Research and Policy Brief No. 11, Mar. 4, 2019, available at https://object.cato.org/sites/cato.org/files/pubs/pdf/irpb-11.pdf (discussing recent data from the American Community Survey on this point); Alex Nowrasteh, "Criminal Immigrants in Texas: Illegal Immigrant Conviction and Arrest Rates for Homicide, Sexual Assault, Larceny, and Other Crimes," Cato Institute, Immigration Research and Policy Brief no. 4, February 26, 2018; and Kaushal, *Blaming Immigrants,* 161–63. For a rare exception to the standard finding that undocumented immigrants have lower levels of criminality than natives, see John R. Lott, "Undocumented Immigrants, US Citizens, and Convicted Criminals in Arizona, " Crime Prevention Research Center, unpublished working paper, (Feb. 2018), available at https://papers.ssrn.com/sol3/papers.cfm?abstract_id=3099992. But this study suffers from a serious methodological problem, on which see Alex Nowrasteh, "The Fatal Flaw in John R. Lott Jr.'s Study on Illegal Immigrant Crime in Arizona," Cato at Liberty, Feb. 5, 2018, available at https://www.cato.org/blog/fatal-flaw-john-r-lott-jrs-study-illegal-immigrant-crime-arizona. The debate continued in John R. Lott, "Responding to Cato's and Others' Attacks on our Research Regarding Crime by Illegal Immigrants," Crime Prevention Research Center, Feb. 6, 2018, available at https://crimeresearch.org/2018/02/responding-catos-attacks-research-regarding-crime-illegal-immigrants/; and Alex Nowrasteh, "Responding to John R. Lott, Jr. on Illegal Immigrant Criminality," *Cato at Liberty*, Feb. 6, 2018, available at https://www.cato.org/blog/responding-john-r-lott-jr-illegal-immigrant-criminality.

52. For a recent overview, see Daniel E. Martinez, Ricardo Martinez-Schulte, and Guillermo Cantor, "Providing Sanctuary or Fostering Crime? A Review of the Research on 'Sanctuary Cities' and Crime," *Sociology Compass* 12 (2018): 1–13.

53. Landegrave and Nowrasteh, "Criminal Immigrants in 2017," 5 (Table 7). The other age groups measured were 25–29, 30–34, 35–39, 40–44, 45–49, and 50–54.

54. See, e.g., Haimin Zhang, "Immigration and Crime: Evidence from Canada," Canadian Labour Market and Skills Researcher Network, Working Paper No. 135 (2014), available

at http://www.clsrn.econ.ubc.ca/workingpapers/CLSRN%20Working%20Paper%20 no.%20135%20-%20Zhang.pdf.

55. This point was brought to my attention by Alex Nowrasteh.

56. See Fabian Dehos, "The Refugee Wave and Its Impact on Crime in Germany," Ruhr Economic Papers No. 737 (December 2017), available at https://www.rwi-essen.de/ media/content/pages/publikationen/ruhr-economic-papers/rep_17_737.pdf.

57. For an extensive overview, see Markus Gehrsitz and Martin Ungerer, "Jobs, Crime, and Votes: A Short-Run Evaluation of the Refugee Crisis in Germany," ZEW Discussion Paper No. 16-086 (2018), 18–20, available at http://ftp.zew.de/pub/ zew-docs/dp/dp16086.pdf.

58. Ibid., 20.

59. "Are Migrants Driving Crime in Germany?" BBC, Sept. 13, 2018, available at https:// www.bbc.com/news/world-europe-45419466.

60. Brian Bell, Francesco Fasani, and Stephen Machin, "Crime and Immigration: Evidence from Large Immigrant Waves," Review of Economics and Statistics 95 (2013): 1278–97.

61. The classic study on this is Jonathan Klick and Alexander Tabarrok, "Using Terror Alert Levels to Estimate the Effect of Police on Crime," Journal of Law and Economics 48 (2005): 267–79.

62. Department of Homeland Security, U.S. Immigrations and Customs Enforcement Budget Review (2018), 11. This does not count some $1.3 billion devoted to "securing" borders (8).

63. The median salary of a police officer in the United States is about $63,000 per year. See Bureau of Labor Statistics, "Police and Detectives," Occupational Research Handbook (2017), available at https://www.bls.gov/ooh/protective-service/ police-and-detectives.htm. That implies that $4 billion can pay the salaries of approximately 63,500 police officers.

64. As of 2012, there were about 1,076 million police officers in the United States. See Department of Justice, National Sources of Law Enforcement Employment Data (2016), available at https://www.bjs.gov/content/pub/pdf/nsleed.pdf.

65. According to the National Weather Service, an average of thirty-one Americans were killed by lightning each year, from 2006 to 2015. National Weather Service, "How Dangerous Is Lightning?," available at http://origin-www.nws.noaa.gov/om/light-ning/odds.shtml. By contrast, the annual incidence of death by immigrant terrorists is far lower. See Alex Nowrasteh, "Terrorism and Immigration: A Risk Analysis, Cato Institute Policy Analysis No. 758 (Dec. 13, 2016), available at https://www.cato.org/ publications/policy-analysis/terrorism-immigration-risk-analysis.

66. See Alex Nowrasteh, "Fatalities and the Annual Chance of Being Murdered in a European Terrorist Attack," Cato Institute, June 21, 2017, available at https://www. cato.org/blog/european-terrorism-fatalities-annual-chance-being-murdered.

67. See, e.g., Andrew C. Forrester, Benjamin Powell, Alex Nowrasteh, and Michelangelo Landegrave, "Do Immigrants Import Terrorism," Cato Institute Working Paper No. 56, July 31, 2019, available at https://www.cato.org/publications/working-paper/ do-immigrants-import-terrorism; Axel Dreher, Martin Gassebner, and Paul Schaudt, "The Effect of Migration on Terror: Made at Home or Imported from Abroad?"

CESifo Working Paper Series No. 6441 (2017), available at https://papers.ssrn.com/sol3/papers.cfm?abstract_id=2976273.

68. See, e.g., Vincent Bove and Tobias Bohmelt, "Does Immigration Induce Terrorism," *Journal of Politics* 78 (2016): 572–88.

69. Richard J. McAlexander, "How Are Immigration and Terrorism Related? An Analysis of Right- and Left-Wing Terrorism in Western Europe, 1980–2004," *Journal of Global Security Studies* 1 (2019): 1–17.

70. See Chapter 5.

71. See, e.g., Salam, *Melting Pot or Civil War?*

72. Ibid.

73. See discussion earlier in this chapter.

74. See, e.g., Samuel P. Huntington, *Who Are We? The Challenges to America's Cultural Identity* (New York: Simon and Schuster, 2005); Krikorian, *The New Case Against Immigration*, ch. 1.

75. For overviews of the evidence, see Waters and Pineau, *The Integration of Immigrants into American Society*; Jacob Vigdor, "The Civic and Cultural Assimilation of Immigrants," in *The Economics of Immigration*, ed. Benjamin Powell (New York: Oxford University Press, 2017); and Legrain, *Immigrants*, 235-39.. Conventional metrics often actually underestimate the extent of assimilation of Hispanic immigrants— the most controversial recent group of migrants—because the most assimilated children and grandchildren of immigrants from this group often do not even identify as members of the group in surveys. Waters and Pineau, *The Integration of Immigrants into American Society*, 259–61.

76. See John Higham, *Strangers in the Land: Patterns of American Nativism, 1860–1925*, 2nd ed. (New York: Athenaeum, 1965).

77. See, e.g., Leon de Winter, "Europe's Muslims Hate the West," *Politico*, Mar. 29, 2016, available at https://www.politico.eu/article/brussels-attacks-terrorism-europe-muslims-brussels-attacks-airport-metro/; cf. Orgad, *Cultural Defense of Nations*, 34–38 (discussing claims to this effect).

78. For overviews of the data on Muslim immigrants' opinions and degree of assimilation in the United States, see, e.g., Pew Research Center, "US Muslims Concerned about Place in Society, but Continue to Believe in the American Dream," July 26, 2017 (Pew Survey of US Muslims), available at http://www.pewforum.org/2017/07/26/findings-from-pew-research-centers-2017-survey-of-us-muslims/; David Bier, "Rapid US Muslim Assimilation Continues Alongside Rapid Muslim Migration," Cato Institute, July 28, 2017, available at https://www.cato.org/blog/rapid-us-muslim-assimilation-continues-alongside-rapid-muslim-immigration; David Bier, "Muslims Rapidly Adopt US Social Values," Cato Institute, Oct. 13, 2016, available at https://www.cato.org/blog/muslims-rapidly-adopt-us-social-political-values.

79. Alex Vandermaas-Peeler et al., "Emerging Consensus on LGBT Issues: Findings From the 2017 American Values Atlas," PRRI (2017), available at https://www.prri.org/wp-content/uploads/2018/05/AVA-2017-FINAL-1.pdf.

80. For evidence that this is an important factor in the case of European Muslims, see, e.g., Shikha Dalmia, "Want to Solve Europe's Jihadi Problem? Reform the Continent's

Toxic Labor Laws," *The Week*, Apr. 5, 2016 (citing relevant studies); Peter Huber, "What Institutions Help Immigrants Integrate," Austrian Institute for Economics Research, Working Paper No. 77 (2015), available at http://www.foreurope.eu/fileadmin/documents/pdf/Workingpapers/WWWforEurope_WPS_no077_MS18.pdf.

81. See, e.g., Legrain, *Immigrants*, 310–17 (discussing some possibilities).

82. See discussion of the similar possible remedy for displacement of native workers, discussed later in this chapter.

83. Robert Putnam, "E Pluribus Unum: Diversity and Community in the Twenty-First Century," *Scandinavian Political Studies* 30 (2007): 137–74.

84. See ibid., 151–53, which finds that diverse American communities have higher distrust almost entirely because African-Americans and Hispanics have lower social trust than whites, which is understandable in a society with a long history of discrimination against these groups. This point about Putnam's results is made by Bryan Caplan, "Trust and Diversity: Not A Bang, but a Whimper," Econlog, June 15, 2017, available at https://www.econlib.org/archives/2017/06/trust_and_diver.html. Other studies find little or no effect of diversity on trust. See, e.g., Christian Bjornskov, "Determinants of Generalized Trust: A Cross-Country Comparison, *Public Choice* 130 (2007): 1–21.

85. For an overview, see, e.g., Peter Nannestad, "What Have We Learned About Generalized Trust, if Anything?" *Annual Review of Political Science* 11 (2008): 413–36.

86. See Felix Roth, "Does Too Much Trust Hamper Economic Growth?" *Kyklos* 62 (2008): 103–28.

87. Orgad, *Cultural Defense of Nations*, 208–12, 226–27. Orgad recognizes that this principle may not apply to refugees. Ibid., 208. For Orgad's rejection of of other cultural justifications for exclusion, see ibid., chs. 5–6.

88. Ibid., 211–12 (emphasis in the original).

89. Ibid., 228–29.

90. Ibid., 211.

91. Ibid.

92. Ibid.

93. Ibid.

94. See discussion of this point in the section on political externalities, earlier in this chapter.

95. Orgad, *Cultural Defense of Nations*, 211.

96. See discussion earlier in this chapter.

97. This is the implication of his suggestion that refusal to accept liberal principles could justify revocation of residency or immigration rights from those to whom they were previously granted. Orgad, *Cultural Defense of Nations*, 208.

98. For a recent defense of such laws, see, e.g., Richard Delgado and Jean Stefancic, *Understanding Words that Wound*, (New York: Routledge, 2019). For a recent critique, see Nadine Strossen, *Hate: Why We Should Resist it with Free Speech, Not Censorship* (New York: Oxford University Press, 2018).

99. See discussion earlier in this chapter.

100. See, e.g., Cafaro, *How Many Is Too Many?*; George Borjas, *Immigration Economics* (Cambridge, MA: Harvard University Press, 2014), chs. 4–7; Krikorian, *The New Case Against Immigration*, ch. 4.

101. See Caglar Ozden et al., *Moving for Prosperity: Global Migration and Labor Markets* (Washington, DC: World Bank, 2018), 17–19; Giovanni Peri and Chard Sparber, "Task Specialization, Immigration, and Wages," *American Economic Journal: Applied Economics* 1 (2009): 135–69; Sari P. Kerr and William Kerr, "Economic Impacts of Immigration: A Survey," NBER Working Paper No. 16736 (2011); Caplan, "Why Restrict Immigration?" 7–8 (surveying studies); Kimberly Clausing, *Open: The Progressive Case for Free Trade, Immigration, and Global Capital* (Cambridge, MA: Harvard University Press, 2019), 192–98; Legrain, *Immigrants*, 138–43.

102. These kinds of examples are discussed in greater detail in Legrain, *Immigrants*, 138–40.

103. See Uuriintuya Batsaikhan, Zsolt Darvas, and Inês Gonçalves Raposo, *People on the Move: Migration and Mobility in the European Union* (Brussels: Bruegel, 2018), 87–88, available at http://bruegel.org/wp-content/uploads/2018/01/People_on_the_move_ONLINE.pdf (summarizing numerous studies with evidence to this effect); Clausing, *Open*, 92–98.

104. Caplan, "Why Restrict Immigration?" 9 (surveying studies).

105. See, e.g., Ozden, *Moving for Prosperity*, 17–18; Caplan, "Why Restrict Immigration?" (summarizing studies); Clausing, *Open*, 192–95. Recently, there has been an ongoing debate between George Borjas and Michael Clemens over the impact on wages of the 1980 Mariel "boatlift"—which transported thousands of Cuban migrants to Miami. See, e.g., George Borjas, "Still More on Mariel: The Role of Race," NBER Working Paper 23504 (2017) (finding a 10–30 percent wage decrease for local workers who are high school dropouts) and Michael Clemens and Jennifer Hunt, "The Labor Market Effects of Refugee Waves: Reconciling Conflicting Results," NBER Working Paper 23433 (2017) (arguing that the Borjas finding is the result of flaws in the data). But even in the worst case scenario, negative effects were confined to high school dropouts—a small segment at the lower end of the labor market.

106. Ozden, *Moving for Prosperity*, 18; Kaushal, *Blaming Immigrants*, 127.

107. For an argument that such protection is unjust, see van der Vossen and Brennan, *Case for Openness*, 32–34.

108. Caplan, "Why Restrict Immigration?," 9.

109. See Joel Achenbach, "Two Mass Murders a World Apart Share a Common Theme: 'Ecofascism,'" *Washington Post*, Aug. 18, 2019, available at https://www.washingtonpost.com/science/two-mass-murders-a-world-apart-share-a-common-theme-ecofascism/2019/08/18/0079a676-bec4-11e9-b873-63ace636af08_story.html.

110. See, e.g., Cafardo, *How Many Is Too Many*, chs. 7–8.

111. Ibid., chs. 7–8.

112. Ibid., ch. 8.

113. For overviews of the relevant literature and evidence, see, e.g., Soumyananda Dinda, "Environmental Kuznets Curve Hypothesis: A Survey," *Ecological Economics* 49 (2004): 431–55; Sun Bo, "A Literature Survey on the Environmental Kuznets Curve," *Energia Procedia* 5 (2011): 1322–25; Gene M. Grossman and Alan B. Krueger, "Economic Growth and the Environment," *Quarterly Journal of Economics* 110 (1995): 353–77; and Ola Honningdal Grytten and Viktoriia Koilo, "Evidence of the Environmental Kuznets Curve in Emerging Eastern European Economies," NHH Dept. of Economics Discussion Paper No. 11 (2019), available at https://papers.ssrn.com/sol3/papers.cfm?abstract_id=3400004.

114. See, e.g., Grytten and Koilo, "Evidence of the Environmental Kuznets Curve."

115. See works cited in Note 113.

116. For a recent statement signed by numerous leading economists across the political spectrum, see, e.g., "Economists' Statement on Carbon Dividends," *Wall Street Journal*, Jan. 16, 2019.

117. For the classic account of tragedies of the commons, see Garrett Hardin, "The Tragedy of the Commons," *Science* 162 (1968): 1243–48.

118. For a leading recent overview of such approaches and relevant empirical evidence, see Terry L. Anderson and Donald R. Leal, *Free Market Environmentalism for the Next Generation* (New York: Palgrave Macmillan, 2015). See also, e.g., Seth W. Norton, "Property Rights, the Environment, and Economic Well-Being," in *Who Owns the Environment?*, ed. Peter J. Hill and Roger E. Meiners (Lanham, MD: Rowman and Littlefield, 1998), 51.

119. For relevant empirical evidence on this, see Anderson and Leal, *Free Market Environmentalism*, ch. 7.

120. See, e.g., Anderson and Leal, *Free Market Environmentalism*, ch. 6.

121. But cf. Jonathan H. Adler, "Taking Property Rights Seriously: The Case of Climate Change," *Social Philosophy and Policy* 26 (2009): 296–316, which explains how the property rights approach can potentially contribute to addressing climate change, by justifying compensation payments to nations harmed by global warming.

122. Neli Esipova, Anita Pugliese, and Julie Ray, "More Than 750 Million Worldwide Would Migrate If They Could," Gallup, Dec. 2018, available at https://news.gallup.com/poll/245255/750-million-worldwide-migrate.aspx.

123. See, e.g., George J. Borjas, "Immigration and Globalization: A Review Essay," *Journal of Economic Literature* 53 (2015): 961–74; Paul Collier, *Exodus: How Migration Is Changing Our World* (New York: Oxford University Press, 2013); Brian Barry, "The Quest for Consistency: A Sceptical View," in *Free Movement: Ethical Issues in the Transnational Migration of People and Money*, ed. Brian Barry and Robert E. Goodin (University Park: University of Pennsylvania Press, 1992), 279–87.

124. See discussion in Chapter 3.

125. For a discussion of such gradual "diaspora" dynamics, see Collier, *Exodus*, ch. 2. His analysis is in some tension with his concern about potential swamping scenarios.

126. Bryan Caplan, "The 'Swamping' that Wasn't: The Diaspora Dynamics of the Puerto Rican Open Borders Experiment," Econlog, Mar. 27, 2014, available at https://www.econlib.org/archives/2014/03/the_swamping_th.html.

127. For a detailed discussion of this point, see Michael Clemens and Lant Pritchett, "The New Economic Case for Migration Restrictions: An Assessment," *Journal of Development Economics* 138 (2018): 153–64.

128. Alex Nowrasteh, Andrew Forrester, and Cole Blondin, "How Mass Immigration Affects Countries with Weak Economic Institutions: A Natural Experiment in Jordan," World Bank Policy Research Working Paper No. 8817 (2019), available at https://papers.ssrn.com/sol3/papers.cfm?abstract_id=3370648.

129. Benjamin Powell, J. R. Clark, and Alex Nowrasteh, "Does Mass Immigration Destroy Institutions? 1990s Israel as a Natural Experiment," *Journal of Economic Behavior and Organization* 141 (2017): 83–95.

130. Jordan had a population of about 3.5 million in 1990, while Israel's stood at 4.8 million. See Central Bureau of Statistics, *The Population of Israel, 1990–2009* (Dec. 2010), available at https://unstats.un.org/unsd/wsd/docs/Israel_wsd_brochure.pdf; Nowrasteh et al., "How Mass Immigration Affects Countries with Weak Economic Institutions."

131. See Nowrasteh et al., "How Mass Immigration Affects Countries with Weak Economic Institutions."

132. See Sam Sokol, "Why Most New Immigrants to Israel are Not Considered Jewish," *Israel Times*, Jan. 4, 2019, available at https://www.timesofisrael.com/why-most-new-immigrants-to-israel-arent-considered-jewish/ (noting that some 400,000 immigrants to Israel from the former Soviet Union are classified as non-Jews by the Israeli government).

133. See generally Luisa Gandolfo, *Palestinians in Jordan: The Politics of Identity* (London: Tauris, 2012).

134. See discussion of these options earlier in this chapter.

135. See discussion of the situation of Estonia earlier in this chapter.

136. Albert O. Hirschman, *Exit, Voice and Loyalty: Responses to Decline in Firms, Organizations, and States* (Cambridge, MA: Harvard University Press, 1970), ch. 4.

137. Ibid. The paradigmatic example employed by Hirschman is that of inner-city schools abandoned by middle-class parents who might have promoted educational reforms had they stayed (45–46, 51–52).

138. Erwin Chemerinsky, "Separate and Unequal: American Public Education Today," *American University Law Review* 56 (2003): 1461–75.

139. See discussion in Chapter 1.

140. Hirschman, *Exit, Voice, and Loyalty*, 45–46, 51–52.

141. For a 2013 review of relevant studies, finding that twenty of twenty-one conclude that there are positive effects, and one finding no effects, see Anna J. Egalite, "Measuring Competitive Effects from School Voucher Programs: A Systematic Review," *Journal of School Choice* 7 (2013): 443–64. A more recent comprehensive international review of economics literature on the effects of school choice concludes that "virtually all" studies from multiple countries indicate that increasing competition from private schools through school choice programs improves the quality of public schools in the relevant area, though the authors caution that it is difficult to fully control for the effects of all relevant variables. See Dennis Epple, Richard E. Romano, and

Miguel Urquiola, "School Vouchers: A Survey of the Economics Literature," *Journal of Economic Literature*, 55 (2017): 441–62, 475–78.

142. See Eric A. Hanushek and Alfred A. Lindseth, *Schoolhouses, Courthouses and Statehouses: Solving the Funding-Achievement Paradox in America's Schools* (Princeton, NJ: Princeton University Press, 2009).

143. Eric Oliver, *Democracy in Suburbia* (Princeton, NJ: Princeton University Press, 2001), 42–52.

144. For evidence that "love marriages" lead to greater male investment in spouses and children than under arranged marriage, see Lena Edlund Nils-Petter Lagerlöf, "Implications of Marriage Institutions for Redistribution and Growth," Center on Democracy, Development, and the Rule of Law, Stanford University working paper (2005), available at https://fsi-live.s3.us-west-1.amazonaws.com/s3fs-public/Nov27_04_No30.pdf.

145. See discussion in Chapter 5.

146. Bill Bishop, *The Big Sort: Why the Clustering of Like-Minded America Is Tearing Us Apart* (New York: Houghton Mifflin, 2008).

147. For data on increasing political polarization in the United States in recent decades, see e.g., Matthew Lewendusky, *The Partisan Sort: How Liberals Became Democrats and Conservatives Became Republicans* (Chicago: University of Chicago Press, 2009). But much of the new polarization is not the result of Americans' becoming more extreme in their views, but of the two major parties becoming more ideologically consistent (chs. 3–4).

148. See Somin, *Democracy and Political Ignorance*, 172–73; Samuel J. Abrams and Morris P. Fiorina, "The 'Big Sort' that Wasn't: A Skeptical Reexamination," *PS: Political Science and Politics* (2009): 203–10.

149. See, e.g., David A. Hopkins, *Red Fighting Blue: How Geography and Electoral Rules Polarize American Politics* (New York: Cambridge University Press, 2017).

150. See Ibid., ch. 4.

151. Somin, *Democracy and Political Ignorance*, 173–74.

152. Sheila Dewan, "Affordable Housing Draws Middle Class to Inland Cities," *New York Times*, Aug. 3, 2014, available at https://www.nytimes.com/2014/08/04/business/affordable-housing-drives-middle-class-to-cities-inland.html.

153. See discussion in Chapter 5.

154. See Xi Liu, Clio Andris, and Bruce A. Desmarais, "Migration and Political Polarization in the U.S.: An Analysis of the County-Level Migration Network," *PLOS ONE* 14 (2019): 1–16.

155. Ibid., 5.

156. Somin, *Democracy and Political Ignorance*, 175.

157. See Heather K. Gerken, "Second-Order Diversity," *Harvard Law Review* 118 (2005): 1099–196.

158. *Dunn v. Blumstein*, 405 U.S. 330 (1972).

159. See discussion earlier in this chapter.

160. See, e.g., Alan Greenblatt, "How California Is Turning the Rest of the West Blue," NPR, Aug. 29, 2013.

161. On the history of such zoning, see Richard Rothstein, *The Color of Law: A Forgotten History of How Our Government Segregated America* (New York: Norton, 2017).

162. This point is noted by Christopher Bertram, *Do States Have the Right to Exclude Immigrants*, (Cambridge: Polity, 2018), 87.

163. For an influential account of the history of such differences in the United States, see David Hackett Fischer, *Albion's Seed: Four British Folkways in America* (New York: Oxford University Press, 1989).

164. *Buchanan v. Warley*, 245 U.S. 60 (1917). On the spread of residential segregation laws prior to *Buchanan*, see, e.g., David Bernstein and Ilya Somin, "Judicial Power and Civil Rights Reconsidered," *Yale Law Journal* 114 (2004): 591–657, 626–39; David E. Bernstein, "Philip Sober Controlling Philip Drunk: *Buchanan v. Warley* in Historical Perspective," *Vanderbilt Law Review* 51 (1998): 797–879.

165. This point also applies to arguments holding that migration restrictions can be imposed on interjurisdictional migrants in a federal system, but not similarly situated migrants who move between different parts of the same subnational jurisdiction.

Chapter 7

1. For more detailed discussion, see Ilya Somin, *Democracy and Political Ignorance: Why Smaller Government Is Smarter*, 2nd ed. (Stanford, CA: Stanford University Press, 2016), 176–78, 192–95.

2. On the importance of hard budget constraints for these purposes, see Barry Weingast, "The Economic Role of Political Institutions: Market-Preserving Federalism and Economic Development," *Journal of Law, Economics, and Organization* 11 (1995): 1–31; Barry Weingast, "Second Generation Fiscal Federalism: Implications of Fiscal Incentives," *Journal of Urban Economics* 65 (2009): 279–93; James Buchanan and Geoffrey Brennan, *The Power to Tax: Analytical Foundations of a Fiscal Constitution* (Cambridge: Cambridge University Press, 1980), 211–17; Ilya Somin, "Foot Voting, Federalism, and Political Freedom," *Nomos: Federalism and Subsidiarity*, ed. James Fleming and Jacob Levy (New York: New York University Press, 2014); Clayton P. Gillette, "Fiscal Federalism as a Constraint on States," *Harvard Journal of Law and Public Policy* 102 (2012): 101–14.

3. See, e.g., Jonathan Rodden, *Hamilton's Paradox: The Promise and Peril of Fiscal Federalism* (Cambridge: Cambridge University Press, 2006), ch. 4.

4. I discussed some of the potential advantages of this approach in Ilya Somin, "Closing the Pandora's Box of Federalism: The Case for Judicial Restriction of Federal Subsidies to State Governments," *Georgetown Law Journal* 90 (2002): 461–502, 477–80.

5. On red jurisdictions in blue states, see Glenn Reynolds, "Splitsylvania: State Secession and What to Do about It," University of Tennessee Legal Studies Research Paper No. 343 (2018), available at https://papers.ssrn.com/sol3/papers.cfm?abstract_id=3130497; on blue jurisdictions in red states, see Richard Schragger, "The Attack on

American Cities," *Texas Law Review* 96 (2018): 1163-1233,; and Richard Schragger, "Federalism, Metropolitanism, and the Problem of States," *Virginia Law Review* 105 (forthcoming), available at https://papers.ssrn.com/sol3/papers.cfm?abstract_id=3384084.

6. US Census Bureau, *2012 Census of Governments*, available at https://www.census.gov/newsroom/releases/archives/governments/cb12-161.html.

7. Heather K. Gerken, "Foreword: Federalism All the Way Down," *Harvard Law Review* 124 (2010): 6–83.

8. For a helpful recent overview of the constitutional issues involved, see Schragger, "Attack on American Cities."

9. See, e.g., Clayton P. Gillette, "Fiscal Home Rule," *University of Denver Law Review* 86 (2009): 1241–61; Richard Briffault, "'Mind the Gap': The Promise and Limits of Home Rule in New York," in *New York's Broken Constitution: The Governance Crisis and the Path to Renewed Greatness*, ed. Peter J. Galie, Christopher Bopst, and Gerald Benjamin (New York: State University of New York Press, 2016).

10. See discussion of the problem of scale in Chapter 2.

11. See discussion in Chapter 2, and later in this chapter. See also Ilya Somin, "Federalism and Constitutional Property Rights," *University of Chicago Legal Forum* 2011 (2011): 53–88.

12. See discussion later in this chapter.

13. For well-known arguments that the political safeguards of federalism make judicial intervention unnecessary in the United States, see Larry D. Kramer, "Putting the Politics Back into the Political Safeguards of Federalism," *Columbia Law Review* 100 (2000), 215–311; Jesse H. Choper, *Judicial Review and the National Political Process* (Chicago: University of Chicago Press, 1980); Jesse H. Choper, "The Scope of National Power Vis-à-Vis the States: The Dispensability of Judicial Review," *Yale Law Journal* 86 (1977), 1552–84; Herbert J. Wechsler, "The Political Safeguards of Federalism: The Role of the States in the Composition and Selection of the Federal Government," *Columbia Law Review* 54 (1954), 543–64.

14. These points are elaborated in greater detail in John McGinnis and Ilya Somin, "Federalism vs. States' Rights: A Defense of Judicial Review in a Federal System," *Northwestern University Law Review* 99 (2004): 89–130; See also Somin, *Democracy and Political Ignorance*, chs. 5–6.

15. Barry Weingast, "The Economic Role of Political Institutions: Market-Preserving Federalism and Economic Development," *Journal of Law, Economics, and Organization* 11 (1995):1–31; see also James Buchanan and Geoffrey Brennan, *The Power to Tax: Analytical Foundations of a Fiscal Constitution* (Cambridge: Cambridge University Press, 1980).

16. See Barry Weingast, "Second Generation Fiscal Federalism," 283–84.

17. Ibid., 283–84.

18. See discussion in Chapter 4, and in Ilya Somin, "Taking Dissenting by Deciding All the Way Down," *Tulsa Law Review* 48 (2013): 523–34 (symposium in honor of Heather Gerken).

19. Crandall v. Nevada, 73 U.S. 35 (1867).

20. Williams v. Fears, 179 U.S. 270, 274 (1900).

21. Edwards v. California, 314 U.S. 160 (1941).

22. Buchanan v. Warley, 245 U.S. 60 (1917). On *Buchanan* and its significance, see, e.g., David Bernstein and Ilya Somin, "Judicial Power and Civil Rights Reconsidered," *Yale Law Journal* 114 (2004): 591–657, 626–39; David E. Bernstein, "Philip Sober Controlling Philip Drunk: *Buchanan v. Warley* in Historical Perspective," *Vanderbilt Law Review* 51 (1998): 797–879.

23. See Shapiro v. Thompson, 394 U.S. 618 (1969) (forbidding a one-year exclusion for such migrants); Saenz v. Roe, 526 U.S. 489 (1999) (forbidding the establishment of a one-year period during which migrants are entitled only to as much in welfare payments as they would have received in their previous home state).

24. See discussion in Chapter 6.

25. See, e.g., Paul E. Peterson and Mark Rom, *Welfare Magnets*, (Washington, DC: Brookings Institution, 1990).

26. See discussion in chapters 3 and 6.

27. See discussion in chapters 2 and 3.

28. US Constitution, Amendment I.

29. See Lawrence v. Texas, 539 U.S. 558 (2003) (striking laws banning same-sex sexual activity); Obergefell v. Hodges, 135 S.Ct. 2071 (2015) (striking down laws banning same-sex marriage).

30. See discussion in Chapter 2; and Edward Glaeser, "Reforming Land Use Regulations," Brookings Institution, Apr. 24, 2017, available at https://www.brookings.edu/research/reforming-land-use-regulations/amp/.

31. Euclid v. Amber Realty, 272 U.S. 365 (1926).

32. See discussion in Chapter 2.

33. For an overview of these developments, see Ilya Somin, *The Grasping Hand: Kelo v. City of New London and the Limits of Eminent Domain*, rev. ed. (Chicago: University of Chicago Press, 2016), ch. 3.

34. See essays on various countries collected in Hojun Lee, Iljoong Kim, and Ilya Somin, eds., *Eminent Domain: A Comparative Perspective* (Cambridge: Cambridge University Press, 2017).

35. See Ilya Somin, "Federalism and Constitutional Property Rights," *University of Chicago Legal Forum* 2011 (2011): 53–88.

36. See discussion of their importance to foot voting in Chapter 4.

37. For an overview and defense of these decisions, see Steven Menashi and Douglas H. Ginsburg, "Rational Basis with Economic Bite," *NYU Journal of Law and Liberty* 8 (2014): 1055–104. For arguments for more robust judicial intervention to protect economic liberties, see, e.g., David Mayer, *Liberty of Contract: Rediscovering a Lost Constitutional Right* (Washington, DC: Cato Institute, 2011); and Bernard Siegan, *Economic Liberties and the Constitution* (Chicago: University of Chicago Press, 1980). For defenses of the conventional wisdom that such rights deserve little or no protection, see, e.g., Cass R. Sunstein, "Lochner's Legacy," *Columbia Law Review* 87 (1987): 873–919, and Barbara Fried, *The Progressive Assault on Laissez-Faire: Robert Hale and the First Law and Economics Movement* (Cambridge, MA: Harvard University Press, 2001).

38. See discussion in Chapter 4. For an extended argument that economic liberty is a central element of liberty more generally, see John Tomasi, *Free Market Fairness* (Princeton, NJ: Princeton University Press, 2012).

39. I discuss a range of such justifications in Ilya Somin, "Taking Property Rights Seriously: The Supreme Court and the 'Poor Relation' of Constitutional Law," George Mason Law and Economics Research Paper No. 08-53 (2008).

40. See Williamson v. Lee Optical, 348 U.S. 483 (1955) (ruling that regulations of economic transactions are subject only to the most minimal "rational basis" constitutional scrutiny).

41. Berman v. Parker, 348 U.S. 26 (1954) (ruling that almost any public interest asserted by the government qualifies as a "public use" for which the government can take property).

42. For a classic statement of the argument that judicial review is needed to protect the rights of people who lack influence over the political process, see John Hart Ely, *Democracy and Distrust: A Theory of Judicial Review* (Cambridge, MA: Harvard University Press, 1980).

43. See Somin, *Grasping Hand*, 99–102.

44. See discussion in Chapter 2.

45. This famous phrase comes from United States v. Carolene Products, 304 U.S. 144, 152–53 n.4 (1938).

46. Ely, *Democracy and Distrust*, ch. 6.

47. See Ilya Somin, "Rethinking the Scope of Federal Power over Immigration," (forthcoming paper on file with author); Anna O. Law, "The Historical Amnesia of Immigration Federalism Debates," *Polity* 47 (2015): 302–19.

48. See discussion of these issues in Chapter 5.

49. 138 S.Ct. 2392 (2018).

50. I criticized the Trump travel ban and the idea of special deference on immigration policy in greater detail in Michael Z. Mannheimer and Ilya Somin, "The Bill of Rights Is the Best Defense against a Travel Ban," *The Hill*, Apr. 24, 2018; and Ilya Somin, "Donald Trump's 'Travel Ban' Is Still a 'Muslim Ban' No Matter What the Supreme Court Ruled," *USA Today*, June 26, 2018.

51. See discussion in Chapter 6. The Naturalization Clause of the US Constitution in fact gives Congress the power to constrain eligibility for citizenship, which in most cases is necessary for voting. US Constitution, Art. I, Section 8, cl. 4.

52. See Chapter 6.

53. See Davide Strazzari, "Canada and Immigration Federalism: Beyond Quebec Exceptionalism," *Perspectives on Federalism* 9 (2017): 56–84, available at http://www.on-federalism.eu/attachments/270_download.pdf.

54. See Roslyn Cameron, "Responding to Australia's Regional Skill Shortages through Regional Skilled Migration," *Journal of Economic and Social Policy* 14 (2011): 4–22.

55. See, e.g., Law, "Historical Amnesia"; Gerald Neuman, "The Lost Century of American Immigration Law, 1776–1875," *Columbia Law Review* 93 (1993): 833; Anna O. Law, "Lunatics, Idiots, Paupers, and Negro Seamen—Immigration Federalism and the Early American State, *Studies in American Political Development* 28 (2014): 107–26;

and Hidetaka Hirota, *Expelling the Poor: Atlantic Seaboard States and the 19th Century Origins of American Immigration Policy* (New York: Oxford University Press, 2017).

56. See Jason L. Riley, "On Immigration, Washington Doesn't Know Best," *Wall Street Journal*, May 2, 2017. For my thoughts on this proposal, see Ilya Somin, "A Federalist Approach to Immigration Reform," Volokh Conspiracy, *Washington Post*, May 5, 2017, available at https://www.washingtonpost.com/news/volokh-conspiracy/wp/20 17/05/05/a-federalist-approach-to-immigration-reform/?utm_term=.d0fef9158165.

57. Adam Ozimek, Kenan Fikri, and John Lettieri, "From Managing Decline to Building the Future: Could a Heartland Visa Help Struggling Regions?," Economic Innovation Group, Apr. 2019, available at https://eig.org/wp-content/uploads/2019/04/ Heartland-Visas-Report.pdf.

58. For an overview of Buttigieg's version of the proposal and its potential advantages, see Matthew Yglesias, "Pete Buttigieg's Plan to Use Immigration to Revitalize Shrinking Communities, Explained," *Vox*, Aug. 15, 2019, available at https://eig.org/wp-content/uploads/2019/04/Heartland-Visas-Report.pdf. On Biden's version, see David Bier, "Biden Backs City-Sponsored Visas," Cato at Liberty, Cato Institute, Dec. 12, 2019, available at https://www.cato.org/blog/ biden-backs-city-sponsored-visas.

59. A recent example is the Trump administration's plan to give state and local governments veto power over admission of refugees into their territory. See Griff Witte, "No Refugees Allowed? Trump's Plan to Give States and Cities a Veto Prompts Outcry," *Washington Post*, Oct. 12, 2019, available at https://www.washingtonpost.com/national/no-refugee s-allowed-trumps-plan-to-give-states-and-cities-a-veto-prompts-an-outcry/2019/10 /12/5348bbee-ec41-11e9-bafb-da248f8d5734_story.html.

60. For discussions of this potential political dynamic, see Peter Spiro, "Learning to Live with Immigration Federalism," *Connecticut Law Review* 97 (1997): 1627–59; and Peter Schuck, "Taking Immigration Federalism Seriously," *University of Chicago Legal Forum* 2007 (2007): 57–92.

Chapter 8

1. Convention Relating to the Status of Refugees, Article 1 (1951, as amended in 1967).
2. See 8 U.S.C. § 1101(a)(42) (defining refugee as "any person who is outside any country of such person's nationality or, in the case of a person having no nationality, is outside any country in which such person last habitually resided, and who is unable or unwilling to return to, and is unable or unwilling to avail himself or herself of the protection of, that country because of persecution or a well-founded fear of persecution on account of race, religion, nationality, membership in a particular social group, or political opinion").
3. Convention Relating to the Status of Refugees, Article 33(1).
4. Universal Declaration of Human Rights, Art. 13, Section 2.
5. For a discussion of arguments holding that governments sometimes have a right to block emigration, see Chapter 5.

6. Jill Goldenziel, "Displaced: A Proposal for an International Agreement to Protect Refugees, Migrants, and States," *Berkeley Journal of International Law* 35 (2017): 47–89, 76–77.

7. Ibid., 70–73.

8. Ibid., 47.

9. Michael Walzer, *Spheres of Justice* (New York: Basic Books, 1983), 48–51; Niraj Nithwani, *Rethinking Refugee Law* (The Hague: Martinus Nijhoff, 2003), 7.

10. Walzer, *Spheres of Justice*, 51.

11. Seyla Benhabib, *The Rights of Others: Aliens, Residents, and Citizens* (Cambridge: Cambridge University Press, 2004), 37.

12. See, e.g., Elizabeth Keyes, "Unconventional Refugees," *American University Law Review* 67 (2017): 89–165; Andrew I. Schoenholtz, "The New Refugees and the Old Treaty: Persecutors and Persecuted in the Twenty-First Century," *Chicago Journal of International Law* 16 (2015): 81–126. The latter article argues for an expansive interpretation of the terms of the 1951 treaty rather than additions to them. But its proposals would still substantially expand the range of people protected. See ibid., pp. 108–119 (describing numerous expansions relative to traditional understandings).

13. See Introduction and Chapter 1.

14. See discussion of welfare rights in Chapters 2 and 5.

15. For possible examples of such exigencies, see discussion in Chapter 6.

16. Ilya Somin, "Justice Department Rejects Salvadoran Woman's Application for Asylum because She Provided 'Material Support' to Terrorists—By Working as a Slave Laborer for Them," *Reason*, June 8, 2018, available at https://reason.com/volokh/2018/06/08/justice-department-rejects-salvadoran-wo.

17. For a vivid description of North Korean totalitarianism and the controls it imposes on everyday life, see Barbara Deming, *Nothing to Envy: Ordinary Lives in North Korea* (New York: Random House, 2009).

18. The state-created famine in North Korea accounted for some 3 million deaths in the 1990s, out of a total population of just 23 million. See Jordan Weissman, "How Kim Jong Il Starved North Korea," *The Atlantic*, Dec. 20, 2011, available at https://www.theatlantic.com/business/archive/2011/12/how-kim-jong-il-starved-north-korea/250244/.

19. For a recent defense of the distinction, see, e.g., David Miller, *Strangers in Our Midst: The Political Philosophy of Immigration* (Cambridge, MA: Harvard University Press, 2016), chs. 5–6; see also Goldenziel, "Displaced."

20. On the importance of government policy as a determinant of economic development, see, e.g., Robert D. Cooter and Hans-Bernd Schafer, *Solomon's Knot: How Law Can End the Poverty of Nations* (Princeton: Princeton University Press, 2012); Hernando de Soto, *The Mystery of Capital: Why Capitalism Triumphs in the West and Fails Everywhere Else* (New York: Basic Books, 2000); Daron Acemoglu and James A. Robinson, *Why Nations Fail* (New York: Crown, 2013); and Nathan Rosenberg and L. E. Birdzell, *How the West Grew Rich* (New York: Basic Books, 1986).

21. See Nicholas Casey and William Neumann, "'I Give and You Give': Venezuela Leader Dangles Food for Votes," *New York Times*, May 18, 2018, available at https://www.nytimes.com/2018/05/18/world/americas/venezuela-election-president-maduro-food.html.

22. For previous critiques of world government that emphasize the lack of exit rights, see, e.g., Hannah Arendt, *Crises of the Republic* (Orlando: Harcourt, Brace, 1972), 330; Bryan Caplan, "The Totalitarian Threat," in *Global Catastrophic Risks*, ed. Nick Bostrom and Milan Cirkovic (New York: Oxford University Press, 2008), 512–14, and Ronald Tinnevelt, "Does a World State Really Lead to a Graveyard of Freedom," in *Cosmopolitan Justice and Its Discontents*, ed. C. Baillet and K. F. Aas (New York: Routledge, 2011), 29–50.

23. Arendt, *Crises of the Republic*, 330.

24. See, e.g., Pippa Norris, "Young Voters Are Voting Very Differently than Older Ones in the UK and the US: That's a Big Deal," *Washington Post*, June 14, 2017, available at https://www.washingtonpost.com/news/monkey-cage/wp/2017/06/14/young-an d-old-are-voting-very-differently-in-the-u-k-and-u-s-thats-a-big-deal/?utm_term= bda761c098b2.

25. See, e.g., Adam Harris, "America Is Divided by Education," *The Atlantic*, Nov. 7, 2018, available at https://www.theatlantic.com/education/archive/2018/11/education-ga p-explains-american-politics/575113/; Mark Bovens and Anchrit Wille, *Diploma Democracy: The Rise of Political Meritocracy* (New York: Oxford University Press, 2017), ch. 4; Mark Bovens and Anchrit Wille, "Globalisation Has Made Education the New Political Cleavage in Europe," London School of Economics and Political Science, Oct. 30, 2017, available at http://blogs.lse.ac.uk/brexit/2017/10/30/ globalisation-has-made-education-the-new-political-cleavage-in-europe/.

26. See, e.g., Gideon Rachman, "And Now for a World Government," *Financial Times*, Dec. 8, 2008, available at https://www.ft.com/content/7a03e5b6-c541-11dd-b51 6-000077b07658.

27. See Ilya Somin, *Democracy and Political Ignorance: Why Smaller Government is Smarter* (Stanford, CA: Stanford University Press, 2d ed. 2016), 160–63.

28. For a classic overview, see Robert Dahl and Edward Tufte, *Size and Democracy* (Princeton, NJ: Princeton University Press, 1973).

29. Cf. Robert Dahl, "Can International Organizations Be Democratic? A Skeptic's View," in *Democracy's Edges*, ed. Ian Shapiro and Casiano Hacker-Gordon (Cambridge: Cambridge University Press, 1999): 19–36 (arguing that problems of scale make it impossible for a world government to be democratic).

30. Rochelle DuFord, "Must a World Government Violate the Right to Exit?," *Ethics and Global Politics* 10 (2017): 19–36.

31. Ibid., 33.

32. See discussion in Chapter 1.

33. For recent proposals for a democratic world government, see, e.g., Joe Leinen and Andreas Bummel, *A World Parliament: Governance and Democracy in the 21st Century*, trans. Joe Cunningham (Berlin: Democracy without Borders, 2018). Leinen is a German member of the European Parliament.

34. William Scheuerman, *The Realist Case for Global Reform*, (Cambridge: Polity Press, 2011), 155; see also Scheuerman, "Globalization, Constitutionalism, and Sovereignty," *Global Constitutionalism* 3 (2014): 102–18.

35. For proposals for a federal structure for world government, see, e.g., Daniel H. Deudney, *Bounding Power: Republican Security Theory from the Polis to the Global Village* (Princeton, NJ: Princeton University Press, 2007); James A. Yunker, *Political Globalization: A New Vision of Federal World Government* (Lanham, MD: University Press of America, 2007); Luis Cabrera, *Political Theory of Global Justice: A Cosmopolitan Case for the World State* (New York: Routledge, 2004); and Eric Cavallero, "Federative Global Democracy," in *Global Democracy and Exclusion*, ed. Ronald Tinnevelt and Helder de Schutter (Oxford: Wiley-Blackwell, 2010).

36. For some recent examples, see Ilya Somin, "No More Fair Weather Federalism," *National Review*, Aug. 18, 2017, available at https://www.nationalreview.com/2017/08/limit-federal-power-left-right-can-agree/.

37. For an overview of the history of gradual erosion in the United States, with only relatively modest clawback in recent years, see Ilya Somin, "The Impact of Judicial Review on American Federalism: Promoting Centralization More than State Autonomy," in *Courts in Federal Countries: Federalists or Unitarists?*, ed. Nicholas Aroney and John Kincaid (Toronto: University of Toronto Press, 2017).

38. For a classic analysis of this dynamic in the case of the United States, see Robert Higgs, *Crisis and Leviathan: Critical Episodes in the Growth of American Government* (New York: Oxford University Press, 1987).

39. For more extensive discussion, see Ronald Tinnevelt, "Federal World Government: The Road to Peace and Justice," *Cooperation and Conflict* 47 (2012): 220–38, 233–34.

40. Ibid.

41. For examples, see Chapter 2.

42. See discussion in Chapter 2 and earlier in this chapter.

43. For the claim that my theory requires some form of "supranatinonal" governance, see James Allan, "Reply to 'How Foot Voting Enhances Political Freedom,'" *San Diego Law Review* 56 (2020): 1121–28, 1126–27. As this chapter explains, the exact opposite is closer to the truth.

44. These odds are derived from simple mathematical calculations.

45. See data cited in Chapter 3.

46. See Roberto Stefano Foa and Yascha Mounk, "The Democratic Disconnect," *Journal of Democracy* 27 (2016): 1–14.

47. Caplan, "Totalitarian Threat," 510–16.

48. Ian Shapiro, *Politics against Domination* (Cambridge, MA: Harvard University Press, 2016), 114.

49. For the argument that the precautionary principle must apply to both action and inaction and to multiple types of risks, see Cass R. Sunstein, *Laws of Fear: Beyond the Precautionary Principle* (Cambridge: Cambridge University Press, 2017).

50. George Orwell, *1984* (New York: Houghton Mifflin Harcourt, 2017), 256.

51. For discussions of proposals of this type, see, e.g., Anne-Marie Slaughter, *A New World Order* (Princeton, NJ: Princeton University Press, 2004); and Thomas G. Weiss

and Rorden Wilkinson, eds., *International Organization and Global Governance* (London: Routledge, 2013).

52. See discussion of rational ignorance in Chapter I, and Somin, *Democracy and Political Ignorance*, ch. 3.

53. See, e.g., Campbell Craig, "The Resurgent Idea of World Government," *Ethics and International Affairs* 22 (2008): 133–42; Leinen and Bummel, *World Parliament*, chs. 10, 12, 16.

54. Environmental Protection Agency, "Global Greenhouse Gas Emissions Data," available at https://www.epa.gov/ghgemissions/global-greenhouse-gas-emissions-data.

55. For classic discussion of the relevant economic theory, see Mancur Olson, *The Logic of Collective Action*, rev. ed. (Cambridge, MA: Harvard University Press, 1971), 49–51. For applications of this point to international collective action, see Todd Sandler, *Global Collective Action*, (Cambridge: Cambridge University Press, 2004).

56. For a more detailed discussion of this point, see John O. McGinnis and Ilya Somin, "Should International Law Be Part of Our Law," *Stanford Law Review* 59 (2007): 1175–247, 1241–43.

57. See, e.g., Campbell Craig, "The Resurgent Idea of World Government," *Ethics and International Affairs* 22 (2008): 133–42; Leinen and Bummel, *World Parliament*, ch. 16; Alexander Wendt, "Why a World State Is Inevitable," *European Journal of International Relations* 9 (2003): 491–542.

58. On the role of mutual deterrence in influencing nuclear strategy, see, e.g., Lawrence Freedman, *The Evolution of Nuclear Strategy*, 3d ed. (New York: Palgrave Macmillan, 2003).

59. For an argument along these lines, see Nick Bostrom, "The Vulnerable World Hypothesis," Oxford University Working Paper, Version 3.21 (2018), available at https://nickbostrom.com/papers/vulnerable.pdf.

Conclusion

1. See discussion of interactions between the three types of foot voting in Chapter 4.

2. See Willliam H. Frey, "US Population Hits 80 Year Low, Capping Off a Year of Demographic Stagnation," Brookings Institution, Dec. 21, 2018, available at https://www.brookings.edu/blog/the-avenue/2018/12/21/us-population-growth-hits-80-year-low-capping-off-a-year-of-demographic-stagnation/.

3. David Bier, "No, the U.S. Is Not the Most Generous Country for Refugees and Asylees in the World—Not by a Long Shot," Cato Institute, Sept.19, 2018, available at https://www.cato.org/publications/commentary/no-us-not-most-generous-country-refugees-asylees-world-not-long-shot.

4. Ibid.

5. See discussion of this possibility in Chapter 8.

6. See, e.g., T. Alexander Aleinikoff, "This Is How Private Citizens Could Help Refugees Come to the US," *Time*, Feb. 10, 2017, available at http://time.com/4666342/private-citizens-help-refugees/. Judith Kumin, "Welcoming Engagement: How Private Sponsorship Can Strengthen Refugee Resettlement in the European Union,"

Migration Policy Institute, Dec. 2015, available at https://www.migrationpolicy. org/research/welcoming-engagement-how-private-sponsorship-can-strengthen-refugee-resettlement-european.

7. See David Schleicher, "Stuck! The Law and the Economics of Residential Stability," *Yale Law Journal* 127 (2018): 78–154; Edward Glaeser, "Reforming Land Use Regulations," Brookings Institution, Apr. 24, 2017, available at https://www. brookings.edu/research/reforming-land-use-regulations/amp/.

8. Ilya Somin, "Minneapolis Strikes a Blow for Affordable Housing by Slashing Zoning," *Reason*, Dec. 8, 2018, available at https://reason.com/volokh/2018/12/08/ minneapolis-strikes-blow-for-affordable.

9. See Laura Bliss, "Oregon's Single-Family Zoning Ban was a "Long Time Coming," City Lab, July 2, 2019, available at https://www.citylab.com/equity/2019/07/ oregon-single-family-zoning-reform-yimby-affordable-housing/593137/.

10. See discussion in Chapters 2 and 7.

11. Ilya Somin, "Foot Voting, Federalism, and Development," *Minnesota Law Review* 102 (2018): 1649–70, 1661–62.

12. See Shannon Tiezzi, "China's Plan for 'Orderly' Hukou Reform," *The Diplomat*, Feb. 3, 2016, available at http://thediplomat.com/2016/02/chinas-plan-for-orderly-hukou-reform/.

13. For relevant recent survey data, see, e.g., "Shifting Public Views on Legal Immigration in the U.S.," Pew Research Center, June 28, 2018, available at http://www.people-press. org/2018/06/28/shifting-public-views-on-legal-immigration-into-the-u-s/; Megan Brenan, "Record-High 75 Percent of Americans Say Immigration Is a Good Thing," Gallup, June 21, 2018, available at https://news.gallup.com/poll/235793/record-high-americans-say-immigration-good-thing.aspx. The percentage of Americans who want to see increased immigration (28 percent) is now the highest it has been in many years, and is for the first time roughly equal to the percentage who prefer a decrease (Brenan, "Record-High 75 Percent of Americans").

14. Ipsos MORI survey, July 2017 (data on file with author).

15. Simone Schotte and Hernan Winkler, "Why Are the Elderly More Averse to Immigration When They Are More Likely to Benefit? Evidence Across Countries," *International Migration Review* 52 (2018): 1250–82.

16. See ibid. and discussion in Chapter 8.

17. See, e.g., John B. Judis, *The Nationalist Revival: Trade, Immigration, and the Revolt against Globalization* (New York: Columbia Public Affairs Council, 2018); Eric Kaufmann, *Whiteshift: Populism, Immigration, and the Future of White Majorities* (New York: Abrams Press, 2019).

18. See John Sides, Michael Tesler, and Lynn Vavreck, *Identity Crisis: The 2016 Presidential Campaign and the Battle for the Meaning of America* (Princeton, NJ: Princeton University Press, 2018), 82–85, 234–36.

19. See generally Benjamin Friedman, *The Moral Consequences of Economic Growth* (New York: Knopf, 2005).

20. See Glaeser, "Reforming Land Use Regulations"; Ilya Somin, "The Emerging Cross-Ideological Consensus on Zoning," Volokh Conspiracy, *Washington*

Post, Dec. 5, 2015, available at https://www.washingtonpost.com/news/volokh-conspiracy/wp/2015/12/05/the-emerging-cross-ideological-consensus-on-zoning/?utm_term=.572f6280fc2b.

21. See Ilya Somin, "Progress in the Struggle Against Exclusionary Zoning, *Reason*, Dec. 25, 2018, available at https://reason.com/2018/12/25/progress-in-the-struggle-against-restric/; and Somin, "Progress on Exclusionary Zoning, Regression on Rent Control, *Reason*, Dec. 25, 2019, available at https://reason.com/2019/12/25/progress-on-exclusionary-zoning-regression-on-rent-control/.

22. See Caglar Ozden et al., *Moving to Prosperity: Global Migration and Labor Markets* (Washington, DC: World Bank, 2018), 99–102.

23. Frederick Douglass, "Our Composite Nationality: An Address Delivered in Boston, Massachusetts, 7 December 1869," in John Blassingame and John McKivigan, eds., *The Frederick Douglass Papers: Series One: Speeches, Debates and Interviews*, Vol. 4 (New Haven, CT: Yale University Press, 1991), 240–59; 252.

Index

For the benefit of digital users, indexed terms that span two pages (e.g., 52–53) may, on occasion, appear on only one of those pages.